CONTENTS

4. POULTRY AND GAME 148

5. VEGETABLES AND SALADS 174

6. HERBS AND SPICES 210

7. RICE, PASTA, PULSES AND GRAINS 226

the
essential
cookbook

Consultant editor
Lorraine Turner

Love Food ® is an imprint of Parragon Books Ltd

Parragon
Queen Street House
4 Queen Street
Bath BA1 1HE, UK

ISBN: 978-1-4075-5457-0

Printed in China

Created and produced by The Bridgewater Book Company Ltd
Project editing by Emily Casey Bailey
Internal design by Lisa McCormick
Photography by Clive Bozzard-Hill
Home economy by Philippa Vanstone

Notes for the reader

This book uses both metric and imperial measurements. Follow the same
units of measurement throughout; do not mix metric and imperial. All
spoon measurements are level: teaspoons are assumed to be 5 ml, and
tablespoons are assumed to be 15 ml. Unless otherwise stated, milk is
assumed to be full fat, eggs and individual vegetables such as potatoes
are medium and pepper is freshly ground black pepper. Recipes using
raw or very lightly cooked eggs should be avoided by children, the
elderly, pregnant or breastfeeding women, convalescents and anyone
suffering from an illness. The times given are an approximate guide only.
Preparation times differ according to the techniques used by different
people and the cooking times may also vary from those given. Optional
ingredients, variations or serving suggestions have not been included in
the calculations.

Recipes using raw or very lightly cooked eggs should be avoided by
infants, the elderly, pregnant women, convalescents, and anyone with
a chronic condition. Pregnant and breastfeeding women are advised
to avoid eating peanuts and peanut products. Sufferers from nut allergies
should be aware that some of the ready-prepared ingredients used in
the recipes in this book may contain nuts. Always check the packaging
before use.

Picture Acknowledgements

Parragon Books would like to thank Getty Images for permission to
reproduce the copyright material on the title page.

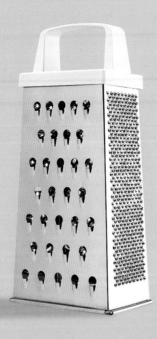

PART ONE

INTRODUCTION

HEALTHY EATING

THE AMERICAN WRITER, MARJORIE RAWLINGS, ONCE SAID THAT FOOD IMAGINATIVELY AND LOVINGLY PREPARED, EATEN IN GOOD COMPANY, WARMS THE SOUL WITH SOMETHING MORE THAN MERE CALORIES. WHILE THIS IS TRUE, IT IS ALSO TRUE THAT THE HUMAN BODY NEEDS A REGULAR AND BALANCED INTAKE OF OVER 70 NUTRIENTS – VITAMINS AND MINERALS – IN ORDER TO KEEP IT WORKING PROPERLY AND PROTECT IT FROM DISEASE.

The five food groups

A healthy and balanced diet needs to contain adequate amounts of five major food groups: protein, carbohydrates, fat, vitamins and minerals.

PROTEIN

This food group provides the building blocks for the body. Everyone's protein requirement differs, depending on health, age and size, but as a rough guide, the average minimum requirement is around 50 g/1¼ oz per day. There are two types of protein: complete protein, which is found in foods of animal origin, such as meat, poultry, fish, eggs, milk and cheese, and incomplete protein, which is found in foods of non-animal origin, such as nuts, seeds, grains, beans and pulses. Complete proteins provide the proper balance of amino acids necessary to build body tissues; incomplete proteins need to be mixed with small amounts of complete protein in order to provide adequate nutrition.

CARBOHYDRATES

The main source of the body's energy is carbohydrates. No official daily requirement exists, but a minimum of 50 g/1¼ oz daily is recommended to avoid an acid condition of the blood called 'ketosis'. This condition occurs when your body has to use fat instead of carbohydrates to provide its energy. Carbohydrates can be found in starchy and sugary foods. There are two types of carbohydrate: complex carbohydrates, which can be found in bread, pasta, rice, cereals, beans, pulses, fruit and vegetables, and simple carbohydrates, which can be found in desserts, puddings, cakes, chocolate, sweets and fizzy drinks. Complex carbohydrates take longer to be broken down in the body, which means they release energy into the body more slowly and gradually. These are the best carbohydrates to eat. The sugary, simple type of carbohydrate will provide a quick boost of energy, but this surge is quickly used up; such 'highs and lows' of energy are not good for maintaining good health and vitality.

FAT

These days we are encouraged to eat a low-fat diet, but to cut fat out completely would be very unhealthy. What we should be doing is eating the types of fat that are good for us, and reducing our intake of the potentially harmful kinds. Saturated fat is potentially harmful in excessive amounts: it can raise our blood cholesterol levels and blood pressure. A good way to remember which foods are high in saturated fat is to think of the fats that stay solid at room temperature, such as lard and butter. It is these kinds of solid fats that clog our arteries and can lead to heart disease. Healthier kinds of fat are polyunsaturated fats, such as sunflower oil and soya oil, and monounsaturated fats, such as olive oil and peanut oil. We also need a regular intake of essential fatty acids (EFAs): these actually help the body to burn off excess fat. Good sources of EFAs include oily fish, sunflower seeds, pumpkin seeds and avocados. So it is not true to say that all fat is bad for you. Restrict saturated fat in your diet by all means, but not the other kinds. Remember also that a low-fat diet is unsuitable for children under 5 years of age.

VITAMINS

This food group comprises organic substances that can be found within the foods we eat. We need only minuscule amounts of these substances in order to be healthy, but a deficiency of even one type of vitamin can cause us to be unhealthy. Vitamins range from the 'fat-soluble' kind, such as A (found in green leafy vegetables, liver and dairy products), D (found in fish liver oils, sardines, tuna and dairy products) and E (found in soya beans, whole wheat and grains, and eggs), to the 'water-soluble' kind, such as C (found in citrus fruits, green leafy vegetables and tomatoes). Some people think that it is possible to live on vitamins only, but this concept is a myth: vitamins are only one of the five main nutrients necessary for a healthy body. It is always preferable to get your vitamins naturally from the foods you eat, rather than from synthetic materials such as tablets, because synthetic vitamins can sometimes cause toxic reactions. Natural vitamins are much safer.

MINERALS

There are about 18 minerals required for healthy body function, and the six most well-known minerals are: calcium (found in milk, cheese and beans), iodine (found in seafood, kelp and onions), iron (found in red meat, egg yolks, oysters, nuts and beans), magnesium (found in figs, lemons, nuts, seeds and apples), phosphorus (found in meat, poultry, fish, whole grains, eggs, nuts and seeds) and zinc (found in steak, wheatgerm, brewer's yeast, eggs and pumpkin seeds). Minerals are essential for maintaining good health. For example, a deficiency of calcium can lead to rickets or osteoporosis, and a deficiency of iron can cause anaemia.

Making the right choices

It is vital to make good food choices and eat sensibly. Did you know, for example, that a diet high in salt and saturated fat can increase the risk of heart disease, while eating other foods, such as beans, can help to reduce cholesterol and prevent heart disease? The message here is that what you absorb into your body plays a crucial role in your health and overall wellbeing. Eating more of the right foods, and reducing your intake of the potentially harmful ones, can contribute enormously to how well you feel and the state of your physical health.

So which are the right foods to eat and which are the wrong ones? It is not always easy to decide. For example, too much salt can lead to higher blood pressure and depleted adrenal glands, but to cut it out completely would be very unwise because we need a certain amount each day in order to stay healthy. Salt actually helps to keep our fluid levels in balance and our muscles healthy. The amount we need, however, is very low – less than 5 g/1 teaspoon per day. Since many foods we buy have salt added already – for example, cheese or ready-prepared foods such as pizzas –

we can usually get the amount we need without having to add extra salt to our meals. It is the habit of adding extra salt to our food that tends to push us over the healthy limit.

Basically, a balanced diet should consist of plenty of fruit, vegetables, whole grains and cereals, dairy products, and smaller quantities of protein foods from animal sources (such as meat, fish, eggs, or dairy products) as well as from non-animal sources (such as beans, peas, nuts and seeds). A vegetarian diet is also perfectly healthy, as long as it is balanced and contains all the essential nutrients.

Dos and don'ts for a healthy diet

Here are some tips to help keep your diet healthy and your body in peak physical condition:

DO eat regular meals – never skip them, especially breakfast. Skipping meals will only encourage your body to go into 'starvation mode' and store up fat.

DO eat at least five portions of fruit and vegetables each day. They can be fresh, frozen or canned, but vary them as much as possible. Not all fruits and vegetables contain the same amount of health-giving nutrients, but when you are in any doubt, you can estimate that one portion is equal to about 85 g/3 oz. Any of the following foods also equal one portion:

• one 150 ml/5 fl oz glass of fruit juice
• one orange, apple, nectarine, peach or banana
• half a grapefruit
• two plums
• a quarter of a cucumber
• one pepper or tomato

• an 85 g/3 oz portion of cauliflower or broccoli
• three heaped tablespoons of any vegetable, for example peas, carrots, sweetcorn, beans or pulses.

DO eat more whole grains, such as oats, barley, rye and corn. Choose wholemeal bread and pasta instead of white varieties, and wholegrain brown rice instead of polished white rice.

DO eat oily fish regularly, at least three times a week if you can.

DO choose organic produce wherever possible; organic foods are free from artificial additives and pesticides, and are a much healthier choice.

DO drink eight glasses of water a day. One glass is equal to 225 ml/8 fl oz, so this means at least 1.8 litres/ 3 pints daily. You need a regular and adequate intake of water in order to flush toxins from the body and replace water lost through urine and sweat. If you do not drink enough water, you will become dehydrated. Dehydration causes symptoms such as headaches,

tiredness and loss of concentration. Prolonged dehydration can lead to constipation and kidney stones.

DON'T eat too much saturated fat. Reduce your intake of greasy fried foods and fatty red meat.

DON'T eat too many sugary foods, such as sweets, chocolate, puddings, desserts and fizzy drinks.

DON'T buy processed foods. Processed foods are often full of artificial additives, such as preservatives, colours and sweeteners – even packaged salad leaves have undergone chemical processing before they reach the retailers' shelves. Instead choose foods that are fresh and in their natural state. The benefits in terms of better flavour and more health-giving nutrients far outweigh the convenience of ready-prepared, packaged foods.

DON'T drink too much caffeine. It is a powerful stimulant and can make you feel lively, but in excess it can lead to health problems. Too much caffeine

can lead to irritability, insomnia and feverish symptoms. Very high doses can cause more serious problems. For example, the British Medical Journal reported that people who drink five or more cups of coffee a day have a 50 per cent higher risk of a heart attack than people who do not drink coffee. The main sources of caffeine are coffee, tea, cola drinks and cocoa, so avoid these drinks as much as possible. Switch to herbal teas and fruit juices instead. Some medicines also contain caffeine, so check the ingredients before you take them, and use an alternative if possible.

DON'T consume too much alcohol. Women should drink no more than 1 unit a day, and men should drink no more than 3 units a day. A unit is equal to one glass of wine, a half-pint of lager or one pub measure of spirits (30 ml/1 fl oz).

DON'T add salt to your food, or at least taste the food before you add salt, then keep added salt to a minimum.

HEALTH AND SAFETY

THE KITCHEN IS OFTEN THE FOCAL POINT OF THE HOME. HOWEVER, IT IS ALSO THE RISKIEST AREA: FIRES ARE MUCH MORE LIKELY TO BREAK OUT IN THE KITCHEN THAN IN ANY OTHER PART OF THE HOME, AND THERE IS A RISK OF INFESTATION BY PESTS OR POTENTIALLY HARMFUL BACTERIA. ADOPTING GOOD HYGIENE HABITS AND TAKING SENSIBLE PRECAUTIONS WILL PROTECT YOUR HOUSEHOLD FROM UNNECESSARY ACCIDENTS AND ILLNESSES.

Kitchen hygiene

Cleanliness is essential in the kitchen. Keep all kitchen surfaces scrupulously clean, and wash your hands thoroughly with soap and water when preparing food. Use a separate towel to dry your hands, not a tea towel. Whenever you go out of the kitchen or touch another surface, such as a door handle or a curtain, even if it is only for a few moments, remember that your hands will quickly pick up bacteria hanging around the home, even if you think your home is scrupulously clean, so always wash your hands again before resuming any food preparation.

Make sure you use different chopping boards and utensils for cooked and raw foods to prevent cross-contamination of bacteria, especially when you are preparing meat or poultry. If you can afford it and have the room to store them, it is a good idea to have several different coloured chopping boards for different purposes. You can keep one for raw meat, one for cooked meat, one for a pet's food, and so on. Wash chopping boards and utensils well in hot, soapy water before and after each use.

Change and wash dish cloths and tea towels regularly. Use a covered rubbish bin and disinfect it on a regular basis.

Food preparation

Make sure that you thoroughly wash any foods that need cleaning, such as soil-covered vegetables, and pat dry with kitchen paper. You should also defrost thoroughly any frozen food that requires it, especially meat and poultry, and do not refreeze once it has thawed. The best place to defrost food is in the refrigerator. However, if you are short of time, you can defrost it in a cool room as long as it is well covered to prevent any potentially harmful bacteria from contaminating it.

Throw away any thawed juices from meat and poultry – do not use them in your dishes. And remember never to reuse a marinade, especially if it has been used for meat or poultry.

When reheating cooked meat dishes, remember that they may be reheated once only, to a temperature of at least 75°C/167°F.

Do not leave cooked rice uncovered at room temperature for any length of time. Potentially harmful bacteria can multiply quickly on cooked rice, so if you have to store it, cover it with clingfilm as soon as possible, and keep it in the refrigerator until you are ready to use it. The same goes for any cooked meats or poultry.

Safe storage

Always buy food as fresh as possible, and from a reputable supplier. Check any 'use by' or 'best before' dates, because sometimes out-of-date items languish on retailers' shelves and are bought by the unwary. Cover all exposed foods with clingfilm before refrigerating. If you buy a whole bird, remove any giblets from the cavity, cover with clingfilm and refrigerate separately from the bird. Store raw and cooked meat and poultry separately in different parts of your refrigerator.

Store your potatoes in a dark place, away from sunlight, or they will turn green – even fluorescent lighting can make them turn green. Green patches in potatoes contain a chemical called solanine. Solanine tastes bitter, and in large concentrations it can give you an upset stomach, so do not buy any potatoes with green patches. If, despite your best efforts, a potato you have

Storing potatoes
Potatoes should be stored away from the sunlight in a dark place to prevent green patches from forming. The green patches contain a substance called solanine, which can upset stomachs.

bought or grown has developed a small green patch, cut the patch out, then use the rest of the potato. If the green covers a large area, you may be better off discarding the whole potato.

Kitchen first aid

Every kitchen should have a basic first-aid kit. Your standard kit should include rubber gloves, antiseptic wipes, burn cream, eye pads, safety pins, different sized dressings, and triangular bandages. Catering establishments use blue plasters in order to make them easier to spot should they fall off. Although you don't have to use this type at home, their deep-blue colouring makes them ideal for home use too.

A fire blanket is also a good precaution in a kitchen. It can be a very useful item to have on hand in case a fire breaks out, and it can also be used to help to keep a shock victim comfortable until help arrives.

Fire safety

As an absolute minimum, fit a battery-operated smoke alarm outside your kitchen, and check the battery regularly. Do not position it in the kitchen itself or over a direct source of smoke or heat, as it may be set off accidentally. Even better, ask a qualified electrician to install smoke and heat detectors throughout your home – for reliability they should be wired up to your mains electricity supply. It is also

a good idea to keep a fire extinguisher in the kitchen. Here are some other tips for kitchen fire safety:
• Keep electrical leads, oven gloves and tea towels away from the cooker.
• Keep your cooker clean, especially the grill and oven. A build-up of fat can catch fire.
• Do not let your sleeves or other loose clothing hang over the stove while you are cooking.

• Never leave pans on the cooker unattended. If you have to leave them, even for a few seconds, perhaps to answer the telephone, remove them from the heat.
• When you've finished cooking, make sure the cooker or oven is turned off.
• If a pan catches fire and you can't put it out easily and quickly, don't take any risks with your safety. Leave the house at once (making sure that you

close all doors behind you as you go), and call the fire brigade immediately. If the fire is small and you are confident you can handle it, put a fire blanket over it, or alternatively run a cloth under the tap, wring it out and then cover the pan with it. Do not throw water into the pan because this action could exacerbate the problem. Turn off the heat as soon as you can get to it safely.

EQUIPMENT

A SELECTION OF CAREFULLY CHOSEN TOOLS IS ESSENTIAL IN THE KITCHEN. IF YOU ARE A BEGINNER, YOU CAN MAKE DO WITH A FEW MULTI-PURPOSE UTENSILS, THEN ADD TO THEM AS YOUR CONFIDENCE GROWS. IF YOU ARE AN EXPERIENCED COOK, YOU MAY WANT TO ADD TO THE BASIC TOOLS WITH SOME MORE SOPHISTICATED ITEMS, SUCH AS A PASTA MACHINE.

Measuring equipment

The items listed here are useful for measuring liquids and solid foods. Note that if you have scales, jugs and spoons in metric and imperial, it is sensible to stick to just one measuring method.

Kitchen scales
Scales come in manual and electric versions. It is best to buy scales that show both metric and imperial measurements.

Measuring jug
Jugs (usually available in both 600-ml/1-pint and 1.2-litre/2-pint sizes) are useful for measuring liquid ingredients. Choose ones that show both metric and imperial measurements.

Measuring spoons
These spoons are ideal for measuring both liquid and dry ingredients accurately.

Measuring cups
Unless you intend to use American recipes, you will not need measuring cups. American cooks use measuring cups instead of kitchen scales. The cups usually come in a nesting set of four different sizes: $1/4$, $1/3$, $1/2$ and 1 cup. They are available in stainless steel or plastic.

Knives

Buy the best quality knives you can afford because they will last longer, and keep them sharp. The first three listed here are the essential knives; the rest can be added later.

Small paring knife
A paring knife is invaluable for cutting vegetables, fruit, meat and cheese. It is 6–9 cm/$2^1/2$–$3^1/2$ inches in length.

Cook's knife
This good multi-purpose knife is 15–30 cm/6–12 inches long, and is essential for slicing and chopping.

Bread knife
This long serrated knife is ideal for slicing bread.

Small serrated knife
This knife is most often used for cutting vegetables and fruit. It is usually about 13 cm/5 inches long.

Measuring jug

Bread knife

Carving knife

Palette knife

Measuring spoons

Cleaver
Its flat, rectangular blade is ideal for cutting meat joints.

Filleting knife
This knife has a flexible blade of about 20 cm/8 inches in length, and is used for vegetables, fruit and raw fish.

Carving knife
This knife has a blade about 30 cm/12 inches long, with a point for easy carving around the bones of joints. It usually comes with a carving fork, which has two long prongs and sometimes a guard to protect against accidents.

Mezzaluna
The mezzaluna has two handles and a curved blade, and is used for chopping herbs and vegetables.

Palette knife
This knife is used for spreading rather than cutting, and it has many uses in the kitchen. It is ideal for icing cakes.

Knife sharpener
Although this has a handle like a knife, instead of a blade it has a long rod of roughened steel. When the edge of a knife is run along the rod at a 45° angle, it sharpens the blade.

Other cutting tools and equipment

In addition to a basic set of knives, you will need some other cutting tools. Some of these tools are very specific, such as the zester, while others are for more general use.

Can opener
This everyday tool comes in many varieties, from hand-operated ones to wall-mounted automatic devices.

Zester
A citrus zester has a rectangular metal head with holes along the top edge. The holes are there to help remove fine shavings of zest without picking up the white pith.

Vegetable peeler
You can buy a swivel-bladed version or one that has a slicing blade in the middle and a sharp tip for coring.

Grater
There are different graters for different purposes, but a good, multi-purpose version to buy is a hollow box-shaped grater with a handle at the top and different cutting holes on each side.

Apple corer
This hollow, cylindrical tool is essential for removing cores from apples and pears quickly and easily.

Pastry cutters
These round circles are available in metal or plastic and are useful for cutting pastry circles. They are also ideal for shaping biscuits.

Kitchen scissors
Choose stainless-steel all-purpose scissors and keep them especially for use in the kitchen.

Small paring knife

Cook's knife

Zester

Vegetable peeler

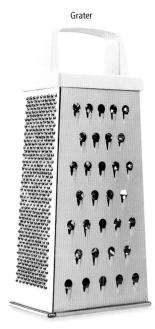

Grater

Pots and pans

When you are buying pots and pans, choose the best quality you can afford. If cared for properly, they will more than repay the extra cost because they will last for many years.

Saucepans
You will need a small, preferably non-stick, milk pan for making sauces and scrambled eggs, and at least three other different-sized saucepans – small, medium and large. Choose saucepans that have secure lids. A large casserole dish with a lid is useful for casseroles, stews and whole birds.

Frying pans
You will need a small omelette pan, and a larger frying pan for more substantial foods. Non-stick varieties are ideal for cooking low-fat meals,

but are not essential. A ridged griddle pan imparts a lovely stripy effect to food and is ideal for chargrilling beef and tuna steaks.

Steamer
Steamers come in different varieties. For example, you can buy a folding metal steamer that adjusts to any size of saucepan. You can also buy metal and bamboo steamers that are placed on top of the saucepan – some have more than one tier so that you can steam more than one food at a time. In addition, there are electric steamers, which are useful if you want to save space on the hob.

Wok
A wok is a deep, rounded, bowl-shaped pan with a handle. It is ideal for cooking stir-fries.

Saucepan

Large saucepan with lid

Frying pan

Ovenware and bakeware

Non-stick baking equipment is useful because it will help you to slide out your culinary creations with ease. Take care not to scour it, however, or you will scratch the non-stick coating.

Baking sheets and trays
Some of these rectangular and square metal sheets are flat and others have a lip around the edges. They are essential for baking a variety of foods, from oven-roasted vegetables and pizzas to meringues and biscuits.

Cake tins
These tins come in different sizes, but, to start with, a couple of 20-cm/8-inch diameter shallow tins will come in handy for making sponges, and a deeper 23-cm/9-inch diameter springform cake tin will be useful for making larger cakes.

Flan/tart tins and dishes
These tins and dishes are usually round, and often have a fluted edge. They are ideal for baking quiches, flans and tarts, and come in a variety of sizes. The best type to buy is the loose-bottomed, stainless steel variety, because it conducts the heat better than ceramic ones and enables food to be lifted out easily.

Pie tins and dishes
These tins come in a variety of shapes and sizes, and are usually fairly deep with a protruding rim for pastry edging.

Roasting tins
These metal tins are deeper than baking trays, and are ideal for roasting meat and poultry.

Muffin tins
These rectangular tins usually come with 12 large, round indentations, which are ideal for making savoury or sweet muffins, individual fruit pies or Yorkshire puddings.

Loaf tins
These rectangular tins have deep sides and come in different sizes. They are useful for baking bread or savoury nut roasts.

Ramekins
These small, round dishes have many uses in the kitchen. They are very handy for making individual soufflés and crème caramels. They also double up nicely as serving dishes for butter, olives and nuts.

Ramekins

Sieves and strainers

The following items are useful in any kitchen. In particular, a sieve is essential for sifting dry ingredients such as flour, while a colander will make light work of draining a variety of foods.

Sieves
These come in metal or plastic, and are useful for sifting flour and straining liquid ingredients.

Colander
A colander is a perforated bowl that is used for draining liquid from foods. Colanders are available in different sizes and different materials, usually metal or plastic. They may have one or two handles and a flat base so that they can sit steadily on a work surface.

Egg separator
Although this small, round, slotted spoon is not essential, new cooks in particular will find it helpful for separating egg yolks from whites.

Dredger
This mesh-covered container is especially useful for sprinkling icing sugar or cocoa powder onto cakes and desserts.

Bowls and basins

You can buy bowls and basins in a variety of different materials and sizes, but metal will react with acid ingredients such as lime juice, so do not use metal bowls for acid-based marinades.

Mixing bowls
Mixing bowls are available in a variety of materials, including ceramic, glass, plastic and stainless steel. At least one large mixing bowl is essential, although several bowls of different sizes are even better. For example, you will need a smaller bowl to whip cream. You can also buy bowls that are sufficiently decorative to double up as serving bowls at the table.

Pudding basins
These come in different sizes and materials, including metal, ceramic, plastic and glass. A large pudding basin is ideal for making a substantial summer pudding or Christmas pudding for a large household, while a set of smaller basins is useful for making individual chilled or steamed puddings. It is often worth recycling basins from shop-bought puddings too.

Sieve

Colander

Large mixing bowl

Pudding basin

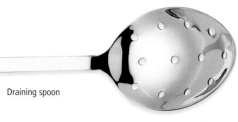

Fish slice

Draining spoon

Serving/basting spoon

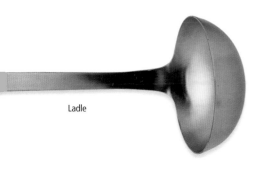

Ladle

Spoons and spatulas

Spoons and spatulas are very helpful for lifting, turning, shaping, draining and serving a variety of foods. Here are some of the utensils you will find most useful.

Fish slice
This slotted lifting tool is essential when lifting floppy food, such as omelettes, fried eggs or fish fillets from frying pans.

Draining spoon
This large, slotted spoon is ideal for lifting solid foods out of liquids so that the liquid drains away, and for skimming scum from the surface of simmering liquids, such as stock, and from jams and marmalade.

Serving/basting spoon
This large spoon is useful for serving food onto plates. It has a groove on one side to direct the flow of juices and sauces.

Ladle
This is helpful for ladling soups into bowls or punch into glasses.

Tongs
A set of tongs is handy for turning hot food on a griddle pan or a barbecue.

Wooden spoon
This type of spoon is available in different sizes and is handy for mixing ingredients evenly, without scratching the delicate surfaces of pans and bowls.

Spatula
This utensil is available in wood or plastic, and is used for folding mixtures such as egg whites. The plastic type is also ideal for scraping down the sides of mixing bowls to get all the mixture out.

Wooden spoons

Spatula

Hot handles

Do not leave spoons and spatulas with metal handles to stand in the pan while cooking on a hot stove. Metal handles can get very hot, and are likely to cause burns.

Hand balloon whisks

Potato masher

Other useful utensils

You can add to your cooking utensils as and when you need them. Here are some of the items you are likely to find most useful and will want to buy sooner rather than later.

Lemon squeezer
These usually come in plastic or glass. They have a strainer to catch any pips, and a bowl underneath to catch the lemon juice.

Corkscrew and bottle opener
You can buy these individually or combined into one utensil. The lever-action corkscrew is the easiest kind to use.

Pastry brush
Brushes are useful for sealing pies with water and for glazing.

Garlic press
A garlic press is not essential but is handy for crushing garlic cloves cleanly and efficiently. Some have a detachable grille for easy cleaning.

Hand whisks
Whisks are available in a variety of shapes and sizes. The most common is the balloon whisk, which is useful for whisking egg whites and cream.

Rolling pin
This long, cylindrical utensil usually comes in wood, glass or ceramic, and is essential for rolling out pastry.

Potato masher
This utensil is essential for mashing potatoes and other vegetables such as swede.

Pestle and mortar
These two utensils come as a pair in a variety of sizes and materials, such as marble and porcelain. They are used for crushing herbs and spices. It is a good idea to buy the largest and sturdiest you can afford.

Chopping boards
If you can, buy several different-coloured boards so that you can keep one for raw meat and poultry, one for cooked meats, and so on.

Wire cooling racks
These metal racks can be round or rectangular, and are ideal for cooling cakes, biscuits and bread. It is often useful to have two racks to accommodate larger batches.

Skewers
Long stainless-steel skewers are a good choice, although other materials, such as wood, are also available. Skewers are essential for cooking kebabs. They are also useful for inserting into cakes and joints of meat to test if they are cooked all the way through.

Pie funnel
This little funnel is available in a variety of shapes and materials, and is used to hold up the pastry in pies. It also prevents the pastry from becoming soggy by allowing the steam to escape.

Ice cream scoop
This tool is useful for scooping neat domes of ice cream or mashed potato onto plates.

Decorative moulds
These moulds are available in many shapes and sizes, and in plastic or metal. They can be used for shaping mousses, ice creams, jellies and creamy desserts.

Piping bags and nozzles
These piping tools come in various sizes and shapes and are useful for creating piped decorations in icing or cream on cakes and desserts.

Thermometers
You can buy thermometers to test the temperature of your refrigerator and oven, and for meat, sugar and deep-fat frying.

Kitchen timers
Timers are available in different designs and sizes, and are useful for monitoring the cooking times of dishes. Many ovens also come with a handy built-in timer.

Lemon squeezer

Garlic press

Pastry brushes

2 1

Machines and electric utensils

There is a wide variety of machines and electrical devices for the kitchen, and these make quick and easy work of preparing food – especially useful when catering for families or parties.

Food processor
This multi-purpose machine has metal blades that chop, shred and grate foods. Usually, it also comes with a selection of other attachments that mix and knead ingredients, such as sponge mixes and pastry dough.

Blender
A blender is useful for puréeing foods and mixing drinks, such as soups, batters, milk shakes and smoothies. It is also known as a liquidizer.

Pasta machine
This machine is not essential because shop-bought pasta is excellent these days. But if you prefer to make your own fresh pasta, you will find it indispensable for rolling and cutting pasta into noodles, ribbons and various decorative shapes.

Grinder
This very useful machine is essential for grinding nuts and coffee beans. It is also ideal for making fresh breadcrumbs, as are food processors and blenders.

Free-standing mixer
This machine, which is also called a food mixer, has a large bowl and a selection of mixing tools, such as a whisk and a dough kneader. It enables you to beat and whisk foods much faster than you can by hand.

Hand-held mixer
This tool, which you can hold over a bowl or saucepan, is more portable than a free-standing mixer. It is suitable for light mixtures, such as eggs and cream, but for more substantial mixtures you will find a free-standing mixer easier to use.

Hand-held blender
This portable version of the blender lets you purée food in a saucepan while it is cooking on the hob.

Deep-fat fryer
This heavy-based machine usually comes with a wire basket that can be hooked onto the side of the machine for easy draining of the cooking oil.

Pressure cooker
This deep, heavy electric saucepan is not essential, but it is useful for steaming food such as rice in about half the normal cooking time.

Slow cooker
This small appliance is very useful for cooking stews and casseroles slowly, and saves you having to use the oven. It also uses less electricity than an oven does. Simply add the food, cover, plug it in, and wait for the lovely aromas to emerge.

Free-standing mixer

Pasta machine

Oven temperatures

Celsius	Fahrenheit	Gas mark	Oven heat
110°	225°	$\frac{1}{4}$	very cool
120°	250°	$\frac{1}{2}$	very cool
140°	275°	1	cool
150°	300°	2	cool
160°	325°	3	moderate
180°	350°	4	moderate
190°	375°	5	moderately hot
200°	400°	6	moderately hot
220°	425°	7	hot
230°	450°	8	very hot
240°	475°	9	very hot

Spoon measurements

1 teaspoon of liquid = 5 ml

1 tablespoon of liquid = 15 ml

Other measurements

Liquid volume		Weight		Linear	
Metric	Imperial	Metric	Imperial	Metric	Imperial
60 ml	2 fl oz	5 g	$\frac{1}{8}$ oz	2 mm	$\frac{1}{16}$ inch
100 ml	$3\frac{1}{2}$ fl oz	10 g	$\frac{1}{4}$ oz	3 mm	$\frac{1}{8}$ inch
150 ml	5 fl oz	25 g	1 oz	5 mm	$\frac{1}{4}$ inch
200 ml	7 fl oz	50 g	$1\frac{3}{4}$ oz	8 mm	$\frac{3}{8}$ inch
300 ml	10 fl oz	75 g	$2\frac{3}{4}$ oz	1 cm	$\frac{1}{2}$ inch
450 ml	16 fl oz	85 g	3 oz	2 cm	$\frac{3}{4}$ inch
500 ml	17 fl oz	100 g	$3\frac{1}{2}$ oz	2.5 cm	1 inch
600 ml	1 pint	150 g	$5\frac{1}{2}$ oz	5 cm	2 inches
700 ml	$1\frac{1}{4}$ pints	225 g	8 oz	7.5 cm	3 inches
850 ml	$1\frac{1}{2}$ pints	300 g	$10\frac{1}{2}$ oz	10 cm	4 inches
1 litre	$1\frac{3}{4}$ pints	450 g	1 lb	20 cm	8 inches
1.5 litres	$2\frac{3}{4}$ pints	500 g	1 lb 2 oz	30 cm	12 inches/1 foot
2.8 litres	5 pints	1 kg	2 lb 4 oz	46 cm	18 inches/$1\frac{1}{2}$ feet
3 litres	$5\frac{1}{4}$ pints	1.5 kg	3 lb 5 oz	50 cm	20 inches/$1\frac{2}{3}$ feet

PREPARATION TECHNIQUES

YOU WILL FIND THIS SECTION A VALUABLE SOURCE OF REFERENCE FOR ALL THE BASIC PREPARATION TECHNIQUES YOU ARE LIKELY TO NEED IN EVERYDAY COOKING. THERE ARE ALSO SOME ADVANCED TECHNIQUES FOR THE MORE EXPERIENCED COOK.

GRIND 1
To crush food, such as nuts or coffee beans, to a powder or into very small pieces. For this job, you can use a pestle and mortar for a coarser result, or a coffee grinder or food processor.

INFUSE
To steep flavourful ingredients, such as herbs or spices, in a liquid in order to flavour it.

BARD
This means to wrap pieces of fat, such as bacon, around lean cuts of meat and poultry to keep them moist and impart more flavour. For example, you can wrap chicken or turkey breasts with rashers of bacon before baking. You can also wrap a meat loaf with bacon rashers to keep it moist during baking.

CRUSH 2
This technique is useful for bringing out the flavour of garlic and herbs, and can be done by pressing the flat side of a knife blade down onto the garlic or herbs. You can also adapt this technique to make biscuit crumbs for cheesecakes. Simply place the biscuits in a polythene bag, tie the end, then use a rolling pin to crush the biscuits inside the bag.

FOLD 3
This technique involves mixing a light mixture into a heavier one using a spoon or spatula in a figure-of-eight movement. This is done to keep the air within the mixture.

BASTE
When you spoon juices or fat over food during cooking, this is known as 'basting'. It helps to keep the food moist and seal in the flavour.

BEAT 4
This technique involves using a fork, spoon or electric mixer in a vigorous

stirring motion to remove any lumps from sauces and incorporate air into omelettes and cake mixtures.

RUB IN

This technique is mainly used when making pastry. Using the fingertips, rub the fat into the flour, lifting it high over the basin in order to trap air in the mixture, making it lighter and giving a better result.

MARINATE

This term means to soak food in a marinade for a few hours or days to tenderize it and give it more flavour. You can marinate meat, poultry, fish and vegetables. Marinades usually consist of oil and perhaps alcohol or vinegar, and are flavoured with different mixtures of herbs and spices.

DEGLAZE

This technique is used after sautéeing food (normally meat). After the food and excess fat have been removed from the pan, a small amount of liquid – such as stock or wine – is stirred in to loosen browned bits of food in the pan. This mixture often forms the base for a sauce to accompany the food.

KNOCK BACK

This entails knocking the air out of bread dough after it has risen.

CLARIFY

You can clarify butter or a liquid. To clarify butter, heat it slowly to separate the milk solids, which sink to the bottom of the pan, skimming any foam off the top. Clarified butter, such as Indian ghee, has a higher smoke point than ordinary butter so you can cook with it at higher temperatures. To clarify a liquid, such as a stock, add egg whites and/or egg shells to it and simmer for 10 minutes then cool and strain it. The egg whites or shells draw out the impurities.

SHRED

This technique involves using a small, sharp knife or grater to cut food into very thin lengths.

LINE

To line a tin with something to prevent food from sticking during cooking. The most common method is to rub butter or oil over the surface of the tin, then cover with baking parchment before adding the food. You can also use bacon rashers as a lining for savoury non-vegetarian dishes.

MARBLE

This technique is used to combine two differently coloured ingredients in order to create a marbled effect. For example, you can mix melted white chocolate into melted plain dark chocolate to create a marbled pattern.

SCORE

This term means to make light incisions on the surface of a food, particularly meat, poultry and fish, in order to facilitate cooking, allow fat to drain and create a decorative effect.

BLEND

Blending involves combining two or more ingredients together by stirring with a spoon or puréeing with an electric blender. It is a useful technique for soups, milk shakes and smoothies.

BUTTERFLY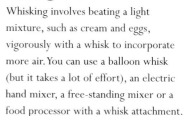

To butterfly a leg of lamb, insert the knife into the cavity of the leg bone and cut to one side to open out the meat; then make a shallow surface cut down the centre to keep the meat open flat. You can also butterfly other foods, such as chicken breasts or large prawns.

KNEAD

This technique uses the heel of the hand to pull and stretch bread dough in order to develop the gluten in the flour so that the bread will keep its shape when it has risen. You can also knead dough in a food processor that has a dough hook.

SKIM

This term means to remove scum or fat from the surface of a simmering liquid with a large slotted spoon or ladle.

WHISK ❷

Whisking involves beating a light mixture, such as cream and eggs, vigorously with a whisk to incorporate more air. You can use a balloon whisk (but it takes a lot of effort), an electric hand mixer, a free-standing mixer or a food processor with a whisk attachment.

ZEST

This means to remove the outer layer of citrus fruit. A zester shaves off the zest without picking up the bitter white pith underneath.

CHIFFONADE ❸

A French term meaning 'made of rags'. It refers to the effect you get when you roll leafy vegetables together, then slice them crossways into ribbons with a sharp knife.

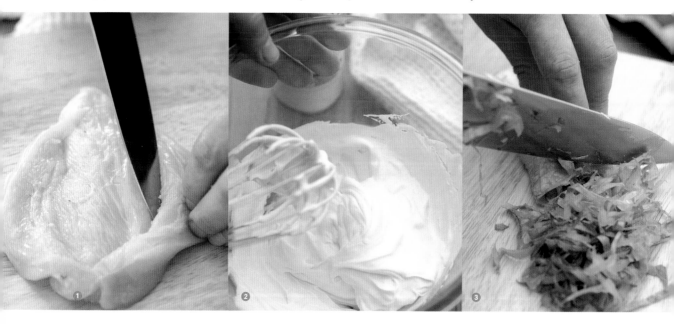

ENRICH

This means adding a rich ingredient to a dish in order to create a richer texture or flavour. For example, you could add butter to a dough, or cream to a sauce.

GLAZE

This involves brushing water, beaten egg or sugar and water onto pastry before baking to give it a glossy shine (and make them crunchy if sugar is added). To glaze a ham, remove the skin from the partly cooked meat then coat the outer surface with sugar and mustard and continue cooking. You can glaze sweet dishes with melted jam or chocolate.

LARD

To lard means to insert strips of pork fat into a lean cut of meat to flavour it and keep it moist.

EMULSIFY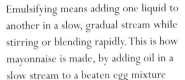

Emulsifying means adding one liquid to another in a slow, gradual stream while stirring or blending rapidly. This is how mayonnaise is made, by adding oil in a slow stream to a beaten egg mixture while whisking or blending vigorously.

TENDERIZE

This involves pounding meat, such as a beef steak, with a mallet in order to break down the tough fibres. You can also tenderize meat by marinating it.

CHOP

This means to cut food into small pieces using a sharp knife. For example, to chop a herb, hold the tip of the knife blade down with one hand, then use your other hand to raise the handle of the knife up and down as you chop the herb. You can chop food roughly or finely, depending on your requirements. Roughly chopped means that the food will be left in larger pieces than when finely chopped.

MASH

Mashing means to reduce food, usually cooked potatoes and other root vegetables, to a pulp using a potato masher or a free-standing mixer.

STEEP

Steeping means to soak an ingredient in hot liquid in order to release its flavour into the liquid.

JULIENNE

This technique involves cutting food, such as carrots and celery, into fine batons or strips.

CUT

This method means to use a sharp knife to make an incision or separate a food into smaller pieces.

DRESS

This can mean to add a dressing to a salad, to decorate a dish before serving or to pluck and truss poultry.

GREASE OR OIL

This is to rub a little butter or oil over the surface of a pan or tin to prevent food sticking to it during cooking.

TRUSS 1

This means to pull poultry or game into shape then secure with string or skewers before cooking. This technique is particularly useful for preventing stuffing from falling out of a bird.

CREAM

Creaming is similar to beating, in that you use a fork, spoon or electric mixer to beat ingredients together until they are smooth. This technique is usually associated with something rich and creamy, such as butter.

SPATCHCOCK

This means to remove the backbone from a bird and secure it so that it can be cooked flat and therefore more rapidly. To remove the backbone, first tuck under the wings and remove the wishbone. Then turn the bird over and cut along each side of the backbone to remove it. Use your hands to push down on the bird's breast and flatten it. Finally, push a metal skewer through the thighs and another through the wings and breast to secure the bird.

PURÉE 2

This describes reducing food to a smooth pulp. You can do this by pushing food through a sieve or using a blender.

MACERATE

To macerate means to soak a food in a liquid, often alcohol, to soften it.

OPEN FREEZE

This technique means to freeze foods, uncovered, in a single layer. For example, you can cut fruit, such as mango, into small pieces, spread them out on a tray and freeze them uncovered. Then transfer individually to a freezer bag and use as required.

CURE

Curing means to preserve a food by salting or smoking it.

DEGORGE

This is soaking meat, poultry or fish in a solution of cold water and salt to remove impurities. It also means salting aubergines to remove their bitter juices.

MINCE

This is to grind food, such as meat, into small pieces using a knife or mincer.

DREDGE

Dredging means to sprinkle flour onto a surface when rolling out pastry, or icing sugar or cocoa powder over desserts.

CRIMP 3

For this technique, use the finger and thumb of one hand and the index finger of the other hand to 'pinch' pastry together around the edge of a pie or pasty. This gives it a decorative effect.

SIFT 4

This technique involves shaking dry ingredients, such as flour, through a sieve to remove lumps and introduce more air into the mixture.

DICE

This means to cut food into small, regular-shaped cubes. You can use a sharp knife or a special dicing utensil.

GRATE

To shred food into small pieces. You can use a box grater or food processor.

PEEL

Peeling involves removing the outer skin or rind from foods such as oranges, avocados or potatoes. Depending on the food, you can use your hands, a sharp knife or a vegetable peeler.

SHUCK

This is how we remove the husks from corn and the shells from peas.

CROSS-HATCH 5

To cross-hatch means to score criss-cross patterns on the surface of foods to allow them to absorb marinades or be removed from their skins. You can cross-hatch the outer layer of fat on a pork joint before cooking to allow the fat to drain and create a decorative effect.

SNIP

This means using kitchen scissors to cut green leafy vegetables or herbs into very small pieces.

SIEVE 6

This involves pushing food through a sieve in order to create a purée.

COOKING METHODS

IN THIS SECTION YOU WILL FIND ALL THE TRADITIONAL COOKING TECHNIQUES, FROM BOILING TO ROASTING, AS WELL AS THE INCREASINGLY POPULAR HEALTH-CONSCIOUS METHODS, SUCH AS STEAMING AND STIR-FRYING.

FRY ①

This method involves cooking food in hot fat, usually oil, in a frying pan. Frying food gives it a delicious flavour. You can shallow-fry or deep-fry food. Deep-frying needs a lot more oil and can be dangerous, so it is always better to shallow-fry food if possible. However, for some foods, such as tempura (a Japanese dish of batter-coated pieces of fish and vegetables) and Scotch eggs, deep-frying is unavoidable. You can also stir-fry food: this method needs only a little oil and is a very healthy way to cook.

DEEP-FRY ②

This technique involves immersing food completely in very hot oil and cooking it at a very high temperature. It is important to choose the correct oil: groundnut and soya bean oil have the highest smoke points (the temperature at which the oil begins to emit smoke) and are therefore the most suitable for deep frying. Rapeseed and corn oil have the next highest, and are also suitable. Sunflower oil has a lower smoke point and should not be used for deep-frying. Deep-frying food is dangerous because it is possible to spill the hot oil or the

pan can catch fire, so great care must be taken and the pan should never be left unattended. A thermostatically controlled deep-fat fryer is a safer and easier option, but still needs care and attention during use. The oil should be heated to a high temperature in order to allow rapid cooking; the high temperature will also help to seal the food and prevent it from absorbing too much oil. When the food is cooked, lift it out carefully using a fish slice or slotted spoon, or the wire basket if using a deep-fat fryer. Let any excess oil drain away from the food on kitchen paper.

DRY-FRY

This method involves cooking food or spices in a frying pan without using fat or oil. For example, you can cook Indian spices, flat breads or Mexican tortillas in a dry frying pan. You can also dry-fry pumpkin seeds or pine kernels until they are golden and lightly toasted.

PAN-FRY

This is another quick and healthy way of cooking food. It involves cooking food quickly in a frying pan with either no fat at all (as in dry-frying) or with the absolute minimum amount of fat necessary. Some foods, such as bacon rashers, have enough fat content of their own, and therefore do not need any added fat. In fact, the fat they emit during cooking can be enough to pan-fry other foods at the same time – in this way, the dish has a minimum amount of fat and maximum flavour.

SHALLOW-FRY

This method of cooking is suitable for foods that will not burn easily – for example, foods that are protected in some way, such as foods coated with flour, breadcrumbs or batter. You will need to add enough oil so that the food will not stick to the pan or burn. Take care to heat the oil to a high temperature because this will help to seal the food when it is added and prevent it from absorbing too much oil. (Food cooked in oil that has not reached the right temperature will be soggy and laden with oil.) Cook the food in the oil for the required time, then turn it over and cook on the other side. Use a fish slice to lift out the food, and let any excess oil drain away from the hot food on kitchen paper. Where this method differs from sautéing is that the food is not moved around the pan, and generally a little more oil is used.

STIR-FRY

This method comes from Asia and is another very healthy way to cook because of the small amount of oil needed. Foods such as meat, poultry and vegetables are cut into small, similar-sized pieces and cooked rapidly, while being tossed constantly, in a wok. You can also use a large frying pan for stir-frying, but a wok is better because the food cooks more rapidly as it comes into contact with the hot sides of the wok. Chinese cooking distinguishes between four or five different methods of stir-frying, but two are the most common. The first is a very rapid technique, where the food is fried in a little oil at the highest heat while being tossed constantly. Foods cooked in this way are often marinated first. The other technique is less vigorous and more moist: the food is cooked in a little liquid, such as a stock, and constantly turned and moved around the pan. Noodles and sauce are often added towards the end of the cooking time. It is important not to overfill the wok, or the food will steam instead of fry.

BOIL ❶
To boil means to cook food in a liquid (usually water, milk or stock) in a saucepan at boiling point (100°C/212°F). Not all foods are boiled continually: sometimes they are 'brought to the boil', then the temperature is reduced and the food is left to simmer (bubble gently). You can cook many foods in this way, such as vegetables, rice, pasta, meat and eggs. You can also boil a liquid rapidly for a period of time in order to evaporate excess moisture (see Reduce).

SIMMER ❷
To simmer means to cook food in liquid that is just below boiling point; there will be very gentle bubbles on the surface of the liquid. This method is often combined with the boiling technique, where a food is first brought to the boil, then the heat is reduced and the food is allowed to simmer for a period of time.

BLANCH
Blanching is a useful technique for loosening skins on foods such as tomatoes, preserving the colour of vegetables, reducing any bitterness in ingredients and preparing foods for freezing. Blanching also helps to reduce the salt content in cured meats. To blanch a food, simply immerse it in boiling water for a few seconds, then plunge it into cold water to prevent further cooking.

REDUCE ❸
This is not really a complete cooking method in its own right, but it is a useful technique, especially for sauces. To reduce a liquid, simply boil it down rapidly in an uncovered pan. This evaporates the liquid and makes the sauce thicker.

STEAM 4

Steaming is a very healthy way to cook, because the food does not come into direct contact with the liquid and therefore more of the nutrients are preserved. Steaming is suitable for a wide range of foods, from poultry and fish to vegetables and puddings. If you use a folding metal steamer, simply bring a small amount of water to the boil in the base of the pan, place the steamer inside, add the food, cover the pan and steam until cooked to your taste. Bamboo steamers are used in a similar way. You can also steam puddings: bring enough water to the boil to come halfway up the side of the pudding basin, then place the basin inside the pan and steam the pudding for the recommended time (taking care to top up with boiling water if necessary during cooking).

SAUTÉ 5

This is similar to frying, but involves moving the food around the frying pan to prevent it browning too rapidly. Usually a small amount of oil or butter is used to oil or grease the pan and prevent the food burning.

CARAMELIZE 6

This term most often refers to the method of caramelizing sugar or onions. To caramelize sugar, heat it until it melts into a syrup. The colour varies from light golden to dark brown, depending on the cooking time. A sugar thermometer is useful here, to get the sugar to the required temperature. When the sugar is removed from the heat, it quickly sets and becomes brittle, but retains its caramelized appearance. You can also sprinkle sugar over a food

and caramelize it under a preheated hot grill or by heating its surface with a kitchen blow torch. To caramelize onions, cook them gently in butter for 30 minutes, or until they turn a rich golden brown.

SEAR ❶

To sear means to brown meat, poultry and fish rapidly over a high heat. This process helps to seal in the juices and keeps the centre of the food moist.

POACH ❷

To poach means to cook food in a liquid at just below boiling point and it is a very gentle method of cooking. The liquids commonly used for poaching are water and alcohol. You can poach poultry, fish, eggs (as long as they are very fresh) and fruit.

SWEAT ❸

This means to cook food (often vegetables such as onions) gently in water or fat until they are softened but not brown.

FLAMBÉ ❹

Strictly speaking, to flambé is more food presentation than cooking method, but since it involves warming an ingredient it is included here. Flambé is a French word meaning 'flamed'. It involves

---

Poaching fruit

Pour enough wine or sugar syrup into a pan to cover the fruit. Bring to a simmer, add the stoned fruit and simmer for 15 minutes, or until tender. Lift out the fruit, reduce the liquid by boiling it down, then pour it over the fruit.

---

sprinkling liqueur over a food, such as a Christmas pudding, then setting the alcohol alight just before serving. It makes a dramatic spectacle at the table, and also burns off the alcohol content.

TOAST

This process uses dry heat to cook foods. For example, you can toast nuts by baking them dry in the oven or cooking them under a preheated hot grill. You can also toast bread under the grill, or you can spear marshmallows on forks and toast them over a fire.

BAKE

To bake means to cook food in an oven using dry heat. For example, you can bake potatoes, cakes, biscuits, breads and custards.

BAKE BLIND **5**

This means to bake a pastry case without a filling. To bake blind, first line a pie tin or flan dish with rolled-out pastry dough, prick it with a fork, place a layer of baking paper over the pastry and weight it down with ceramic or metal baking beans. Then bake it. If you haven't got any baking beans, you can use dried beans or pulses instead. Baking blind helps to ensure that the pastry stays crisp after the filling is added, and is especially necessary if the filling does not need to be cooked, or needs only a very short time to cook.

ROAST **6**

Roasting is similar to baking, in that food is cooked in the oven using dry heat. In this case, however, the process is often used for meat, poultry and vegetables. It is usually necessary to add a little fat when roasting foods to keep them moist. Roasting can really bring out the flavour of a food: for example, peppers that have been roasted are extra sweet and flavourful. You can also roast a wide variety of other vegetables, not just potatoes and parsnips, but also garlic, onions, carrots, fennel, sweet potatoes, aubergines and swede.

BRAISE

This is a long, slow way to cook food. It is especially useful for tough cuts of meat, and for poultry and vegetables. To braise foods, first brown them in oil, then cook them very slowly in a small amount of flavoured liquid, such as stock or wine, in a dish with a tight-fitting lid. You can cook them on a hob or in an oven.

CASEROLE

This method is similar to braising; you can use a large, heavy-based casserole dish with a tight-fitting lid for this. First brown the food in oil, add a small amount of flavoured liquid, cover with a lid, then cook very slowly in the oven. Sometimes a casserole can be likened to a stew, where the food is cut into smaller pieces and more cooking liquid is added. After cooking, you can serve the food directly from the casserole dish.

STEW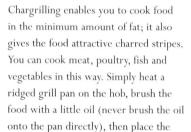

Stewing is a very slow method of cooking. It is similar to braising, except that the food is cut into smaller pieces and more liquid is used. This technique is suitable for meat (especially tough cuts because the long cooking process

helps to tenderize the meat), poultry, fish, vegetables, grains such as barley, and certain fruits such as apples, pears, peaches and nectarines.

POT-ROAST ❷

This technique is very similar to braising in that it involves cooking food (usually meat, especially beef) very slowly in a covered pot in the oven. Only a very little liquid is used.

Chargrilled vegetables

To ring the changes to chargrilled vegetables, mix 1 tablespoon olive oil, 1 teaspoon lemon juice, 1 teaspoon each chopped fresh rosemary and thyme, and season to taste with salt and pepper. Brush the mixture over the vegetables, and chargrill as required.

GRIDDLE

Traditionally, a griddle is a flat, usually rimless, pan, which is used to cook pancakes and drop scones with the minimum of oil. Griddles usually have a long handle and are often made of a heavy metal that conducts heat well, such as cast iron. Nowadays, the term 'griddle' is often confused with chargrill.

CHARGRILL ❹

Chargrilling enables you to cook food in the minimum amount of fat; it also gives the food attractive charred stripes. You can cook meat, poultry, fish and vegetables in this way. Simply heat a ridged grill pan on the hob, brush the food with a little oil (never brush the oil onto the pan directly), then place the food on the heated pan. Cook according

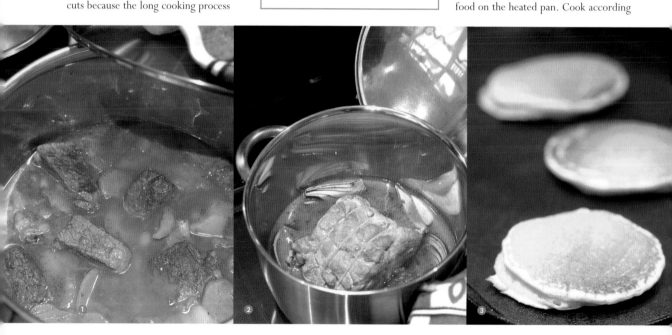

to the recipe, turning the food over once to cook on the other side. You can also chargrill food on a metal grid set over hot coals.

BARBECUE ⑤

With this method the food is usually cooked on a mesh over hot coals. The barbecue apparatus can range from a simple portable tray consisting of a mesh with flammable, slow-burning paper underneath, to an elaborate electric barbecue. Foods are often marinated first, in order to give them more flavour and to aid the cooking process. Always barbecue your food outdoors in the open air in order to waft away any carbon monoxide fumes given off by the lit charcoal. Also, in order to prevent burns, use long-handled utensils to lift and turn the food.

GRILL ⑥

Grilling is a quick and healthy way to cook food. Modern cookers usually have an integral grill; they also come with a grill pan with a wire mesh to allow excess fat to drain away. A grill should always be preheated before use. Grilling is a very versatile method of cooking: you can cook meat, poultry, fish and vegetables under a grill, and toast other foods such as bread and cheese. Grilling food involves cooking it directly under the heat source, which ensures that the outside of the food is browned quickly, while the inside stays moist.

BLOW TORCH

One of the cook's best-kept secrets is blow-torching food. This method of cooking is simple, quick and effective. You can buy a kitchen blow torch from any reputable kitchen equipment store, and you will find it inexpensive and convenient. It has a variety of uses. For example, to make a crunchy, caramelized topping for crème brûlées, simply sprinkle them generously with white sugar until the surfaces are completely covered. Now ignite your blow torch and adjust the air for a blue flame. Apply the flame to the sugar until it caramelizes and turns golden brown. You can also skin a pepper by blow-torching instead of roasting it. This method is especially suitable if you are short of time or have only one or two peppers to skin. Simply spear the pepper with a fork, then turn it over the flame of the blow torch until the skin is charred and black. Transfer the pepper to a plastic bag, leave it for 15 minutes, then peel off the skin in the usual way.

STORECUPBOARDS

A GOOD STORE OF NON-PERISHABLE FOOD STUFFS IS AN ESSENTIAL PART OF EVERY COOK'S KITCHEN. WELL-STOCKED KITCHEN CUPBOARDS, AND PERHAPS A LARDER, ENSURE THAT YOU ALWAYS HAVE A GOOD SELECTION OF STAPLE ITEMS ON HAND FOR EVERY OCCASION. MAKE SURE YOU CHECK THE USE-BY DATES OF YOUR STORED ITEMS REGULARLY, AND DISCARD ANY THAT HAVE BECOME OUT OF DATE.

Oils

There are many different varieties of oil available these days, but it is not necessary to buy them all. You simply need oil that is suitable for drizzling and for cooking at high temperatures.

Olive oil

This mildly fruity oil is ideal for drizzling over salads. It can range from a champagne colour to bright green. The best oils are cold-pressed – this is a chemical-free process that uses only pressure and produces a low level of acidity. You can also flavour it with different ingredients – for example, try adding some herbs, such as basil leaves, or some garlic to it – after a day or two the oil will become infused with their flavour. Its smoke point (the temperature at which it begins to smoke) is 210°C/410°F.

Extra virgin olive oil

Produced from the first cold-pressing of the olives, this oil has a very low acid level. It is the most expensive type of olive oil, and has a peppery, fruity flavour. You can use it for drizzling over salads and hot dishes such as pizzas. Its smoke point is 210°C/410°F.

Sunflower oil

This is a good multi-purpose oil that can be used for most cooking purposes. However, it is not recommended for deep-frying because this method needs an oil with a higher smoke point. The smoke point of sunflower oil is 199°C/390°F. Sunflower oil has a very light flavour and is therefore ideal in dressings.

Sesame seed oil

This oil comes in two varieties: one has a light colour and a nutty flavour, the other is darker and has a stronger flavour. The darker one is most often used in Asian dishes. This oil is excellent for frying and stir-frying. Its smoke point is 210°C/410°F.

Vegetable oil

A blend of various oils, mainly rapeseed, soya, coconut and palm. It is best used for frying rather than in salads because it is quite greasy.

Groundnut oil

A combination of a very mild flavour and a high smoke point of 232°C/450°F makes groundnut oil extremely versatile. It is therefore suitable for dressings and mayonnaise, and for drizzling over dishes, as well as for all forms of cooking, including deep-frying.

Corn oil

This oil is economical to buy, and therefore is a good choice for cooking. However, it has a strong, distinctive flavour that makes it unsuitable for dressings and drizzling over dishes. Its smoke point is 210°C/410°F.

Olive oil

Extra virgin olive oil

Sunflower oil

Rapeseed oil

This oil is gaining in popularity because it is lower in saturated fat than other oils. It also contains the omega-3 essential fatty acid, which is now widely believed to help reduce cholesterol levels. It has a mild flavour and so is suitable for salad dressings as well as for cooking. Its smoke point is 229°C/444°F.

Soya oil

This economical oil is extracted from soya beans and has a light yellow colour. Like rapeseed oil, its popularity is growing because it is low in saturated fat. Its smoke point is 232°C/450°F, which makes it ideal for all types of cooking, including deep-frying. However, it has a strong taste and is therefore not suitable for dressings or for drizzling over finished dishes.

Nut oil

Corn oil

Vinegars

Vinegar adds a lovely, pungent kick to dressings, marinades, sauces and a wide range of dishes. It is available in different varieties, and here are some of the most popular types.

Malt vinegar

This is made from malted barley and is available in two varieties: a colourless form, which is very strong and is used for pickling, and a dark brown variety, which is used in chutneys and on traditional British fish and chips. This vinegar is not suitable for dressings.

Cider vinegar

This vinegar is made from apples and has a strong, sharp taste. It is best used with meats and in pickles and chutneys.

Wine vinegars

These are available in different varieties, mainly red, white and sherry. They can be used in dressings, marinades and sauces, and can be sprinkled over food.

Balsamic vinegar

This delicious vinegar is thick, dark and slightly sweet. It is made from grape juice that is aged in barrels over a period of years.

Speciality vinegars

These vinegars can be made with fruits such as berries, nuts or a wide variety of herbs. Other popular favourites are rice vinegar (used in Asian cooking) and cane vinegar, which has a rich, slightly sweet taste.

Vegetable oil

Basil-flavoured olive oil

Malt vinegar

Red wine vinegar

Balsamic vinegar

Flour

Keep your flour fresh by storing it in an airtight container with a tight-fitting lid in a cool, dry place. You can store white flours for 6–8 months, and wholemeal flours for up to 2 months.

Cornflour
This powdery flour is made from corn kernels and is used for thickening sauces, soups and desserts. It is usually mixed with a small quantity of cold liquid to make a smooth paste before being added to hot dishes.

Plain flour
This flour is used for thickening sauces as well as for making batters and pastry.

Self-raising flour
Plain flour that has had baking powder and salt added is known as self-raising flour. It is used for making cakes and biscuits.

Wholemeal flour
This flour has a stronger flavour than white flour and contains wheatgerm, which means it has a higher fibre, fat and nutrient content. However, since it has a higher fat content, it should be stored in the refrigerator to prevent it from going rancid.

Strong bread flour
This flour is used for making bread. It contains a high level of gluten, which helps to give the bread dough its elasticity. If you are using a wholemeal variety, keep it in an airtight container in the refrigerator.

Rice flour
This powdery flour is made from white rice, and is used mainly in baked foods and to make Asian rice-flour noodles.

1 Plain wholemeal flour
2 Cornflour
3 Plain flour
4 Malted brown flour
5 Strong bread flour
6 Self-raising flour

Pasta, noodles and grains

All these different dried pasta shapes, noodles and grains keep well in the storecupboard. They are ideal for cooking quick, satisfying meals at short notice.

Spaghetti

Long-shaped pasta

There are different varieties of dried long-shaped pastas, including spaghetti, fettuccine (narrow ribbons), tagliatelle (slightly wider ribbons) and vermicelli (very fine, hair-like lengths). These pastas are usually made with durum wheat or wholewheat flour, and may be coloured using ingredients such as spinach (green), beetroot juice (red), tomatoes (orange-red) or even squid ink (black).

Short-shaped pasta

Dried short shapes of pasta include conchiglie (shells), fusilli (spirals), farfalle (bows) and tubular varieties such as penne and macaroni. These shapes are particularly good for holding chunky sauces.

Other shapes of dried pasta

Other favourite shapes to keep in your storecupboard include lasagne (rectangular sheets) and cannelloni (large tubes).

Dried noodles

Most noodles are associated with Asian cooking. The main difference between noodles and long-shaped pasta is that noodles usually have egg added, such as Chinese egg noodles. Alternatively, sometimes they are made from rice flour. Noodles are very popular in stir-fries and soups. Many varieties need no cooking – you simply soak them in hot water for a few minutes before adding to the dish of your choice.

Long-grain rice

You can buy white and brown varieties of long-grain rice. When cooked, the grains stay dry and separate and do not clump together. This rice is used in savoury dishes.

Medium-grain rice

These grains are a little shorter than long-grain rice, and more moist. They tend to clump together when cooked. This rice is used in savoury dishes such as Spanish paella and Japanese sushi.

Short-grain rice

This rice has short, fat grains that are more starchy and moist than medium- and long-grain rice. There are different varieties, including pearl rice (used in Asian cooking) and arborio rice (used in risottos).

Easy-cook rice

The grains in easy-cook rice are polished and partly boiled so that they are quick and easy to cook and stay fluffy and separate. Easy-cook rice is a convenient alternative to white or brown rice, but does not have as much flavour.

Wild rice

Despite its name, wild rice is not actually a rice – it is a marsh grass that is cultivated in the United States and Canada. The grains are long and black and have a nutty flavour. Wild rice is expensive, so for economy reasons it is often mixed with less-expensive brown long-grain rice.

Bulgar wheat

This comprises wheat kernels that have had the bran removed. They are then steamed, dried and ground into different degrees of coarseness. The result is a golden-brown grain that has a nutty flavour. It can be cooked like rice and is also excellent in salads.

Couscous

This is not a true grain, but pieces of semolina dough that have been rolled, dampened and coated with a fine wheat flour. It makes a fine accompaniment to savoury dishes.

Polenta

This yellow grain is made from cornmeal and is very popular in Italian cooking. It can be eaten hot or cold. It can also be cooked in a slab then cut into squares and grilled or fried.

Noodles

Long-grain brown rice

Assorted dried pasta shapes

Pulses

Beans, lentils and peas are known as pulses, and they are good sources of protein. All pulses except lentils and split peas need soaking for at least 8 hours, then boiling rapidly for 10 minutes before cooking for around 45 minutes. The exception is soya beans, which need even longer. It is a good idea to keep some ready-to-use canned pulses to hand for impromptu meals.

Cannellini beans
A type of haricot bean, these long, creamy white beans are excellent in soups and salads.

Red kidney beans
These red, kidney-shaped beans can be added to soups, salads, stews and other savoury dishes such as Chilli con Carne.

Aduki beans
These beans are small and red and are popular in Japanese cooking, especially coated with sugar. They are also good in savoury dishes such as soups and salads.

Butter beans
These white, kidney-shaped beans are excellent in soups and salads.

Black-eyed beans
These beans are small and beige and have a circular black 'eye'. They are commonly found in Chinese cooking, and are particularly popular in sauces, stir-fries and soups.

Borlotti beans
These oval-shaped beans have pale pink to maroon streaked skin. They are creamy when cooked and are excellent in soups, dips and other savoury dishes.

Soya beans
Although most soya beans are yellow, they can also be black, brown or green. They are much richer in nutrients than the other pulses, and are particularly full of protein, as well as iron and calcium. Soya beans are used to make cooking oils and margarine, flour, soya milk and cheeses, soy sauce, tofu, miso and textured vegetable protein. They are good in soups and other savoury dishes, particularly curries. They should be soaked for at least 12 hours, drained and rinsed, then covered with fresh water and brought to the boil. Boil them for the first hour of cooking, then simmer them for the remaining 2–3 hours that it takes to cook them.

Chickpeas
These round, beige pulses have a nutty flavour and are excellent in soups, stews and salads, as well as ground up in dips such as hummus. Like soya beans, they need a longer soaking and cooking time than many pulses, so it is good to keep some canned chickpeas on hand for when you are short of time.

Lentils
These tiny, disc-shaped pulses are available in different varieties and colours. Red and orange lentils become mushy when cooked, and are therefore ideal puréed and used in soups and sauces. The green and continental brown varieties (Puy lentils) keep their shape when cooked and are ideal in warm winter salads, sauces, stews and other savoury dishes.

Split peas
These small peas are disc-shaped and split along a natural seam. They can be yellow or green, and are excellent cooked and puréed. They are also good in soups, bakes and other savoury dishes.

Red kidney beans

Red lentils

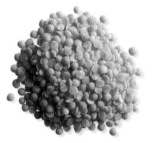

Aduki beans

Chickpeas

Cannellini beans

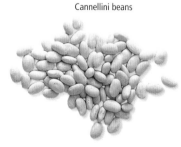

Nuts and seeds

Nuts and seeds have a high oil content, and can quickly go rancid. If they have shells, store them in a cool, dry place. If they do not have shells, refrigerate them in airtight containers.

Almonds

These lozenge-shaped nuts have a thin brown covering and a cream centre. They come in two types, sweet and bitter, but it is the sweet variety that is normally used. Available whole, blanched, chopped and crystallized, they are excellent in both savoury and sweet dishes, from salads and savoury bakes to cakes, biscuits and marzipan.

Hazelnuts

These small, round nuts have a brown covering and a cream interior, and a rich, sweet flavour. They are especially popular in muesli and cereals, savoury dishes and bakes, such as nut loaf, as well as sweet dishes including cakes and biscuits.

Walnuts

These nuts have a large, round, wrinkled shell and two double lobes inside. The nuts have a delicious creamy taste and are good in salads and savoury bakes, as well as sweet dishes and cakes. They also make a very flavourful oil.

Pecan nuts

These nuts are golden brown with a beige interior. They have a very high fat content. They are used in a variety of savoury dishes, and desserts such as pecan pie.

Cashew nuts

These creamy, butter-flavoured kidney-shaped nuts have a high fat content and are delicious roasted and added to stir-fries and bakes.

Pistachio nuts

These pale green nuts have a delicate flavour. They are often used in stuffings and also to decorate desserts.

Pine kernels

These small, oval nuts are creamy in colour and in flavour. They are excellent toasted or dry-fried, and are used in salads and rice dishes, sauces such as pesto, and also savoury and sweet dishes.

Peanuts

Despite their name, peanuts are not actually nuts, they are legumes and very versatile. They are used to make oil and also peanut butter, which in turn makes a delicious satay sauce. They are also good in salads, side dishes and stir-fries.

Seeds

A selection of seeds can be very useful in your storecupboard. Sunflower seeds, for example, are rich in essential fatty acids and are delicious sprinkled into muesli and salads. Pumpkin seeds are also nutritious and make a good snack. Sesame seeds are popular in Asian cooking and are delicious toasted and in stir-fries. Dill seeds have an aniseed flavour and are good with fish and vegetables. Caraway seeds have a pungent flavour and are used in soups, stews, vegetable dishes and in bread. Poppy seeds are slightly sweet and make an attractive decoration sprinkled over salads and bread rolls.

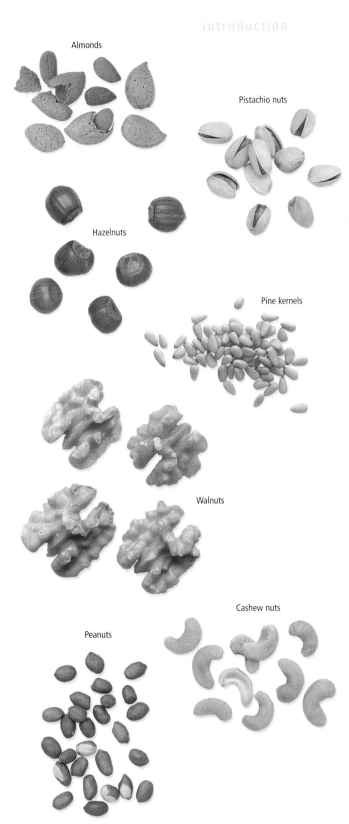

Almonds

Pistachio nuts

Hazelnuts

Pine kernels

Walnuts

Cashew nuts

Peanuts

Dried herbs

It is always worthwhile having a collection of dried herbs. They are especially useful for dishes that require a long cooking time, such as casseroles. Use half the recommended fresh quantity.

Oregano
This herb has a strong flavour and is perfect sprinkled on pizzas and in pasta sauces.

Basil
This popular herb is delicious in sauces and is particularly good with tomatoes.

Sage
This herb is good in egg, cheese, poultry and meat dishes.

Dill
This is an excellent herb with vegetables and fish.

Rosemary
A pungent herb that goes well with poultry and meat, and also root vegetables, especially potatoes.

Mixed herbs
This combination usually consists of oregano, rosemary and thyme, plus one or two other herbs. Mixed herbs can be used in a variety of savoury dishes, including sauces and Italian dishes such as pizza and pasta.

Spices and seasonings

A selection of spices in your storecupboard is extremely useful for enhancing the flavour of dishes. Some spices, such as ginger and turmeric, are also said to aid digestion.

Ginger
This hot, pungent spice has a lemony flavour when fresh, but a sweeter flavour when dried. It is particularly used in Indian cooking, as well as in chutneys, desserts and baked goods such as cakes, notably gingerbread, and biscuits.

Turmeric
A peppery spice with a distinctive yellow colour. Turmeric is often used instead of the more expensive saffron. It is especially good in curries and rice dishes such as paella.

Saffron
This yellow spice has a slightly bitter flavour and a pungent aroma. It is sold in strands and is used in dishes to colour and flavour them.

Coriander
This spice has an aromatic flavour and is excellent with meat, poultry and vegetables.

Cumin
This spice has a strong, slightly bitter flavour, and is particularly good with poultry and vegetables.

Cloves
A sweet spice with a strong flavour. Use whole cloves to stud hams and fruits, and ground cloves to add flavour to desserts.

Nutmeg
This spice has a sweet flavour and is used in savoury and sweet dishes.

Mace
This spice has a sweet flavour and is excellent in soups and sauces.

Paprika

Basil

Cumin

Sage

Oregano

Rosemary

Cloves

Cinnamon

A very popular spice. Cinnamon is sweet and fragrant and is used in desserts and baked foods such as cakes, sweet pies and biscuits.

Curry powder

This is a blend of spices, and the flavour varies from mild to hot. It adds a distinctive flavour to sauces and savoury dishes.

Mixed spice

A mixture of sweet spices, such as cinnamon, cloves, mace and nutmeg, plus one or two others. It gives a delicious flavour to desserts, cakes, biscuits and drinks.

Chilli powder

This is a blend of dried chillies. It adds a kick to sauces and savoury dishes.

Turmeric

Ground ginger

Five-spice powder

This blend of five spices usually contains cinnamon, cloves, fennel seed, Szechuan peppercorns and star anise. It is very popular in Chinese cooking, and gives a wonderful flavour to stir-fries.

Paprika

This has a hot flavour and an attractive red colour. It is ideal as a garnish.

Peppercorns

These come in different varieties. Ground black or white peppercorns are an extremely popular seasoning for a wide variety of savoury foods and also some sweet dishes such as balsamic strawberries. You can also buy green peppercorns.

Salt

This is a great favourite as a seasoning, but care must be taken not to overuse it or it will overpower the food, and be bad for health.

Peppercorns

Sugars and syrups

Store your sugar in a dry place at room temperature. Syrups should be kept in tightly sealed containers at room temperature or in the refrigerator.

Granulated sugar

This basic, cheap sugar is essential in your storecupboard. Use it to sweeten drinks and cereals and to sprinkle on desserts.

Caster sugar

This sugar is finer than granulated sugar and dissolves quickly, so it is ideal for meringues and cakes.

Icing sugar

This very fine sugar is ideal for making icing and for dusting cakes and desserts.

Soft brown sugar

This stronger-flavoured sugar comes in various shades from light to dark.

Demerara sugar

This crunchy brown sugar is delicious sprinkled over desserts and cakes before being grilled or baked.

Honey

This comes in a variety of flavours and colours, as either clear, liquid honey or opaque, set honey. It has many uses, from glazing ham and flavouring vegetables to sweetening desserts and drinks.

Golden syrup

This clear, golden syrup is made from evaporated sugar cane juice. It is used in a variety of dishes, and to top pancakes and ice cream.

Maple syrup

This syrup has a delicious sweet flavour and can be used in a wide variety of savoury and sweet dishes. It is very popular on pancakes.

1 Icing sugar
2 Soft brown sugar
3 Caster sugar
4 Demerara sugar
5 Granulated sugar

Sauces, pastes and condiments

A good selection of sauces and condiments is invaluable in the kitchen, and will ensure you always have the right ingredient on hand to add exciting and interesting flavours to your dishes.

Tomato ketchup
This sauce is popular in British cooking and is added to cooked foods such as chips and hamburgers. It is also good as an ingredient in dressings and relishes.

Brown sauce
This strongly flavoured sauce is a traditional British accompaniment to a fried breakfast.

Soy sauce
This popular sauce is essential for stir-fries and other Asian dishes. You can buy the Chinese version, which is salty, or the Japanese type, which is slightly sweeter.

Worcestershire sauce
This strongly flavoured sauce is made with onions, molasses and anchovies, and is used to season meats, gravies and soups, and occasionally cocktails.

Pesto sauce
Pesto is made from basil, garlic, pine kernels, Parmesan cheese and olive oil. It is ideal for quick pasta meals.

Tabasco sauce
This very hot chilli sauce is used in dishes to give them a kick, such as Mexican salsas. It is also used to season certain cocktails.

Hoisin sauce
This sweet soya-based sauce with a sticky texture is very popular in Chinese cooking. It is known by various names such as Peking sauce.

Thai fish sauce (nam pla)
This salty sauce is made from fermented fish and has a very strong taste and smell. It is used to flavour Thai dishes and as a table condiment.

Horseradish sauce
Horseradish is a root with a very hot flavour. It makes an excellent creamy white sauce, which is very good with meat, poultry, fish and egg dishes.

Plum sauce
This fruity sauce is popular in Chinese cooking and is traditionally served with spring rolls and also Peking duck.

Harissa
This North African condiment is made from oil, garlic, herbs and spices, and is served with soups and couscous.

Tahini
A thick paste made from finely ground sesame seeds. It is used to flavour Middle Eastern dishes.

Thai curry paste
This is available in different varieties: green is the hottest, yellow is the mildest and red varies in the amount of heat. It is a popular ingredient in Thai dishes.

Miso
A paste made from fermented soya beans. It is used in Japanese cooking to thicken and flavour soups and other dishes.

Tomato purée
This is a tomato paste that is useful in sauces and soups because of its intense flavour.

Passata
This is simply sieved tomatoes. It is ideal for soups and sauces, and for spreading over pizzas.

Mustards
You can buy different types of mustard. Dijon mustard has a strong flavour and is used in dips and dressings. English mustard is very hot and useful in dips and dressings. Coarse-grain mustard is usually milder, and is good with a variety of savoury dishes, especially meats.

1 Soy sauce
2 Coarse-grain mustard
3 Tabasco sauce
4 Thai fish sauce
5 Pesto sauce
6 Horseradish sauce

Canned and bottled foods

Keep a selection of cannned and bottled foods on hand, such as pulses, fish, vegetables and pickled items, and you will never be short of ingredients for delicious meals at short notice.

Canned pulses

You can buy a wide variety of canned beans, such as red kidney beans and chickpeas, which will save you time because you do not have to soak them or cook them. Tins of baked beans in tomato sauce are indispensable for quick meals.

Canned fish

Canned fish, such as tuna, salmon, crab, anchovies, sardines and pilchards, are versatile items to have in the storecupboard. They are particularly useful when added to pastas and salads.

Canned tomatoes

Canned tomatoes can be used in a wide variety of dishes, from sauces and soups to stews and casseroles.

Coconut milk

Canned coconut milk is very useful for cooking Thai dishes, particularly creamy curries and desserts.

Sweetcorn

Canned sweetcorn is deliciously sweet and ideal in salads, soups, bakes and casseroles.

Canned sardines

Water chestnuts

These are popular in Chinese cooking, and are particularly good in stir-fries.

Olives

It is always useful to keep a tin or bottle of olives on hand. They make ideal tapas for unexpected guests and are delicious in salads and pastas and on pizzas.

Sun-dried tomatoes

These are very good in Italian recipes, particularly salads, pastas and bread.

Pickled foods

Onions, gherkins and capers make perfect accompaniments and garnishes for meat and vegetable dishes.

Dried fruits and berries

A selection of dried fruits and berries is very useful to keep on hand. They make ideal snacks and can be used in a wide variety of savoury and sweet dishes, from muesli, vegetable curries and meat dishes to desserts and sweet pies. Dried fruits and berries include currants, raisins, sultanas, apricots, prunes, figs, dates, mangoes, pears, apples, bananas, cranberries and blueberries.

Other items

Here is a selection of other items you will find useful to keep in your storecupboard.

Stock cubes

These are very convenient for soups, casseroles and other dishes, particularly if you have do not have enough time to make fresh stock.

Gelatine

You will need gelatine to set mousses and jellies. You can also buy a vegetarian equivalent, such as agar agar.

Chocolate and cocoa powder

These are useful for desserts and baked goods, and also for some savoury dishes.

Vanilla

You can buy vanilla in pod or liquid form (essence and extract) as a flavouring. Vanilla is particularly delicious in desserts.

Alcohol

White wine, red wine and sherry are handy for a variety of savoury and sweet dishes. Although not essential, flavoured liqueurs are also useful, such as orange, coffee and almond.

Vanilla pods

Refrigerator and freezer essentials

Your chilled essentials should include eggs, milk, yogurt and crème fraîche. You should also keep some butter, including an unsalted variety for baking and desserts. Bread is another essential, not just as an accompaniment, but for making breadcrumbs and recipes such as crostini. Cheeses should include an all-purpose firm variety, such as Cheddar, and also Parmesan, as well as cream cheese. You may find bacon rashers useful. Tofu is full of protein: it is good in stir-fries and is useful for vegetarian meals. In the freezer, you might like to keep frozen prawns and fish fillets, vegetables and ice cream.

PART TWO

MAIN COMMODITIES AND RECIPES

1

EGGS AND DAIRY

EGGS AND DAIRY PRODUCTS, SUCH AS MILK, BUTTER
AND CHEESE, ARE EXCELLENT SOURCES OF PROTEIN.
THEY ARE ALSO VERY VERSATILE FOODS AND CAN
BE USED TO ENRICH A WIDE RANGE OF SWEET AND
SAVOURY DISHES. IN THIS SECTION YOU WILL FIND A
MOUTHWATERING ARRAY OF EGG AND DAIRY RECIPES
TO DELIGHT EVERY MEMBER OF YOUR HOUSEHOLD.

INTRODUCTION

NOWADAYS WE CAN BUY A WIDE RANGE OF DELICIOUS EGGS, FROM WHITE AND BROWN, ORGANIC AND FREE-RANGE, TO MORE EXOTIC TYPES, SUCH AS THE DISTINCTIVE BLUE EGGS FROM THE OAKHAM BLUE HEN. LIKEWISE, MORE DAIRY PRODUCTS ARE AVAILABLE THAN BEFORE, AND WE CAN CHOOSE FROM AN EVER-INCREASING ARRAY OF MILK, YOGURT, CREAM, BUTTER AND CHEESE, WHICH ARE FULL OF PROTEIN AND VERY EASY TO PREPARE AND COOK.

Buying and storing eggs

Always buy your eggs from a reputable supplier, and do not buy any with cracked shells. Ensure the eggs are as fresh as possible by checking the 'best before' date on the carton. In many cases the 'best before' date is also printed on the eggshells themselves. You can also check an egg's freshness by floating it in water: if it sinks to the bottom of the bowl horizontally, it is very fresh; if it stays vertical with its tip on the bottom, it is less fresh; if it floats to the top it is stale and should be discarded.

Store your eggs, pointed ends down, in their carton in the door of your refrigerator or in a cool place in your kitchen. Separated egg whites will keep in the refrigerator in a lidded container for a week, and in the freezer for three months. Egg yolks or whole beaten eggs will keep in the refrigerator for up to 2 days, or in the freezer for up to 3 months (add a little salt to them before freezing). When freezing eggs, or indeed any food, always label the container with the date of freezing and what it contains.

Eggs are best cooked at room temperature, so get them out of the refrigerator 2–3 hours before they are needed, if possible.

Whisking egg whites

Eggs that are 3–5 days old are best for whisking. Make sure that everything is clean and that your bowl is free of grease. Put the egg whites in a large bowl. If you are whisking by hand, use a large balloon whisk in an upward, circular movement. Alternatively, use a hand-held electric whisk or free-standing food mixer. If the recipe calls for a 'soft peaks' consistency, the mixture should form peaks that are soft and will flop over. If you need 'firm peaks', the peaks should stand rigid.

Scrambling eggs

Allow 2 eggs and 1 tablespoon of milk per person. Whisk together the eggs and milk in a bowl, then season with salt and pepper. Melt 1 tablespoon of butter in a non-stick pan, then pour in the egg mixture. Stir constantly over a low heat for 5–7 minutes until almost set, then remove from the heat. Stir for 1 more minute, then serve.

Boiling eggs

To boil eggs, bring a small saucepan of water to the boil. Lower the heat to a simmer, add a pinch of salt, then carefully add the eggs (if they have been

Safety

Eggs can carry harmful bacteria and may cause food poisoning if not thoroughly cooked, so do not give dishes with raw or lightly cooked eggs to people who may be particularly vulnerable, such as pregnant or breastfeeding women, babies and toddlers, the elderly, people who are ill or convalescents.

Free-range hen egg

Khaki Campbell duck egg

Aylesbury duck egg

refrigerated, bring them out about an hour beforehand to allow them to come to room temperature). Simmer gently for 4–5 minutes for soft-boiled, and 9–10 minutes for hardboiled (no longer, or a dark ring will appear around the yolk). Remove with a slotted spoon and plunge into cold water to prevent further cooking. Serve as required.

Frying eggs

Heat 1–2 tablespoons of oil in a frying pan until hot (but not smoking). Break the eggs carefully into the pan so that the yolks remain intact. Cook over a medium heat, occasionally basting with the hot oil to help the yolk set, for 3–4 minutes. Use a fish slice to lift out the eggs and allow the oil to drain away. Serve immediately.

Poaching eggs

Eggs need to be very fresh for poaching or they will break up in the water. You can use a non-stick egg poacher for this, or alternatively use the following method. Take a small frying pan and fill it with enough water to cover an egg.

Bring the water to the boil, then lower the heat to a simmer. Add a pinch of salt. Break the egg carefully into a cup, then pour it gently into the boiling water so that the yolk does not break. Cook for 3–4 minutes, depending on how you like your eggs; you may find it helpful to baste the egg with a little of the cooking liquid to ensure it is cooked. Lift it out with a slotted spoon and serve.

Separating eggs

There are some clever devices available for separating yolks from egg whites – for example, you can buy a spoon-shaped implement that has holes in to allow the egg white to pass through, leaving the egg yolk intact. If you don't have a separating gadget, you can use the shell method (using cold eggs makes this method easier). ❶ Crack the egg shell gently on the edge of a bowl. ❷ Open the shell slowly, allowing the white to drip into the bowl. ❸ Taking care not to break the yolk, pass it from one shell half to the other. ❹ Repeat until the yolk and white are fully separated.

Alternatively, open the egg into your hand and let the white drip through your fingers to separate.

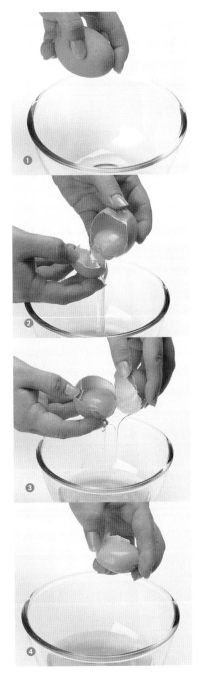

Coll duck egg

Goose egg

Quail egg

Buying and storing milk

Milk is a good source of protein and calcium. The most commonly available is fresh cow's milk, which comes in full-fat (4% fat), semi-skimmed (less than 2% fat) and skimmed (less than 1% fat). Other varieties include homogenized, which has the fat spread throughout the milk so that there is no creamy layer on top, and long-life (UHT) milk, which has been heated quickly to around 149°C/300°F, then cooled and vacuum-packed to ensure a shelf-life without refrigeration of around six months. You can also buy condensed milk, which is very thick and sweet; evaporated milk, which is sterilized in tins and often used to replace full-fat milk; buttermilk, which tastes like yogurt or thickened low-fat milk; and powdered milk, which you can reconstitute with water and use

in place of fresh milk. If you are sensitive to cow's milk, you can buy goat's milk or sheep's milk, or milk made from soya or rice instead.

Most fresh milk is pasteurized (heated then quickly cooled) these days in order to kill off any harmful bacteria, although some unpasteurized milk is available, often straight from the farm (see Safety box, opposite).

Always check the 'best before' date on milk before you buy it, and store fresh milk in the refrigerator. Keep it covered to prevent contamination.

Buying and storing yogurt

Yogurt is made by fermenting milk with healthy bacteria. It has a slightly tangy taste and is a healthy choice because it is thick and creamy yet low in fat. Greek-style yogurt is the thickest and has the

creamiest consistency. You can also freeze yogurt for a healthy low-fat alternative to ice cream. Check the 'best before' date before buying, and store it in the refrigerator. Keep it covered when not in use.

Buying and storing butter

Butter is made by churning cream until it separates into semi-solids. It comprises at least 80% fat and the other 20% is made up of milk solids and water. Sometimes it is coloured with annatto (a natural colour made from the paste of seeds). Butter is available in salted and unsalted varieties: unsalted is essential for sweet dishes. You can also buy 'spreadable' butter: this has been blended with oil so that it will stay soft and can be spread more easily. Make sure your butter is always tightly

Fresh milk

Clotted cream

Yogurt

Butter

wrapped to prevent it from absorbing odours. Check the 'best before' date on the packaging. Butter also freezes well, for up to 6 months in the freezer.

Buying and storing cream

Cream is made from the fattiest part of milk. It therefore has a higher fat content than milk, and a milder flavour. Half-fat and single cream have the lowest fat contents: the former is useful for pouring into drinks such as coffee, and the latter is ideal for sauces and soups. Soured cream (around 18–20% fat) has a slightly tangy taste and is ideal in savoury dishes, as is the higher fat crème fraîche (up to 50% fat). Whipping cream has a high fat content (30–35%) and, as its name suggests, is ideal for whipping and piping into decorative shapes. Double cream has a very high fat content (over 40%) and should therefore be used sparingly. It is a delicious luxury for special occasions, perhaps to enrich a sauce or accompany a dessert. Clotted cream has the highest fat content of all (around 60%) and is very thick. It is ideal on scones or as an accompaniment for special desserts.

All cream should be kept covered and stored in the refrigerator. Use it by the 'best before' date on the carton.

Buying and storing cheese

Cheese is made from milk that is allowed to thicken and then separate into curds (semi-solids) and whey (a liquid). Fresh cheeses are rindless and vary in consistency. Typical cheeses in this category are cream cheese and cottage cheese. Soft and semi-hard cheeses are firmer, and range from creamy soft cheeses with rinds, such as Brie, to firmer cheeses such as Port Salut. Generally, the harder the cheese, the higher the fat content, and hard cheeses have the highest fat of all. They are often easy to grate, and range from Cheddar cheese to Parmesan. Blue cheeses are also available: these have blue veins running through them and a strong flavour and aroma (the veins are made by a friendly bacteria). Blue cheese varieties include Gorgonzola and Stilton. You can also buy cheese made from goat's milk and sheep's milk.

Keep your cheese tightly wrapped. Store fresh cheese in the coldest part of the refrigerator, and the other cheeses in the warmest part. Hard cheeses can be grated ready for use and kept in the refrigerator for up to one week. Use cheeses by the 'best before' date. You can also freeze hard cheeses, but they will have a crumblier texture when they are defrosted. Grated cheese also freezes well but is only suitable for cooking, not for adding to salads.

Cheddar

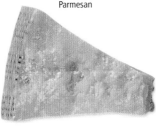

Parmesan

Stilton

Curd cheese

EGGS BENEDICT WITH QUICK HOLLANDAISE SAUCE

THIS DELICIOUS RECIPE IS QUICK AND EASY TO PREPARE. IT MAKES AN EXCELLENT BREAKFAST, LUNCH OR SUPPER, OR A TASTY SNACK AT ANY TIME OF DAY. YOU CAN ALSO SUBSTITUTE BACON FOR THE HAM, OR USE SPINACH IF YOU ARE CATERING FOR VEGETARIANS.

serves
4

preparation
30 minutes

cooking
12–15 minutes

ingredients
- 1 tbsp white wine vinegar
- 4 eggs
- 4 English muffins
- 4 slices good-quality ham

QUICK HOLLANDAISE SAUCE
- 3 egg yolks
- 200 g/7 oz butter
- 1 tbsp lemon juice
- pepper

1 Fill a wide frying pan three-quarters full with water and bring to the boil over a low heat. Reduce the heat to a simmer and add the vinegar. When the water is barely simmering, carefully break the eggs into the pan. Leave for 1 minute, then, using a large spoon, gently loosen the eggs from the base of the pan. Leave to cook for a further 3 minutes, or until the white is cooked and the yolk is still soft, basting the top of the egg with the water from time to time.

2 Meanwhile, to make the hollandaise sauce, place the egg yolks in a blender or food processor. Melt the butter in a small saucepan until bubbling. With the motor still running, gradually add the hot butter in a steady stream until the sauce is thick and creamy. Add the lemon juice, and a little warm water if the sauce is too thick, then season to taste with pepper. Remove from the blender or food processor and keep warm.

3 Split the muffins and toast them on both sides. To serve, top each muffin with a slice of ham, a poached egg and a generous spoonful of hollandaise sauce.

cook's tip

For best results when poaching eggs, break them into a cup first, then slide into the hot water. If you prefer firmer yolks, poach for a little longer than the suggested three minutes.

EGGS FLORENTINE

THIS TASTY DISH IS RICH IN PROTEIN AND MINERALS, INCLUDING IRON, CALCIUM AND ZINC. IT ALSO WORKS VERY WELL FOR VEGETARIANS, AS LONG AS YOU USE A CHEDDAR THAT IS MADE FROM NON-ANIMAL RENNET. IF NECESSARY, YOU CAN REPLACE THE WHOLEMEAL FLOUR WITH WHITE FLOUR.

serves
2–4
(2 as a light snack or 4 as part of a brunch)

preparation
50 minutes

cooking
45–55 minutes

ingredients
- 450 g/1 lb fresh spinach leaves, thoroughly washed
- 55 g/2 oz unsalted butter
- 55 g/2 oz button mushrooms, sliced
- 55 g/2 oz pine kernels, toasted
- 6 spring onions, chopped
- 4 eggs

- 25 g/1 oz plain wholemeal flour
- 300 ml/10 fl oz milk, warmed
- 1 tsp English mustard
- 85 g/3 oz mature Cheddar cheese, grated
- salt and pepper

1 Preheat the oven to 190°C/375°F/Gas Mark 5. Shake off any excess water from the spinach, place in a large saucepan with the water clinging to the leaves and sprinkle with a little salt. Cover and cook over a medium heat for 2–3 minutes, or until wilted. Drain, pressing out any excess liquid, then chop.

2 Heat 15 g/½ oz of the butter in a small saucepan over a medium heat. Add the mushrooms and cook for 2 minutes, stirring frequently. Add the pine kernels and spring onions and cook for a further 2 minutes. Remove, season to taste with salt and pepper and scatter over the spinach. Reserve.

3 Meanwhile, fill a frying pan with cold water and bring to the boil, then reduce the heat to a gentle simmer. Carefully break an egg into a cup and slip into the water. Add the remaining eggs and cook for 4–5 minutes, or until set. Carefully remove the eggs with a slotted spoon and arrange on top of the spinach mixture.

4 Melt the remaining butter in a saucepan and stir in the flour. Cook for 2 minutes, then remove from the heat and gradually stir in the milk. Return to the heat and cook, stirring constantly, until the mixture comes to the boil and has thickened. Stir in the mustard, then 55 g/2 oz of the cheese. Continue stirring until the cheese has melted. Add salt and pepper to taste, then pour over the eggs, completely covering them. Sprinkle with the remaining cheese.

5 Cook in the preheated oven for 20–25 minutes, or until piping hot and the top is golden brown and bubbling.

SWEET SOUFFLÉ OMELETTE

THE MOUTH-WATERING FILLING OF SWEET CHERRY TOMATOES, MUSHROOMS AND BABY SPINACH
LEAVES IS A WONDERFUL CONTRAST TO THE LIGHT FLUFFY OMELETTES, WHICH HAVE TO BE COOKED
ONE BY ONE. MAKE SURE THE OIL IS REALLY HOT BEFORE YOU COOK THE OMELETTES.

serves
4

preparation
50 minutes

cooking
20–25 minutes

ingredients
- 175 g/6 oz cherry tomatoes
- 225 g/8 oz mixed
  mushrooms (such as button,
  chestnut, shiitake, oyster
  and wild mushrooms)
- 4 tbsp fresh vegetable stock
- small bunch fresh thyme
- 8 eggs, separated (for 4 egg
  yolks and 8 egg whites)
- 8 tbsp water
- 4 tsp olive oil
- 25 g/1 oz baby spinach
  leaves, rinsed
- salt and pepper
- fresh thyme sprigs,
  to garnish

1 Halve the tomatoes and place
them in a saucepan. Wipe the
mushrooms with kitchen paper,
trim if necessary and slice if large.
Place in the saucepan.

2 Add the stock and thyme to the
pan. Bring to the boil, cover and
simmer for 5–6 minutes until
tender. Drain, remove the thyme and
discard, and keep the mixture warm.

3 Meanwhile, whisk the egg yolks
with the water until frothy. Mix the
8 egg whites in a clean, grease-free
bowl until stiff and dry.

4 Spoon the egg yolk mixture into
the egg whites and, using a metal
spoon, fold the whites and yolks
into each other until well mixed.
Take care not to knock out too
much of the air.

5 For each omelette, brush a small
omelette pan with 1 teaspoon oil
and heat until hot. Pour in a quarter
of the egg mixture and cook for
4–5 minutes, or until the mixture
has set. Preheat the grill to medium.

6 Slide the omelette pan under the
grill and finish cooking the omelette
for 2–3 minutes until set.

7 Transfer the omelette to a warmed
serving plate. Fill the omelette with
a few baby spinach leaves and a
quarter of the mushroom and tomato
mixture. Flip over the top of the
omelette, garnish with thyme sprigs
and serve immediately.

SPANISH TORTILLA

THERE IS HARDLY A TAPAS BAR IN SPAIN THAT DOESN'T SERVE THIS SIMPLE, BUT DELICIOUS, THICK OMELETTE. IT'S SO WELL LOVED IN SPAIN THAT, GENERATIONS AGO, IT WAS SAID THAT COUNTRY GIRLS COULD IMPROVE THEIR CHANCE OF MARRYING EARLY BY MAKING AN EXCELLENT TORTILLA.

makes
8–10 slices

preparation
30 minutes, plus 15 minutes' resting

cooking
35–40 minutes

ingredients
- 125 ml/4 fl oz olive oil
- 600 g/1 lb 5 oz potatoes, peeled and thinly sliced
- 1 large onion, thinly sliced
- 6 large eggs
- salt and pepper
- fresh flat-leaf parsley sprigs, to garnish

1 Heat a 25-cm/10-inch frying pan, preferably non-stick, over a high heat. Add the oil and heat. Reduce the heat, then add the potatoes and onion and cook for 15–20 minutes until the potatoes are tender.

2 Beat the eggs in a large bowl and season generously with salt and pepper. Drain the potatoes and onion through a sieve over a heatproof bowl to reserve the oil. Very gently stir the vegetables into the eggs; leave to stand for 10 minutes.

3 Use a wooden spoon or spatula to remove any crusty bits stuck to the base of the frying pan. Reheat the frying pan over a medium–high heat with 4 tablespoons of the reserved oil. Add the egg mixture and smooth the surface, pressing the potatoes and onions into an even layer.

4 Cook for about 5 minutes, shaking the frying pan occasionally, until the base is set. Use a spatula to loosen the side of the tortilla. Place a large plate over the top and carefully invert the frying pan and plate together so the tortilla drops onto the plate.

5 Add 1 tablespoon of the remaining reserved oil to the frying pan and swirl around. Carefully slide the tortilla back into the pan, cooked side up. Run the spatula around the tortilla, to tuck in the edge.

6 Continue cooking for 3 minutes, or until the eggs are set and the base is golden brown. Remove the frying pan from the heat and slide the tortilla onto a plate. Leave to stand for at least 5 minutes before cutting. Garnish with parsley sprigs and serve warm or at room temperature.

cook's tip

If you are worried about inverting the tortilla, finish cooking it in the frying pan under a medium–high grill, about 10 cm/4 inches from the heat source, until the runny egg mixture on top is set. The tortilla will not, however, have its characteristic 'rounded' edge.

QUICHE LORRAINE

THIS ELEGANT VERSION OF THE CLASSIC FRENCH TART IS DELICIOUS AS IT IS, OR IT CAN FORM THE BASIS OF AN EVEN MORE ELABORATE QUICHE. YOU CAN, FOR EXAMPLE, ARRANGE COOKED OR CANNED ASPARAGUS SPEARS ON THE TOP, OR SMOTHER IT WITH A LAYER OF SAUTÉED MUSHROOMS.

makes
1 x 23-cm/
9-inch quiche
preparation
30 minutes, plus
45 minutes'
chilling and
cooling
cooking
40–50 minutes

ingredients
PASTRY
• 175 g/6 oz plain flour, plus
  extra for dusting
• pinch of salt
• 115 g/4 oz butter, diced
• 25 g/1 oz pecorino cheese,
  grated
• 4–6 tbsp iced water

FILLING
• 115 g/4 oz Gruyère cheese,
  thinly sliced
• 55 g/2 oz Roquefort
  cheese, crumbled
• 175 g/6 oz rindless lean
  bacon, grilled until crisp
• 3 eggs
• 150 ml/5 fl oz double
  cream
• salt and pepper

1 To make the pastry, sift the flour with the salt into a bowl. Add the butter and rub it in with your fingertips until the mixture resembles breadcrumbs. Stir in the grated cheese, then stir in enough of the water to bind. Shape the dough into a ball, wrap in foil and chill in the refrigerator for 15 minutes.

2 Preheat the oven to 190°C/375°F/Gas Mark 5. Unwrap and roll out the dough on a lightly floured work surface. Use to line a 23-cm/9-inch quiche tin. Place the tin on a baking sheet. Prick the base of the pastry case all over with a fork, line with foil or greaseproof paper and fill with baking beans. Bake in the preheated oven for 15 minutes until the edges are set and dry. Remove the beans and lining and bake the pastry case for a further 5–7 minutes, or until golden. Leave to cool slightly.

3 For the filling, arrange the cheese over the base of the pastry case, then crumble the bacon evenly on top. Place the eggs and cream in a bowl and beat together until thoroughly combined. Add salt and pepper to taste. Pour the mixture into the pastry case and return to the oven for 20 minutes, or until the filling is golden and set.

4 Remove from the oven and cool the quiche in the tin for 10 minutes. Transfer to a wire rack to cool completely. Cover and store in the refrigerator, but return to room temperature before serving.

CHEESE FONDUE (BLUE CHEESE)

IT'S GOOD TO SEE THE CLASSIC SWISS FONDUE RETURNING TO POPULARITY – IT'S EASY, INEXPENSIVE AND DELICIOUS. AS A TRADITIONAL FORFEIT, YOU HAVE TO DRINK A GLASS OF WINE EVERY TIME YOUR DIPPER FALLS OFF THE FORK, SO THE EVENING SHOULD GO WITH A SWING.

serves
4

preparation
10 minutes

cooking
20 minutes

ingredients
- 1 garlic clove, peeled and halved
- 425 ml/15 fl oz dry white wine
- 5 tbsp brandy
- 350 g/12 oz Gruyère cheese, grated
- 350 g/12 oz dolcelatte cheese, crumbled
- 1 tbsp cornflour
- 2 tbsp single cream
- salt and pepper

DIPPERS
- fresh crusty bread, cut into bite-sized pieces
- bite-sized pieces of lightly cooked vegetables wrapped in cooked ham or strips of lightly cooked bacon

1 Rub the inside of a flameproof fondue pot with the garlic. Discard the garlic. Pour in the wine and 3 tablespoons of the brandy, then transfer to the hob and bring to a gentle simmer over a low heat. Add a small handful of the cheeses and stir constantly until melted. Continue to add the cheese gradually, stirring constantly after each addition, until all the cheese has been added. Continue to stir until thoroughly melted and bubbling gently.

2 Mix the cornflour with the remaining brandy in a small bowl. Stir the cornflour mixture into the fondue and continue to stir for 3–4 minutes until thickened and bubbling. Stir in the cream and season to taste with salt and pepper.

3 Using protective gloves, transfer the fondue pot to a lit tabletop burner. To serve, allow your guests to spear pieces of bread and ham-wrapped vegetables onto fondue forks and dip them into the fondue.

cook's tip

It is important to add the cheese gradually and stir constantly until it has completely melted before adding any more. Otherwise, the mixture will 'split'– that is, the fat will separate. Keep the heat very low and, ideally, use an earthenware fondue pot rather than a metal one.

AUBERGINE GRATIN

THIS DISH IS FULL OF MEDITERRANEAN FLAVOURS, AND IS RICH IN VITAMINS, INCLUDING VITAMIN C, AS WELL AS MINERALS AND PROTEIN. IT MAKES AN EXCELLENT APPETIZER, OR A SATISFYING LUNCH OR SUPPER IF ACCOMPANIED BY SOME FRESH CRUSTY BREAD.

serves
4 as a starter

preparation
15 minutes

cooking
40 minutes

ingredients
- 4 tbsp olive oil
- 2 onions, finely chopped
- 2 garlic cloves, very finely chopped
- 2 aubergines, thickly sliced
- 3 tbsp chopped fresh flat-leaf parsley
- ½ tsp dried thyme
- 400 g/14 oz canned chopped tomatoes
- 175 g/6 oz mozzarella cheese, coarsely grated
- 6 tbsp freshly grated Parmesan cheese
- salt and pepper

1 Heat the oil in a frying pan over a medium heat. Add the onion and cook for 5 minutes, or until softened. Add the garlic and cook for a few seconds, or until just beginning to colour. Using a slotted spoon, transfer the onion mixture to a plate. Cook the aubergine slices in batches in the same pan until they are just lightly browned.

2 Preheat the oven to 200°C/400°F/Gas Mark 6. Arrange a layer of aubergine slices in the base of a shallow ovenproof dish. Sprinkle with some of the parsley, thyme, salt and pepper. Add a layer of onion, tomatoes and mozzarella, sprinkling parsley, thyme, salt and pepper over each layer.

3 Continue layering, finishing with a layer of aubergine slices. Sprinkle with the Parmesan cheese. Bake, uncovered, in the preheated oven for 20–30 minutes, or until the top is golden and the aubergines are tender. Serve hot.

cook's tip

It is a good idea to salt the aubergine slices first in order to draw out some of their bitterness. Simply sprinkle them with salt and leave them in a colander for an hour. Then rinse well, carefully squeeze out the moisture, and pat dry with kitchen paper.

PANCAKES

IN BRITAIN PANCAKES ARE ALWAYS ASSOCIATED WITH SHROVE TUESDAY, OR 'PANCAKE DAY', WHEN WE ARE MEANT TO USE UP ANY RICH FOODS – PARTICULARLY EGGS – WHICH SHOULD NOT BE EATEN DURING LENT. IN OTHER COUNTRIES THE DAY IS KNOWN AS 'MARDI GRAS' OR 'FAT TUESDAY'.

makes
10

preparation
10 minutes,
plus 30 minutes'
resting

cooking
15 minutes

ingredients
- 100 g/3 ½ oz plain flour
- pinch of salt
- 1 egg, beaten
- 300 ml/10 fl oz milk
- 10 tsp butter (for sweet pancakes) or oil (for savoury ones)

TO SERVE
- lemon wedges
- caster sugar
- warmed honey or jam

1 Place the flour and salt in a mixing bowl. Make a well in the centre and add the egg and half the milk. Using a whisk, beat the egg and milk together and gradually incorporate the flour. Continue beating until the mixture is smooth and there are no lumps. Gradually beat in the remaining milk. Pour the batter mixture into a jug and leave to stand for 30 minutes.

2 Heat an 18-cm/7-inch heavy-based frying pan over a medium heat. Add 1 teaspoon of the butter or oil, depending on what you are going to eat with the pancakes.

3 Pour in enough batter to just cover the base and swirl the batter around the frying pan while tilting it so that you have a thin, even layer. Cook for about 30 seconds and then lift up the edge of the pancake and see if it is brown. Loosen the pancake around the edges and flip it over with a spatula or palette knife. Alternatively, have a go at tossing the pancake by flipping the pan quickly with a deft flick of the wrist and catching it carefully.

4 Cook on the other side until golden brown, then turn out onto a warmed plate, cover with foil and keep warm while you cook the pancakes in the remaining butter or oil. Layer the pancakes with greaseproof paper so you can separate them at the end.

5 Serve the pancakes with lemon and sugar, warmed honey or jam, or a filling of your choice.

MERINGUES

THESE ARE JUST AS MERINGUES SHOULD BE – AS LIGHT AS AIR AND AT THE SAME TIME CRISP, WITH A MELT-IN-THE-MOUTH QUALITY. MAKE SURE THAT THE BOWL YOU USE TO THE WHISK EGG WHITES IS COMPLETELY CLEAN AND GREASE-FREE, OR YOUR MERINGUE MIXTURE WILL COLLAPSE.

makes
13

preparation
15 minutes, plus
8 hours' cooling

cooking
1½ hours

ingredients
• 4 egg whites
• salt
• 125 g/4½ oz granulated sugar
• 125 g/4½ oz caster sugar
• 300 ml/10 fl oz double cream, lightly whipped, to serve

1 Preheat the oven to 120°C/250°F/Gas Mark ½. Line 3 baking trays with sheets of baking paper.

2 Place the egg whites and a pinch of salt in a large clean bowl and, using an electric hand-held whisk or balloon whisk, whisk until stiff. (You should be able to turn the bowl upside down without any movement from the whisked egg whites.)

3 Whisk in the granulated sugar, a little at a time; the meringue should begin to look glossy at this stage.

4 Sprinkle in the caster sugar, a little at a time, and continue whisking until all the sugar has been incorporated and the meringue is thick, white and forms peaks.

5 Transfer the meringue mixture to a piping bag fitted with a 2-cm/¾-inch star nozzle. Pipe about 26 small whirls of the mixture onto the prepared baking trays.

6 Bake in the preheated oven for 1½ hours, or until the meringues are pale golden in colour and can be easily lifted off the paper. Leave them to cool overnight in the turned-off oven.

7 Just before serving, sandwich the meringues together in pairs with the cream and arrange on a serving plate.

variation
For a finer texture, replace the granulated sugar with caster sugar.

LEMON MERINGUE PIE

A SWEET, TANGY FILLING AND A MELT-IN-THE-MOUTH TOPPING CONTRAST SUPERBLY WITH A CRISP
PASTRY CASE. THIS POPULAR DESSERT LOOKS EVERY BIT AS LOVELY AS IT TASTES. IT'S USUALLY
SERVED HOT AND THERE'S RARELY ANY LEFT OVER, BUT, IF THERE IS, IT'S ALSO DELICIOUS COLD.

serves
4

preparation
25 minutes,
plus 30 minutes'
resting

cooking
1 hour

ingredients

PASTRY
- 200 g/7 oz plain flour, plus
  extra for dusting
- 100 g/3¾ oz butter, diced,
  plus extra for greasing
- 50 g/1¾ oz icing
  sugar, sifted
- finely grated rind of
  1 lemon
- 1 egg yolk, beaten
- 3 tbsp milk

FILLING
- 3 tbsp cornflour
- 300 ml/10 fl oz cold water
- juice and grated rind of
  2 lemons
- 175 g/6 oz caster sugar
- 2 eggs, separated

1 To make the pastry, sift the flour into a large bowl. Add the butter and rub it in until the mixture resembles breadcrumbs. Mix in the remaining ingredients. Knead briefly on a lightly floured work surface. Leave to rest for 30 minutes.

2 Preheat the oven to 180°C/350°F/Gas Mark 4. Grease a 20-cm/8-inch ovenproof flan dish with butter.

3 Roll out the pastry to a thickness of 5 mm/¼ inch and line the dish

with it. Prick with a fork, then line with greaseproof paper and fill with baking beans. Bake for 15 minutes. Remove from the oven, then reduce the oven temperature to 150°C/300°F/Gas Mark 2.

4 To make the filling, mix the cornflour with a little water to form a paste. Pour the remaining water into a saucepan. Stir in the lemon juice and rind and cornflour paste. Bring to the boil, while stirring, and cook for 2 minutes. Cool slightly,

then stir in 5 tablespoons of the sugar and the egg yolks and pour into the pastry case. Whisk the egg whites in a separate bowl until stiff. Gradually whisk in the remaining sugar and spread over the pie. Bake in the oven for 40 minutes, or until the meringue is light brown. Remove and serve.

cook's tip

When making meringue it is important to use a clean, dry, grease-free bowl. To produce a perfectly smooth meringue, whisk in the sugar a tablespoon at a time.

CRÈME BRÛLÉE TARTS

CARAMELIZED SUGAR MAKES A CONTRASTING AND DECORATIVE TOPPING ON THE CREAMY, MELT-IN-THE-MOUTH FILLING IN THESE TARTS. IT'S FUNNY THAT WE ALL THINK CRÈME BRÛLÉE IS FRENCH BECAUSE IT WAS ACTUALLY INVENTED IN THE ENGLISH UNIVERSITY TOWN OF CAMBRIDGE.

serves
6

preparation
25 minutes, plus
2½ hours' cooling
and chilling

cooking
30 minutes

ingredients

PASTRY
- 150 g/5½ oz plain flour, plus extra for dusting
- 25 g/1 oz caster sugar
- 125 g/4½ oz butter, cut into small pieces
- 1 tbsp water
- demerara sugar, for sprinkling
- fresh redcurrants, to decorate

FILLING
- 4 egg yolks
- 50 g/1¾ oz caster sugar
- 400 ml/14 fl oz double cream
- 1 tsp vanilla essence

1 To make the pastry, place the flour and sugar in a large bowl. Add the butter and rub it in with your fingertips until it resembles breadcrumbs. Add the water and mix to a soft dough. Wrap the dough in clingfilm and leave to chill for 30 minutes.

2 Roll out the dough on a lightly floured work surface and use to line 6 x 10-cm/4-inch tart tins. Prick the base of the pastry with a fork and leave to chill for 20 minutes.

3 Preheat the oven to 190°C/375°F/Gas Mark 5. Line the pastry cases with foil and baking beans and bake in the oven for 15 minutes. Remove the foil and beans and cook for a further 10 minutes until crisp and golden. Leave to cool.

4 Meanwhile, make the filling. Place the egg yolks and caster sugar in a bowl and beat together until thick and pale. Heat the cream and vanilla essence in a saucepan until just below boiling point, then pour it onto the egg mixture, whisking constantly.

5 Return the mixture to a clean saucepan and bring to just below boiling point, stirring, until thick. Do not boil or it will curdle.

6 Leave the mixture to cool slightly, then pour it into the tart tins. Leave to cool then leave to chill overnight.

7 Preheat the grill to medium. Sprinkle the tarts with the demerara sugar. Place under the hot grill for a few minutes until browned on top. Cool, then leave to chill for 2 hours before serving with fresh redcurrants.

cook's tip

The secret of crisp, light pastry is to handle it as little as possible. When you're rubbing in the butter, use only the tips of your fingers, as the palms of your hands will warm up and partially melt the butter. If it's a hot day — or the kitchen is well heated — rinse your hands under cold running water, then dry before you start. Place the water for mixing the dough in the refrigerator to chill before using.

CRÈME CARAMEL

THIS CREAMY DESSERT WITH ITS CARAMELIZED TOPPING IS A FAVOURITE THROUGHOUT EUROPE –
CALLED CRÈME CARAMEL IN FRANCE, FLAN IN SPAIN AND BAKED CUSTARD IN BRITAIN. THE
CONTRASTING TEXTURES AND FLAVOURS MAKE IT A TOP CHOICE FOR ADULTS AND KIDS ALIKE.

serves
4–6
preparation
15 minutes, plus
24 hours' chilling
cooking
1½–1¾ hours

ingredients
- butter, for greasing
- 175 g/6 oz plus 2 tbsp
  caster sugar
- 4 tbsp water
- ½ lemon
- 500 ml/18 fl oz milk
- 1 vanilla pod
- 2 large eggs
- 2 large egg yolks

TO DECORATE
- sugared fruit
- fresh mint sprigs

1 Preheat the oven to 160°C/
325°F/Gas Mark 3. Lightly grease
the side of a 1.2-litre/2-pint soufflé
dish. To make the caramel, place
75 g/2¾ oz sugar with the water in
a saucepan over a medium–high heat
and cook, stirring, until the sugar
dissolves. Boil until the syrup turns
a deep golden brown.

2 Immediately remove from the heat
and add in a few drops of lemon
juice. Pour into the soufflé dish and
swirl around. Reserve.

3 Pour the milk into a saucepan.
Slit the vanilla pod lengthways and
add it to the milk. Bring to the boil,
remove the saucepan from the heat
and stir in the remaining sugar,
stirring until it dissolves. Reserve.

4 Beat the eggs and egg yolks
together in a bowl. Pour the milk
mixture over them, whisking.
Remove the vanilla pod. Strain
the egg mixture into a bowl, then
transfer to the soufflé dish.

5 Place the dish in a roasting tin with
enough boiling water to come two-
thirds up the side.

6 Bake in the preheated oven for
75–90 minutes, or until a knife
inserted in the centre comes out
clean. Leave to cool completely.
Cover with clingfilm and leave
to chill for at least 24 hours.

7 Run a round-bladed knife around
the edge. Place an up-turned serving
plate on top of the soufflé dish, then
invert the plate and dish, giving a
sharp shake halfway over. Lift off
the soufflé dish and serve, decorated
with sugared fruit and mint sprigs.

RICH VANILLA ICE CREAM

THIS RICH ICE CREAM PROVIDES A DELICIOUS FINISH TO A MEAL. YOU CAN SERVE IT EITHER AS IT IS, OR WITH A TOPPING OF YOUR CHOICE, SUCH AS A CHOCOLATE OR FRUIT SAUCE. IT ALSO MAKES AN EXCELLENT ACCOMPANIMENT TO FRUIT DESSERTS AND SWEET PIES.

serves
4–6
preparation
20 minutes, plus 30 minutes' infusing and 4–6 hours' cooling and freezing
cooking
15–20 minutes

ingredients
- 300 ml/10 fl oz single cream
- 300 ml/10 fl oz double cream or 600 ml/1 pint whipping cream
- 1 vanilla pod
- 4 large egg yolks
- 115 g/4 oz caster sugar

1 Pour the single and double cream or whipping cream into a large heavy-based saucepan. Split open the vanilla pod and scrape out the seeds into the cream, then add the whole vanilla pod. Bring almost to the boil, then remove the pan from the heat and leave to infuse for 30 minutes.

2 Place the egg yolks and sugar in a large bowl and whisk together until pale and the mixture leaves a trail when the whisk is lifted. Remove the vanilla pod from the cream, then slowly add the cream to the egg mixture, stirring constantly with a wooden spoon. Strain the mixture into the rinsed-out saucepan or a double boiler and cook over a low heat for 10–15 minutes, stirring constantly, until the mixture thickens enough to coat the back of the spoon. Do not allow the mixture to boil or it will curdle. Remove the custard from the heat and leave to cool for at least 1 hour, stirring occasionally to prevent a skin from forming.

3 If using an ice cream machine, churn the cold custard in the machine following the manufacturer's instructions. Alternatively, freeze the custard in a freezerproof container, uncovered, for 1–2 hours, or until it begins to set around the edges. Turn the custard into a bowl and stir with a fork or beat in a food processor until smooth. Return to the freezer and freeze for a further 2–3 hours, or until firm or required. Cover the container with a lid for storing.

CHOCOLATE CHIP ICE CREAM
WITH HOT CHOCOLATE FUDGE SAUCE

THE ADDITION OF CHOCOLATE PIECES AND THE CHOCOLATE FUDGE SAUCE IN THIS RECIPE
PROVIDES A PERFECT COUNTERPOINT TO THE CREAMINESS OF THE ICE CREAM. THIS IS A POPULAR
DESSERT WITH CHILDREN AND ADULTS ALIKE.

serves
4–6

preparation
20 minutes, plus
30 minutes'
infusing and 4–6
hours' cooling
and freezing

cooking
15–20 minutes

ingredients
- 300 ml/10 fl oz full-fat milk
- 1 vanilla pod
- 115 g/4 oz milk chocolate
- 85 g/3 oz caster sugar
- 3 egg yolks
- 300 ml/10 fl oz whipping cream

CHOCOLATE FUDGE SAUCE
- 50 g/1¾ oz milk chocolate, broken into pieces
- 25 g/1 oz butter
- 4 tbsp full-fat milk
- 225 g/8 oz soft light brown sugar
- 2 tbsp golden syrup

1 Pour the milk into a heavy-based saucepan. Add the vanilla pod and bring almost to the boil. Remove from the heat and leave to infuse for 30 minutes. Meanwhile, chop the chocolate into small pieces.

2 Place the sugar and egg yolks in a large bowl and whisk together until pale and the mixture leaves a trail when the whisk is lifted. Remove the vanilla pod from the milk, then slowly add the milk to the sugar mixture, stirring constantly with a wooden spoon. Strain the mixture into the rinsed-out saucepan or a double boiler and cook over a low heat for 10–15 minutes, stirring constantly, until the mixture thickens enough to coat the back of the spoon. Do not boil or it will curdle.

3 Remove the custard from the heat and leave to cool for at least 1 hour, stirring occasionally to prevent a skin

from forming. Meanwhile, whip the cream until it holds its shape. Chill in the refrigerator until required.

4 If using an ice cream machine, fold the cold custard into the whipped cream, then churn in the machine following the manufacturer's instructions. Just before the ice cream freezes, add the chocolate pieces. Alternatively, freeze the custard in a freezerproof container, uncovered, for 1–2 hours, or until it begins to set around the edges. Turn the custard into a bowl and stir with a fork or beat in a food processor until smooth. Fold in the whipped cream and chocolate pieces. Return to the freezer and freeze for a further 2–3 hours, or until firm or required. Cover with a lid for storing.

5 Make the sauce just before serving the ice cream. Place the chocolate,

butter and milk in a heatproof bowl set over a saucepan of simmering water and heat gently, stirring occasionally, until the chocolate has melted and the sauce is smooth. Transfer the mixture to a heavy-based saucepan and stir in the sugar and syrup. Heat gently until the sugar has dissolved, then bring to the boil and boil, without stirring, for 5 minutes. Serve the hot sauce poured over the ice cream.

TIRAMISÙ

LITERALLY MEANING 'PICK ME UP', THIS MELT-IN-THE-MOUTH DESSERT HAS A REPUTATION FOR DOING EXACTLY THAT. IT'S NOT A TRADITIONAL DISH, BUT SINCE ITS INVENTION ABOUT THIRTY YEARS AGO IT HAS BECOME A FIRM FAVOURITE ACROSS THE GLOBE.

serves
4

preparation
20 minutes, plus
2 hours' chilling

cooking
none

ingredients
- 200 ml/7 fl oz strong black coffee, cooled to room temperature
- 4 tbsp orange liqueur, such as Cointreau
- 3 tbsp orange juice
- 16 Italian sponge fingers
- 250 g/9 oz mascarpone cheese
- 300 ml/10 fl oz double cream, lightly whipped
- 3 tbsp icing sugar
- grated rind of 1 orange
- 60 g/2 ¼ oz plain dark chocolate, grated

TO DECORATE
- chopped toasted almonds
- crystallized orange peel
- chocolate shavings

1 Pour the cooled coffee into a jug and stir in the orange liqueur and orange juice. Place 8 of the sponge fingers in the base of a serving dish, then pour over half of the coffee mixture.

2 Place the mascarpone in a separate bowl together with the cream, icing sugar and orange rind and mix well. Spread half of the mascarpone mixture over the coffee-soaked sponge fingers, then arrange the remaining sponge fingers on top. Pour over the remaining coffee mixture then spread over the remaining mascarpone mixture. Scatter over the grated chocolate and leave to chill in the refrigerator for at least 2 hours. Serve decorated with chopped toasted almonds, crystallized orange peel and chocolate shavings.

 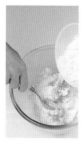 

cook's tip
You can decorate this dessert with chopped mixed nuts instead of chopped toasted almonds. Alternatively, try replacing the orange liqueur with the same quantity of almond-flavour liqueur, such as Amaretto.

CHOCOLATE MILK SHAKE

A CHOCOLATE MILK SHAKE IS A SPECIAL TREAT AT ANY TIME OF DAY, AND THIS ONE IS THE ULTIMATE INDULGENCE. IT HAS A RICH, DEEP MOCHA FLAVOUR, AND THE CHOCOLATE ICE CREAM MAKES IT THICK ENOUGH TO EAT WITH A SPOON. UNSURPRISINGLY, IT IS VERY POPULAR WITH CHILDREN.

serves
4

preparation
10 minutes

cooking
none

ingredients
- 300 ml/10 fl oz milk
- 2 tbsp chocolate syrup
- 2 tbsp coffee syrup
- 800 g/1 lb 12 oz chocolate ice cream

TO DECORATE
- 150 ml/5 fl oz double cream, whipped
- cocoa powder, for sprinkling

1 Pour the milk, chocolate syrup and coffee syrup into a food processor or blender and gently process until blended. Add the ice cream and process to a smooth consistency.

2 Pour the mixture into tall glasses.

3 To decorate, spoon the cream into a piping bag fitted with a large, star-shaped nozzle. Pipe generous amounts of cream on top of the milk shakes. Sprinkle over the cocoa powder and serve with straws.

NECTARINE MELT

MANGO AND NECTARINE IS AN INSPIRED COMBINATION, MADE ALL THE MORE SPECIAL WITH THE CLEVER ADDITION OF LEMON SORBET. NOT ONLY DOES THIS MAKE A DELICIOUS DRINK THAT CAN BE SERVED AS A DESSERT, IT IS ALSO A NUTRITIOUS AND HEALTHY CHOICE.

serves
2

preparation
10 minutes

cooking
none

ingredients
- 250 ml/9 fl oz milk
- 350 g/12 oz lemon sorbet
- 1 ripe mango, stoned and diced
- 2 ripe nectarines, stoned and diced

1 Pour the milk into a food processor, add half of the lemon sorbet and process gently until combined. Add the remaining sorbet and process until smooth.

2 When the mixture is thoroughly blended, gradually add the diced mango and nectarines and process until smooth.

3 Pour the mixture into tall glasses, add straws and serve.

2

FISH AND SHELLFISH

WHO CAN RESIST THE AROMA AND FLAVOUR OF FRESH
FISH AND SHELLFISH, LOVINGLY PREPARED? YOU CAN
COOK AND SERVE SEAFOOD IN A MULTITUDE OF WAYS,
FROM STIR-FRIES AND CHARGRILLS TO BAKES AND
BARBECUES. THIS SECTION PRESENTS A STUNNING
COLLECTION OF DISHES THAT YOU WILL WANT TO
MAKE AGAIN AND AGAIN.

INTRODUCTION

FISH AND SHELLFISH ARE VERY GOOD FOR YOU: THEY ARE FULL OF PROTEIN, IODINE AND MAGNESIUM, WHICH ARE ESSENTIAL FOR BUILDING TISSUE, REGULATING THE METABOLISM AND KEEPING THE BOWEL HEALTHY. OILY FISH IN PARTICULAR ARE RICH IN ESSENTIAL FATTY ACIDS, WHICH HELP TO LOWER CHOLESTEROL AND SUPPORT THE IMMUNE SYSTEM.

Buying and storing fresh fish

Nowadays there is a wide variety of fish available. You can buy fresh flat fish, such as plaice, sole or halibut, or round fish, such as cod, haddock, salmon or trout. You can also buy preserved fish, which have been smoked, dried or salted. When buying fresh whole fish, choose those that smell fresh or that smell of the sea. Avoid any that smell of ammonia. They should have moist, full eyes and shiny, firm bodies. You can ask your fishmonger to skin, gut and fillet whole larger fish for you. Refrigerate the fish as soon as you get home. Fresh fish is best eaten on the day of purchase, but it will keep for a day or two if necessary. Frozen fish will keep for up to six months in the freezer, but will need thawing in the refrigerator for at least 8 hours before use. Oily fish, such as mackerel, should be wrapped well in clean damp cloths and stored in the refrigerator. Lower-fat white fish, such as cod and haddock, can be covered with clingfilm. Use it by the 'best before' date on the packaging.

Smoked fish

You can buy a wide variety of smoked fish. Smoked salmon is very popular and is usually served cold with slices of lemon. Smoked trout has a mild flavour and is best partnered with horseradish or slices of lemon. Smoked mackerel has a rich flavour and needs a sharp sauce, such as dill or mustard. Smoked haddock is delicious served with a creamy sauce or in kedgerees, while smoked cod is popular in pies. Kippers are best grilled or poached. Fresh smoked fish should be wrapped well in clingfilm and stored in the refrigerator. Smoked fish is often bought vacuum-packed. Store it in the refrigerator and use by the 'best before' date.

Brown trout

Dover sole

White fish

There is a wide range of white fish available these days. Some are low in fat, such as cod and haddock, while others are rich in healthy essential fatty acids, such as sardines.

Cod

This round fish has firm, white, flaky flesh and a mild flavour. It can be baked, grilled, poached, pan-fried or deep-fried in batter or breadcrumbs.

Haddock

Like cod, this round fish has firm, white flesh and a mild flavour. It can be baked, grilled, poached, pan-fried or deep-fried, and in many recipes is interchangeable with cod.

Hake

Milder-flavoured than cod, this round fish can be fried, baked or steamed and is also useful in soups.

Trout

Like salmon, this round fish is available farmed or wild, but the wild variety is rare. It can be pan-fried, grilled, poached, steamed, barbecued or baked. This is an oily fish, which means that it is rich in essential fatty acids.

Halibut and turbot

These large flat fish both have firm flesh and an excellent flavour and are interchangeable in many recipes. You can fry, poach, steam, grill or bake both these fish.

Sole

This flat fish comes in two varieties – lemon sole and Dover sole – and in different sizes. Dover sole has an excellent flavour and needs little added flavouring to bring out its best qualities. Lemon sole has less flavour, but is improved with the addition of other flavourings. You can pan-fry, deep-fry, bake, steam or grill both types.

Herrings, sardines, sprats and whitebait

These small fish have lots of bones, so it is best to ask your fishmonger to remove the innards and as many bones as possible. They can be barbecued, deep-fried, baked or grilled. They are also oily fish, and therefore rich in essential fatty acids.

Mackerel

This is a round fish with a delicious flavour. It is at its best when simply grilled, but can also be fried or barbecued. It is another oily fish that is good for your health.

Plaice

This flat fish needs extra flavouring but is very good when pan-fried or deep-fried, baked, grilled, poached or steamed.

Salmon

This round fish is available farmed or wild. A popular fish, it can be pan-fried, grilled, poached, steamed, barbecued or baked. Salmon en croûte or en papillote (salmon baked in pastry or in parchment) are particularly popular dishes. Salmon is another oily fish.

Tuna

This is a round oily fish with firm, 'meaty' flesh that makes wonderful steaks with only a very mild fish flavour. The steaks are excellent chargrilled for 2–3 minutes each side (do not overcook). You can also bake, barbecue, grill, braise or stew fresh tuna.

Herring

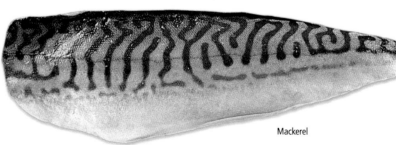

Mackerel

Buying and storing shellfish

Shellfish can cause food poisoning, so always buy them as fresh as possible from a reputable supplier. Shellfish should smell fresh or sweet – avoid any that smell of chlorine or sulphur. If you are buying mussels, clams or oysters, the shells should be tightly closed and not cracked or damaged.

Refrigerate shellfish in a covered container as soon as you get home and use on the day of purchase. If you buy live lobster or crabs, place something heavy on top of the container to stop them escaping. Handle shellfish as little as possible and prepare with thoroughly clean equipment and hands.

Preparation and cooking techniques

Preparation techniques vary enormously depending on the type of shellfish you are using. If you are in any doubt, your local fishmonger will be able to give you advice. Shellfish does not need to cook for long periods of time so stick to the recommended cooking times. Do not overcook it or you could impair the texture and/or taste. Squid, for example, becomes unpleasantly rubbery if cooked for too long.

Crab

Fresh and frozen shellfish

You can buy fresh shellfish from fishmongers and many shops and supermarkets. In some cases, prawns for example, you can also buy them ready prepared, cooked and frozen.

Crab and lobster

You can buy crabs and lobsters alive or cooked. If you buy them live, make sure the claws are tied with string to keep them still. Put them in the freezer for 1 hour before cooking to desensitize. To cook, take a large saucepan and pour in enough water or stock to cover the crab or lobster. Bring it to the boil, add the crab or lobster, cover the pan and boil until it turns red. Allow 5 minutes of cooking for every 450 g/1 lb) of crab. For a lobster, allow 5 minutes for the first 450 g/ 1 lb, plus an extra 3 minutes for each further 450 g/1 lb. To remove the cooked meat from the crab, crack the claws and remove and reserve the white meat. Snap off the tail, then use your hands to break the shell. Lift out the body, cut it in half lengthways and scoop out the meat. Then lift out the brown meat from the shell. The edible parts of a lobster are the meat in the tail and claws, the liver, and the roe if the lobster is female. Cooking a lobster and removing the meat can be fiddly, however, so it is usually best to ask your fishmonger to do this for you.

Mussels

Mussels

Use mussels on the day of purchase and keep them in lightly salted water before use. To clean and debeard them, use a small knife to scrape off any barnacles from the shells, then pull out and discard any clumps of hair (these are called 'beards'). Use a stiff brush to scrub the shells under cold running water, then tap them all with the handle of the knife and discard any that do not close tightly. To steam them, heat a little liquid (water, stock or wine) in a large saucepan, add the cleaned mussels, cover the pan and steam them, shaking the pan occasionally, for 5–6 minutes. Remove from the heat and discard any mussels that remain closed. You can also grill or bake them half-shelled, or stew them shelled.

Oysters

These shellfish are usually eaten raw. Use a stiff brush to scrub the shells under cold running water, and discard any that are open. To open an oyster, insert a knife blade between the two shell halves and twist it to prise them open. Use a spoon to lift out the oyster inside (you will need to cut it from the muscle underneath). Serve it on a half-shell. You can also bake or grill oysters in their half-shells, or stew them shelled.

Prawns

These come in different sizes and you can buy them peeled or unpeeled, cooked or raw. Cooked, peeled prawns are also available frozen. To peel and devein a raw prawn, carefully peel off the shell (you can remove the tail or leave it on for decorative effect). Using a small knife, make a shallow cut along the dark vein to reveal it, then remove it with the knife's tip. Discard the vein, then rinse the prawn under cold running water and pat dry with kitchen paper. Prawns require very little cooking – for example, you need to stir-fry them for only 2–3 minutes until they turn pink. You can pan-fry, stir-fry, grill, bake, barbecue or steam them.

Scallops

These have a delicate flavour and are becoming increasingly popular. They should be creamy-white with pink corals. They need a minimal amount of cooking, usually 1–2 minutes on each side if you are pan-frying them shelled. You can also grill or bake them in their half-shells.

Squid

You can buy squid whole or already prepared. The edible parts are the tentacles, fins, pouch and the ink. Sauté the squid for 2–3 minutes only – do not overcook it or it will be rubbery. You can also deep-fry, bake, poach and stew it.

Clams

Use a stiff brush to scrub the shells under cold running water, and discard any that open. To open a clam, insert a knife blade between the two shell halves and twist it to prise them open. Use a spoon to lift out the soft flesh inside. You can eat clams raw, or you can steam them in their shells for 4 minutes or until they have opened. You can also bake or grill them in their half-shells, or stew them shelled.

Prawns

Lobster

Squid

Oyster

SALMON COULIBIAC

THIS DELICIOUS FISH PIE IS IDEAL FOR ENTERTAINING. THE RECIPE ORIGINATED IN RUSSIA AND TRADITIONALLY CONTAINED BUCKWHEAT INSTEAD OF RICE. THE ORIGINAL VERSION WAS ALSO MUCH LARGER AND NEEDED MORE THAN ONE PERSON TO CARRY IT TO THE TABLE.

serves
4

preparation
40 minutes

cooking
50–60 minutes

ingredients
- 50 g/1¾ oz long-grain rice
- pinch of salt
- 3 eggs
- 2 tbsp vegetable oil
- 1 onion, finely chopped
- 1 garlic clove, crushed
- 1 tsp finely grated lemon rind
- 2 tbsp chopped fresh parsley
- 1 tbsp chopped fresh dill
- 450 g/1 lb salmon fillet, skinned and cubed
- 500 g/1 lb 2 oz puff pastry
- butter, for greasing
- beaten egg, to glaze

QUICK HOLLANDAISE SAUCE
- 175 g/6 oz butter
- 1 tbsp wine vinegar
- 2 tbsp lemon juice
- 3 egg yolks
- salt and pepper

1 Preheat the oven to 200°C/400°F/Gas Mark 6. Cook the rice with the pinch of salt in plenty of boiling water for 7–8 minutes until tender. Drain well and reserve. Bring a small saucepan of water to the boil and add the eggs. Cook for 8 minutes from when the water returns to the boil. Drain and refresh under cold water. When cool enough to handle, shell and slice thinly.

2 Heat the oil in a frying pan. Add the onion and cook gently for 5 minutes, or until softened. Add the garlic and cook for a further 30 seconds. Add to the rice with the lemon rind, parsley, dill and salmon.

3 Roll out the pastry to a rectangle measuring 40 x 30 cm/16 x 12 inches. Lift the pastry onto a lightly greased baking sheet. Spoon half the filling onto one half of the pastry, leaving a border of about 2 cm/¾ inch. Top with the sliced eggs, then the remaining filling.

4 Dampen the outside edges of the pastry with a little beaten egg then fold over the remaining pastry. Crimp the edges to seal well. Mark the pastry using a small sharp knife, taking care not to cut through the pastry. Decorate with pastry trimmings and brush with beaten egg.

5 Bake in the preheated oven for 30–35 minutes, or until the pastry is risen and golden.

6 For the sauce, place the butter in a small saucepan and melt slowly. Place the wine vinegar and lemon juice in another saucepan and bring to the boil. Meanwhile, place the egg yolks and a pinch of salt in a food processor or blender and blend together. With the motor still running, gradually add the hot vinegar and lemon juice. When the butter begins to boil, start to pour this into the machine in a steady stream until all the butter has been added and the sauce has thickened. Season to taste with salt and pepper.

7 Keep warm by placing in a bowl over hot water. Serve the pie with the hollandaise sauce on the side.

FISH CAKES

THESE MOUTHWATERING FISH CAKES ARE FULL OF EXCITING ASIAN FLAVOURS TO TEMPT THE TASTE BUDS. THEY ARE IDEAL FOR ENTERTAINING BECAUSE YOU CAN MAKE THE FISH CAKES AND DIPPING SAUCE IN ADVANCE, THEN FRY THE FISH CAKES AND REHEAT THE SAUCE WHEN NEEDED.

serves
4

preparation
25 minutes,
plus 30 minutes'
cooling

cooking
20 minutes

ingredients
- 450 g/1 lb white fish fillets, skinned and cut into cubes
- 1 egg white
- 2 kaffir lime leaves, roughly torn
- 1 tbsp green curry paste
- 55 g/2 oz French beans, finely chopped
- 1 fresh red chilli, deseeded and finely chopped
- bunch of fresh coriander, chopped
- 2 tbsp vegetable or groundnut oil, for frying
- 1 fresh green chilli, deseeded and sliced, to serve

DIPPING SAUCE
- 115 g/4 oz caster sugar
- 1½ tbsp water
- 50 ml/2 fl oz white wine vinegar
- 1 small carrot, cut into thin batons
- 5-cm/2-inch piece cucumber, peeled, deseeded and cut into thin batons

1 Place the fish in a food processor with the egg white, lime leaves and curry paste and process until smooth. Transfer the mixture to a bowl and stir in the French beans, red chilli and coriander.

2 With dampened hands, shape the mixture into small patties, about 5 cm/2 inches across. Place them on a large plate in a single layer and chill for 30 minutes.

3 Meanwhile, make the dipping sauce. Place the sugar in a saucepan with the water and vinegar and heat gently, stirring until the sugar has dissolved. Add the carrot and cucumber, then remove from the heat and leave to cool.

4 Heat the oil in a frying pan and shallow fry the fish cakes, in batches, until golden brown on both sides. Drain on kitchen paper and keep warm while you cook the remaining batches. If you like, reheat the dipping sauce. Top the fish cakes with chilli slices and serve immediately with the dipping sauce.

GRILLED TROUT FILLETS

THESE LIGHTLY GRILLED TROUT FILLETS HAVE A DELICIOUS CRISPY COATING OF TOASTED NUTS AND MELTED CHEESE. THEY ARE RICH IN PROTEIN, AND ARE DELICIOUS SERVED WITH COOKED RICE AND TWISTS OF LEMON, OR FRESHLY BAKED WEDGES OF POTATO AND OTHER ROOT VEGETABLES.

serves
4

preparation
20 minutes

cooking
5 minutes

ingredients
- 2 tbsp chopped toasted hazelnuts
- 2 tbsp ground almonds
- 115 g/4 oz Cheddar cheese, grated
- 4 tbsp fresh breadcrumbs, white or wholemeal
- 1 egg
- 1 tbsp milk
- 4 brown trout fillets, about 175 g/6 oz each
- 2 tbsp plain flour
- salt and pepper
- fresh flat-leaf parsley sprigs, to garnish
- freshly cooked rice, to serve

1 Preheat the grill to medium. Place the hazelnuts and almonds in a large bowl. Add the cheese and breadcrumbs and mix together. Place the egg and milk in a separate bowl and beat together. Season to taste with salt and pepper.

2 Rinse the fish fillets and pat dry with kitchen paper. Coat the fillets in the flour, then dip them into the egg mixture. Transfer them to the bowl containing the nuts and cheese, and turn the fillets in the mixture until thoroughly coated.

3 Cook the fish under the hot grill for 5 minutes, turning once during the cooking time, or until golden and cooked through. Remove from the grill and transfer to warmed plates. Garnish with parsley sprigs and serve with freshly cooked rice.

GRILLED SARDINES

WHEN YOU DRIVE ALONG THE MEDITERRANEAN COAST, YOU'LL COME ACROSS SMALL HARBOURSIDE RESTAURANTS GRILLING THE DAY'S CATCH OF SARDINES. THIS RECIPE MAKES FULL USE OF THE WONDERFUL FLAVOURS OF THE MEDITERRANEAN, WITH A HINT OF CHILLI SPICE IN THE DRESSING.

serves
4–6

preparation
30 minutes plus
2½ hours' cooling
and chilling

cooking
3–5 minutes

ingredients
- 12 sardines
- olive oil
- fresh flat-leaf parsley sprigs, to garnish
- lemon wedges, to serve

DRESSING
- 150 ml/5 fl oz extra virgin olive oil
- finely grated rind of 1 large lemon
- 4 tbsp lemon juice, or to taste
- 4 shallots, thinly sliced
- 1 small fresh red chilli, deseeded and finely chopped
- 1 large garlic clove, finely chopped
- salt and pepper

1 Preheat the grill to medium. To make the dressing, place all the ingredients in a screw-top jar, season with salt and pepper, then shake until blended. Pour into a non-metallic baking dish that is large enough to hold the sardines in a single layer. Reserve until required.

2 To prepare the sardines, chop off the heads and make a slit all along the length of each belly. Pull out the insides, rinse the fish inside and out with cold water and pat dry with kitchen paper.

3 Line the grill pan with foil, shiny side up. Brush the foil with a little olive oil to prevent the sardines sticking. Arrange the sardines

on the foil in a single layer and brush with a little of the dressing. Grill under the hot grill for 90 seconds.

4 Turn the fish over, brush with a little more dressing and continue grilling for 90 seconds, or until they are cooked through and flake easily.

5 Transfer the fish to the dish with the dressing. Spoon the dressing over the fish and leave to cool completely. Cover and chill for at least 2 hours to allow the flavours to blend.

6 Transfer the sardines to a serving platter and garnish with parsley. Serve with lemon wedges for squeezing over.

GRILLED SEA BASS WITH STEWED ARTICHOKES

IN THIS IDEAL DISH FOR A LUNCH OR LIGHT SUPPER, BABY GLOBE ARTICHOKES ARE SLOWLY
COOKED WITH OLIVE OIL, GARLIC, THYME AND LEMON TO CREATE A SOFT BLEND OF FLAVOURS
THAT HARMONIZE VERY WELL WITH THE FISH, WITHOUT BEING OVERPOWERING.

serves
6

preparation
30 minutes

cooking
35–45 minutes

ingredients
- 1.8 kg/4 lb baby globe artichokes
- 2 ½ tbsp fresh lemon juice, plus the cut halves of the lemon
- 150 ml/5 fl oz olive oil
- 10 garlic cloves, finely sliced
- 1 tbsp fresh chopped thyme, plus extra to garnish
- 6 x 115 g/4 oz sea bass fillets
- 1 tbsp olive oil
- salt and pepper
- crusty bread, to serve

1 Peel away the tough outer leaves of each artichoke until the yellow-green heart is revealed. Slice off the pointed top at about halfway between the point and the top of the stem. Cut off the stem and pare off what is left of the dark green leaves around the bottom of the artichoke.

2 Submerge the prepared artichokes in water containing the cut halves of the lemon to prevent them browning. When all the artichokes have been prepared, turn them choke side down and slice thickly.

3 Heat the oil in a large saucepan. Add the artichoke pieces, garlic, thyme, lemon juice and seasoning, cover and cook the artichokes over a low heat for 20–30 minutes, without colouring, until tender.

4 Meanwhile, preheat a ridged grill pan or light a barbecue. Brush the sea bass fillets with the 1 tablespoon olive oil and season well. Cook on the grill pan or over hot coals for 3–4 minutes on each side until just tender.

5 Divide the stewed artichokes between plates and top each with a fish fillet. Garnish with chopped thyme and serve with crusty bread.

variation
Artichokes cooked this way also suit cod, halibut or salmon.

DOVER SOLE À LA MEUNIÈRE

DOVER SOLE À LA MEUNIÈRE, OR 'IN THE STYLE OF A MILLER'S WIFE', GETS ITS NAME FROM THE LIGHT DUSTING OF FLOUR THAT THE FISH IS GIVEN BEFORE COOKING. THE COMBINATION OF CHOPPED FRESH PARSLEY, LEMON AND MELTED BUTTER COMPLEMENTS THE FISH PERFECTLY.

serves
4

preparation
20 minutes

cooking
15 minutes

ingredients
- 4 tbsp plain flour
- 1 tsp salt
- 4 x 400 g/14 oz Dover sole, cleaned and skinned
- 150 g/5½ oz butter
- 3 tbsp lemon juice
- 1 tbsp chopped fresh parsley
- ¼ of a preserved lemon, finely chopped (optional)
- fresh parsley sprigs, to garnish
- lemon wedges, to serve

1 Preheat the grill to medium. Mix the flour with the salt and place on a large plate or tray. Drop the fish into the flour, one at a time, and shake well to remove any excess. Melt 40 g/1½ oz of the butter in a small saucepan and use to brush the fish liberally all over.

2 Place the fish under the hot grill and cook for 5 minutes on each side.

3 Meanwhile, melt the remaining butter in a pan. Pour cold water into a bowl that is large enough to take the base of the pan. Keep nearby.

4 Heat the butter until it turns a golden brown and begins to smell nutty. Remove immediately from the heat and immerse the base of the pan in the cold water, to stop cooking.

5 Place the fillets on individual plates, drizzle with the lemon juice and sprinkle with the parsley and preserved lemon, if using. Pour over the browned butter, garnish with parsley sprigs and serve immediately with lemon wedges for squeezing over.

cook's tip

If you have a large enough frying pan (or two) you can fry the floured fish in butter, if you prefer.

PAELLA

PAELLA IS A RUSTIC SPANISH DISH OF SHELLFISH, SAUSAGE (CHORIZO), POULTRY, VEGETABLES
AND RICE, SEASONED WITH GOLDEN SAFFRON. IT IS BEST TO USE STARCHY RICE, SUCH AS ARBORIO,
TO ENSURE YOU RECREATE THE TRADITIONAL CREAMINESS THAT IS THE HALLMARK OF THIS DISH.

serves
4

preparation
15 minutes

cooking
30 minutes

ingredients
- 3 tbsp olive oil
- 2 tbsp butter
- 2 garlic cloves, chopped
- 1 onion, chopped
- 2 large tomatoes, deseeded
  and diced
- 85 g/3 oz frozen peas
- 1 red pepper, deseeded
  and chopped
- 150 g/5 ½ oz arborio rice
- 2 tsp dried mixed herbs
- 1 tsp saffron powder
- 425 ml/15 fl oz chicken
  stock
- 4 skinless, boneless
  chicken breasts
- 150 g/5 ½ oz lean
  chorizo, skinned
- 200 g/7 oz cooked
  lobster meat
- 200 g/7 oz prawns, peeled
  and deveined
- 1 tbsp chopped fresh
  flat-leaf parsley
- salt and pepper

TO GARNISH
- pinch of cayenne pepper
- red pepper strips

1 Heat the oil and butter in a
large frying pan over a medium heat.
Add the garlic and onion and cook,
stirring, for 3 minutes, or until
slightly softened.

2 Add the tomatoes, peas, red
pepper, rice, mixed herbs and saffron
and cook, stirring, for 2 minutes.
Pour in the stock and bring to the
boil. Reduce the heat to low and
cook, stirring, for 10 minutes.

3 Chop the chicken into bite-sized
pieces and add to the frying pan.
Cook, stirring occasionally, for

5 minutes. Chop up the chorizo,
add to the frying pan and cook for
3 minutes. Chop up the lobster meat
and add to the pan with the prawns
and parsley. Season with salt and
pepper and cook, stirring, for a
further 2 minutes.

4 Remove the frying pan from the
heat, transfer the paella to a large
serving platter or individual plates,
garnish with cayenne and red pepper
strips and serve.

TRADITIONAL GREEK BAKED FISH

THE TRADITIONAL GREEK WAY OF BAKING FISH IS TO COOK IT WHOLE WITH TOMATOES AND LEMONS (WHICH ARE EATEN WITH THE RIND ON), ALTHOUGH BOTH THE GREEKS AND THE TURKS CLAIM TO HAVE ORIGINATED THE METHOD. A VARIETY OF FISH CAN BE COOKED THIS WAY SO TAKE YOUR PICK.

serves
4–6

preparation
30 minutes

cooking
1 hour 20
minutes–1 hour
40 minutes

ingredients
- 5 tbsp olive oil
- 2 onions, thinly sliced
- 2 garlic cloves, finely chopped
- 2 carrots, thinly sliced
- 2 celery sticks, thinly sliced
- 150 ml/5 fl oz dry white wine
- 400 g/14 oz canned chopped tomatoes
- pinch of sugar
- 1 large lemon, thinly sliced
- 2 tbsp chopped fresh flat-leaf parsley
- 1 tsp chopped fresh marjoram
- 1–1.3 kg/2–3 lb round whole fish, such as sea bream, sea bass, John Dory, red snapper, or red or grey mullet, scaled and gutted
- butter, for greasing
- salt and pepper

1 Preheat the oven to 180°C/350°F/ Gas Mark 4. Heat 4 tablespoons of the oil in a large saucepan. Add the onions and garlic and fry for 5 minutes until softened. Add the carrots and celery and fry for 5–10 minutes until slightly softened.

2 Pour the wine into the saucepan and bring to the boil. Add the tomatoes and their juice, the sugar, half the lemon slices, salt and pepper and simmer for 20 minutes. Add the parsley and marjoram.

3 Place the fish in a greased, shallow ovenproof dish. Pour the vegetables around the fish, arranging some of the lemon slices on top. Sprinkle with the remaining oil and season to taste with salt and pepper.

4 Bake the fish, uncovered, in the preheated oven for 45 minutes– 1 hour depending on the thickness of the fish, until tender. Serve immediately, straight from the oven.

SEAFOOD GRATIN

A DISH THAT IS COOKED 'AU GRATIN' IS TRADITIONALLY TOPPED WITH BREADCRUMBS AND/OR CHEESE, AND THEN BAKED UNTIL GOLDEN BROWN. USUALLY IT IS THEN SERVED IN THE BAKING DISH. THIS SEAFOOD GRATIN IS MADE WITH A WONDERFUL COMBINATION OF FRESH FISH AND SHELLFISH.

serves
4

preparation
15 minutes

cooking
1 hour

ingredients
- 450 g/1 lb cod fillets
- 225 g/8 oz prawns, peeled and deveined
- 225 g/8 oz scallops
- 3 tbsp extra virgin olive oil
- 1 garlic clove, chopped
- 4 spring onions, chopped
- 1 courgette, sliced
- 425 g/15 oz canned plum tomatoes
- 2 tbsp chopped fresh basil
- 50 g/1¾ oz fresh breadcrumbs
- 75 g/2¾ oz Cheddar cheese, grated
- salt and pepper
- freshly cooked broccoli and cauliflower, to serve

1 Preheat the oven to 190°C/375°F/ Gas Mark 5. Bring a large saucepan of water to the boil, then reduce the heat to medium. Rinse the cod, pat dry with kitchen paper and add to the pan. Cook for 5 minutes. Add the prawns and cook for 3 minutes, then add the scallops and cook for 2 minutes. Drain, refresh under cold running water and drain again.

2 Heat 2 tablespoons of the oil in a frying pan over a low heat. Add the garlic and spring onions and cook, stirring, for 3 minutes. Add the courgette and cook for 3 minutes, then add the tomatoes with their juice, and the basil. Season to taste with salt and pepper and leave to simmer for 10 minutes.

3 Brush a shallow baking dish with the remaining oil and arrange the seafood in it. Remove the saucepan from the heat and pour the sauce over the fish. Scatter over the breadcrumbs and top with cheese. Bake in the oven for 30 minutes until golden. Serve with freshly cooked broccoli and cauliflower.

PRAWN & PINEAPPLE CURRY

THIS DELICIOUS CURRY EXUDES EXCITING THAI AROMAS AND FLAVOURS. IT LOOKS VERY IMPRESSIVE, YET IT TAKES ONLY A FEW MINUTES TO PREPARE AND COOK. IT HAS THE PERFECT PARTNER IN FRESHLY COOKED JASMINE RICE, BUT YOU COULD ALSO SERVE IT WITH COCONUT RICE.

serves
4
preparation
10 minutes
cooking
10–15 minutes

ingredients
- 450 ml/16 fl oz coconut cream
- ½ fresh pineapple, peeled and chopped
- 2 tbsp Thai red curry paste
- 2 tbsp Thai fish sauce
- 2 tsp sugar
- 350 g/12 oz raw tiger prawns
- 2 tbsp chopped fresh coriander
- edible flower, to garnish
- steamed jasmine rice, to serve

1 Place the coconut cream, pineapple, curry paste, fish sauce and sugar in a large frying pan. Heat gently over a medium heat until almost boiling. Peel and devein the prawns. Add the prawns and chopped coriander and simmer gently for 3 minutes, or until the prawns are cooked.

2 Garnish with a fresh flower and serve with steamed jasmine rice.

SQUID & RED ONION STIR-FRY

SQUID REALLY IS WONDERFUL IF QUICKLY COOKED AS IN THIS RECIPE – IT IS NOT TOUGH AND
RUBBERY UNLESS IT IS OVERCOOKED. THE ADDITION OF THE GREEN PEPPER AND SLICED RED ONION
IN THIS DISH PROVIDES AN IDEAL CONTRAST TO THE SQUID IN TERMS OF TEXTURE AND FLAVOUR.

serves
4

preparation
10 minutes

cooking
12–15 minutes

ingredients
- 450 g/1 lb squid rings
- 2 tbsp plain flour
- ½ tsp salt
- 1 green pepper
- 2 tbsp groundnut oil
- 1 red onion, sliced
- 160 g/5¾ oz jar black bean sauce

1 Rinse the squid rings under cold running water and pat dry with kitchen paper.

2 Place the plain flour and salt in a bowl and mix together. Add the squid rings and toss until they are finely coated.

3 Using a sharp knife, deseed the pepper. Slice the pepper into thin strips.

4 Heat the groundnut oil in a large preheated wok.

5 Add the pepper and red onion to the wok and stir-fry for 2 minutes, or until the vegetables are just beginning to soften.

6 Add the squid rings to the wok and cook for a further 5 minutes, or until the squid is cooked through.

7 Add the black bean sauce to the wok and heat through until the juices are bubbling. Transfer to warmed bowls and serve immediately.

cook's tip

Serve this dish with fried rice or noodles tossed in soy sauce for a complete meal.

TEMPURA WHITEBAIT

TEMPURA IS A CLASSIC JAPANESE BATTER MADE WITH EGG, FLOUR AND WATER. THE BATTER IS VERY COLD AND LUMPY, WHICH GIVES THE FINISHED DISH ITS CHARACTERISTIC APPEARANCE. IDEALLY, IT SHOULD BE EATEN STRAIGHT AWAY WHILE STILL HOT.

serves
4

preparation
15 minutes

cooking
10 minutes

ingredients
- 450 g/1 lb whitebait, thawed if frozen
- 100 g/3 ½ oz plain flour
- 50 g/1 ¾ oz cornflour
- ½ tsp salt
- 200 ml/7 fl oz cold water
- 1 egg
- a few ice cubes
- vegetable oil, for deep-frying
- lemon wedges, to serve

CHILLI AND LIME MAYONNAISE
- 1 egg yolk
- 1 tbsp lime juice
- 1 fresh red chilli, deseeded and finely chopped
- 2 tbsp chopped fresh coriander
- 200 ml/7 fl oz light olive oil
- salt and pepper

1 For the mayonnaise, place the egg yolk, lime juice, chilli, coriander and seasoning in a food processor and process until foaming. With the machine still running, gradually add the olive oil, drop by drop, until the mixture begins to thicken. Continue adding the oil in a steady stream until all the oil has been incorporated. Taste and adjust the seasoning and add a little hot water if the mixture is too thick. Reserve.

2 For the tempura whitebait, rinse the fish and pat dry. Reserve on kitchen paper. Sift together the plain flour, cornflour and salt into a large bowl. Whisk together the water, egg and ice cubes then pour onto the flour mix. Whisk briefly until the mixture is runny, but still lumpy with dry bits of flour still apparent.

3 Meanwhile, fill a deep saucepan about a third full with vegetable oil and heat to 190°C/375°F, or until a cube of bread browns in 30 seconds.

4 Dip the whitebait, a few at a time, into the batter and carefully drop into the hot oil. Deep-fry for 1 minute until the batter is crisp but not browned. Drain on kitchen paper and keep warm while you cook the remaining fish. Serve hot with the mayonnaise and lemon wedges.

COD & CHIPS

THIS IS THE GENUINE ARTICLE – A CRUNCHY, DEEP GOLDEN BATTER SURROUNDING PERFECTLY
COOKED FISH, SERVED WITH GOLDEN CRISPY CHIPS. IF YOU'VE NEVER HAD CHIPS WITH
MAYONNAISE, TRY THEM WITH THIS LOVELY MUSTARDY VERSION AND YOU'LL BE CONVERTED.

serves
4
preparation
30 minutes, plus
1 hour resting
cooking
40–50 minutes

ingredients
- 900 g/2 lb potatoes
- 4 x 175 g/6 oz thick pieces
  cod fillet, preferably from
  the head end
- vegetable oil, for
  deep-frying
- salt and pepper
- fresh parsley sprigs,
  to garnish
- lemon wedges, to serve

BATTER
- 15 g/$\frac{1}{2}$ oz fresh yeast
- 300 ml/10 fl oz beer
- 225 g/8 oz plain flour
- 2 tsp salt

MAYONNAISE
- 1 egg yolk
- 1 tsp wholegrain mustard
- 1 tbsp lemon juice
- 200 ml/7 fl oz light olive oil
- salt and pepper

1 For the batter, cream the yeast
with a little of the beer to a smooth
paste. Gradually stir in the rest of the
beer. Sift the plain flour and salt into
a bowl, make a well in the centre and
add the yeast mixture. Gradually
whisk to a smooth batter. Cover
and leave at room temperature for
1 hour.

2 For the mayonnaise, place the
egg yolk, mustard, lemon juice
and seasoning in a food processor.
Process for 30 seconds until frothy.
With the machine still running,
gradually add the olive oil, drop by
drop, until the mixture begins to
thicken. Continue adding the oil in
a steady stream until all the oil has
been incorporated. Taste and adjust
the seasoning if necessary. Thin with
a little hot water if the mayonnaise is
too thick. Chill until needed.

3 For the fish and chips, cut the
potatoes into chips about 1.5 cm/
$\frac{1}{2}$ inch thick. Heat a large saucepan
half filled with vegetable oil to
140°C/275°F, or until a cube of
bread browns in 1 minute. Cook the
chips in 2 batches for 5 minutes, or
until they are cooked through but
not browned. Place the chips to
drain on kitchen paper and reserve.

4 Increase the heat to 160°C/325°F,
or until a cube of bread browns in
45 seconds. Season the fish then dip
into the batter. Deep-fry 2 pieces at
a time for 7–8 minutes until deep
golden brown and cooked through.
Drain on kitchen paper and keep it
warm while you cook the remaining
fish. Keep all the fish warm while
you finish cooking the chips.

5 Increase the heat to 190°C/375°F,
or until a cube of bread browns in
30 seconds. Deep-fry the chips again,
in 2 batches, for 2–3 minutes until
crisp and golden. Drain on kitchen
paper and sprinkle with salt.

6 Serve the fish with the chips,
mayonnaise and lemon wedges, and
garnished with parsley sprigs.

CRISPY BAKED PLAICE

THIS CRISPY GOLDEN FISH DISH IS VERY EASY AND QUICK TO PREPARE, AND BAKES BEAUTIFULLY.
ONCE IT IS IN THE OVEN YOU CAN LEAVE IT AND GET ON WITH OTHER THINGS, SO IT IS IDEAL FOR
COOKS WHO ARE ON A TIGHT SCHEDULE OR WHO HAVE A BUSY LIFESTYLE.

serves
2

preparation
10 minutes

cooking
25 minutes

ingredients
- 115 g/4 oz plaice fillet
- 4 tbsp butter, diced
- 1 tbsp lemon juice
- salt and pepper

TOPPING
- 4 tbsp fresh white breadcrumbs
- 1 tsp dried herbs, such as parsley, oregano or thyme
- 1 tsp mustard powder (optional)
- 1 tbsp Cheddar cheese, grated

1 Preheat the oven to 180°C/350°F/Gas Mark 4.

2 Arrange the fish in a single layer in a shallow ovenproof dish.

3 Dot 2 tablespoons of butter over the fish. Sprinkle with lemon juice and season with salt and pepper.

4 To make the topping, combine the breadcrumbs with the herbs, mustard (if using) and grated cheese. Spoon the topping over the fish and dot with the remaining butter.

5 Bake in the oven for 20 minutes. If necessary, flash the dish under a hot grill for an extra 3–4 minutes to brown the topping before serving.

cook's tip

To vary the ingredients and flavours, try using the same quantity of fresh cod or haddock fillet instead of the plaice. You can also vary the herbs – for example, try using 1 teaspoon dried dill instead of the parsley, oregano or thyme.

SMOKED FISH PIE

THIS IS A CLASSIC VERSION OF A FISH PIE WITH BEAUTIFULLY FLAVOURED SMOKED FISH, AND PRAWNS AND VEGETABLES. IT IS VERY EASY TO PREPARE AND COOK, AND THE TANTALIZING AROMAS AND FLAVOURS WILL HAVE EVERY MEMBER OF YOUR HOUSEHOLD CLAMOURING FOR MORE.

serves
6

preparation
10 minutes

cooking
1½ hours

ingredients
- 2 tbsp olive oil
- 1 onion, finely chopped
- 1 leek, thinly sliced
- 1 carrot, diced
- 1 celery stick, diced
- 115 g/4 oz button mushrooms, halved
- grated rind 1 lemon
- 350 g/12 oz skinless, boneless smoked cod or haddock fillet, cubed
- 350 g/12 oz skinless, boneless white fish, cubed
- 225 g/8 oz cooked peeled prawns
- 2 tbsp chopped fresh parsley
- 1 tbsp chopped fresh dill, plus sprigs to garnish
- cooked vegetables, to serve

SAUCE
- 4 tbsp butter
- 4 tbsp plain flour
- 1 tsp mustard powder
- 600 ml/1 pint milk
- 85 g/3 oz Gruyère cheese, grated

TOPPING
- 675 g/1 lb 8 oz potatoes, unpeeled
- 4 tbsp butter, melted
- 25 g/1 oz Gruyère cheese, grated
- salt and pepper

1 For the sauce, heat the butter in a large saucepan and when melted add the flour and mustard powder. Stir until smooth and cook over a very low heat for 2 minutes without colouring. Slowly beat in the milk until smooth. Simmer gently for 2 minutes then stir in the cheese until smooth. Remove from the heat and place some clingfilm over the surface of the sauce to prevent a skin from forming. Reserve.

2 Meanwhile, for the topping, boil the whole potatoes in plenty of salted water for 15 minutes. Drain well and leave until the potatoes are cool enough to handle.

3 Preheat the oven to 200°C/ 400°F/Gas Mark 6. Heat the oil in a clean saucepan. Add the onion and cook for 5 minutes until softened. Add the leek, carrot, celery and mushrooms and cook for a further 10 minutes, or until the vegetables have softened. Stir in the lemon rind and cook briefly.

4 Add the softened vegetables with the fish, prawns, parsley and dill to the sauce. Season to taste with salt and pepper and transfer to a greased 1.7-litre/3-pint casserole dish.

5 Peel the cooled potatoes and grate them coarsely. Mix with the melted butter. Cover the filling with the grated potato and sprinkle with the grated Gruyère cheese.

6 Cover loosely with foil and bake in the preheated oven for 30 minutes. Remove the foil and bake for a further 30 minutes, or until the topping is tender and golden and the filling is bubbling. Garnish with dill sprigs and serve with your favourite selection of vegetables.

cook's tip

White fish such as haddock, monkfish or hake would be suitable to use in this dish.

CHARGRILLED TUNA WITH CHILLI SALSA

A FIRM FISH SUCH AS TUNA IS AN EXCELLENT CHOICE FOR BARBECUES, BECAUSE IT IS QUITE MEATY
AND DOES NOT BREAK UP DURING COOKING. HERE IT IS SERVED WITH A COLOURFUL AND SPICY
CHILLI SALSA. IT MAKES AN EXCELLENT CHOICE FOR PEOPLE ON A LOW-FAT DIET.

serves

4

preparation

15 minutes, plus
1 hour marinating

cooking

20 minutes

ingredients

- 4 tuna steaks, about
  175 g/6 oz each
- grated rind and juice
  of 1 lime
- 2 tbsp olive oil
- salt and pepper
- fresh coriander sprigs,
  to garnish

CHILLI SALSA

- 2 orange peppers
- 1 tbsp olive oil
- juice of 1 lime
- juice of 1 orange
- 2–3 fresh red chillies,
  deseeded and chopped
- pinch of cayenne pepper

1 Rinse the tuna thoroughly under
cold running water and pat dry with
kitchen paper, then place in a large
shallow non-metallic dish. Sprinkle
the lime rind and juice and the oil
over the fish. Season to taste with
salt and pepper, cover with clingfilm
and leave to marinate in the
refrigerator for up to 1 hour.

2 Preheat the barbecue. To make
the salsa, brush the peppers with
the olive oil and cook over hot coals,
turning frequently, for 10 minutes,
or until the skin is blackened and

charred. Remove from the barbecue
and leave to cool slightly, then peel
off the skins and discard the seeds.
Place the peppers in a food processor
with the remaining salsa ingredients
and process to a purée. Transfer to
a bowl and season to taste with salt
and pepper.

3 Cook the tuna over hot coals for
4–5 minutes on each side until
golden. Transfer to plates, garnish
with coriander sprigs and serve
immediately with the salsa.

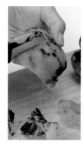

cook's tip

*You can make the chilli salsa in advance.
Halve the orange peppers and cook, skin-
side upwards, under a preheated hot grill.
Cook until blackened and charred, then
continue as in Step 2.*

3

MEAT

RED MEAT IS VERY NUTRITIOUS AND CAN PLAY A
VALUABLE PART IN A HEALTHY DIET, ESPECIALLY IF YOU
CHOOSE LEAN CUTS TO KEEP THE SATURATED FAT
LEVELS TO A MINIMUM. IT IS FULL OF VITAMINS AND
MINERALS, ESPECIALLY IRON AND PROTEIN. ON THE
FOLLOWING PAGES YOU WILL FIND SOME DELICIOUS
RECIPES TO MAKE THE MOST OF ANY CUT OF MEAT.

INTRODUCTION

MEAT IS RICH IN PROTEIN AND EASY TO COOK. IT MAKES AN EXCELLENT CENTREPIECE TO ANY MEAL, AND YOU CAN CHOOSE FROM A WIDE RANGE OF JOINTS AND CUTS, FROM THE ECONOMICAL TO THE INDULGENT, TO SUIT ANY OCCASION.

Buying and storing meat

Always buy your fresh meat from a reputable supplier. For lamb, choose firm, pinkish, marbled meat; avoid any that looks dark and soggy. The fat should be cream-coloured, not yellow. For pork, choose moist, pinkish meat with white fat. Avoid any meat that looks oily or that has yellow fat. For beef, look for meat that is deep burgundy red, not bright red; the fat should be cream-coloured, not yellow. Choose beef that has a marbling of fat through it – this will ensure that the meat stays moist during cooking. For veal, the flesh should be a very pale pink and the fat white. If it is turning red, it means that the meat is older than it should be.

If you are buying a joint of meat, allow 175–350 g/6–12 oz per person, depending on whether the meat is on or off the bone.

As soon as you get the meat home, unwrap it and transfer it to a clean dish (the dish should have a lip deep enough to catch any juices). Cover it with clingfilm and store in the refrigerator away from any cooked meats in order to prevent cross-contamination. Leave any prepackaged meat in its wrapping in the refrigerator and use by the 'best before' date. Unpackaged minced lamb, beef and pork is best used within 1–2 days of purchase. Fresh cuts of beef and pork will keep in the refrigerator for 2–3 days, and cooked beef and pork can be refrigerated for 4–5 days. Fresh lamb cuts will keep for up to 4 days in the refrigerator. Before cooking, bring out the meat (keep it covered) and allow it to come back to room temperature for about 30 minutes before cooking. You can freeze small cuts of beef or pork for up to 6 months, and lamb for up to 3 months. Make sure you thaw the meat thoroughly in a refrigerator or cool room before cooking: allow 6 hours per 450 g/1 lb.

Preparation techniques

There is a range of techniques you can use to prepare and/or improve your chosen cuts of meat before cooking. Some of them are done purely for presentation, while other techniques help to tenderize the meat or facilitate thorough cooking.

LAMB CHOPS
Use a sharp knife to remove the excess fat around the edge.

PORK CHOPS AND RUMP STEAKS
Use a sharp knife to make incisions in the fat at intervals of 2.5 cm/1 inch around the edge.

BRAISING STEAK
Use a sharp knife to remove any excess fat. Slice the meat across the grain, then cut across the slices to form smaller pieces or cubes of meat.

TENDERIZE THIN CUTS OF MEAT
Put them between sheets of greaseproof paper and pound with either a meat mallet or the base of a saucepan.

STUFF AND TIE A BONELESS JOINT
Put it skin-side down and arrange the stuffing evenly over the surface. Roll up the joint from the thick end, tie a piece of clean string lengthways around the joint, then knot it and trim off the ends. Now tie further pieces of string cross-ways around the joint at intervals of about 2.5 cm/1 inch. Knot each one in turn and trim the ends.

BUTTERFLY A LEG OF LAMB
Push a chef's knife into the cavity of the bone, then cut sideways to part the meat. Open it out and make a light incision down the centre of the meat so that it stays open and flat.

PREPARE A RACK OF LAMB
Remove the skin and excess fat, leaving a layer of fat about 1.5-cm/³/₄-inch thick. Cut off the bone at the back, then remove the fat from the ends of the bones (to a length of about 5 cm/ 2 inches). Use a knife to scrape out the meat from between the bones.

Choosing cuts of meat

There are many different cuts of meat available. Choosing the right cut will help to ensure the perfect result for your chosen recipe. When in doubt, ask your local butcher for advice.

Beef

For roasting, choose sirloin, topside fillet and rib. Fillet and steaks are excellent for grilling, pan-frying or barbecuing. For braising and stewing, use chuck or topside.

Pork

For roasting, choose the belly, leg, loin, shoulder, fillet, chops or steaks. For grilling, use the belly, escalopes, loin, shoulder, fillet, chops or steaks. The belly, loin, fillet, chops or steaks are excellent for barbecues. For frying, use the loin, fillet, chops and steaks, and also bacon. To stew or braise, use the leg, shoulder or loin.

Veal

The breast, loin and shoulder are best for roasting, while the loin, topside and cutlets are ideal for grilling and barbecuing. For pan-frying, choose the loin or topside, and for stewing or braising use the knuckle, shoulder or breast.

Lamb

The leg is the most popular choice for roasting, but you can also roast the shoulder, saddle, breast and best end of neck. For grilling, try chops, noisettes, leg and best end of neck. The leg or chops are ideal for barbecues, and for pan-frying use noisettes or the middle neck. Finally, for stewing, braising or casseroles, use the shoulder, shank or middle neck.

Beef

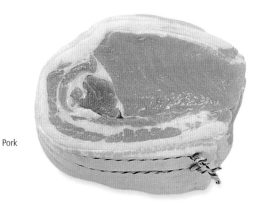

Pork

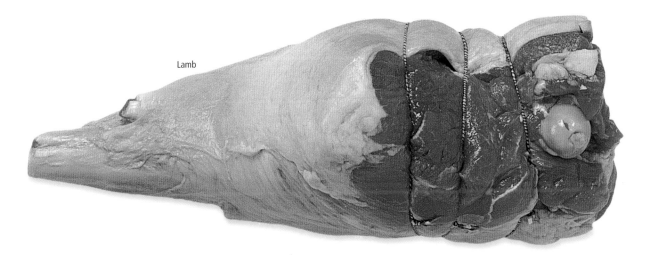

Lamb

Cooking and carving techniques

Techniques for cooking and carving joints of meat are not difficult, but they do have to be performed properly in order to get the best out of the meat. Follow the instructions given here for perfect results every time.

ROASTING AND CARVING A BONED JOINT

This technique is suitable for boned joints of lamb, pork and beef. Rub the surface with a little oil, followed by some salt and some crushed peppercorns (use a pestle and mortar for this). Place on a rack in a roasting tin, then roast in the oven, basting once or twice during cooking. Remove from the oven and cut off the strings. Wrap the meat in foil and leave to stand for 15–20 minutes. To carve, steady the meat with a fork, then carve slices downwards from one end.

ROASTING AND CARVING A LEG OF LAMB

Using a sharp knife, score a criss-cross pattern in the fat, then rub all over the surface with a little oil, followed by some salt and freshly ground black pepper. Put the meat on a rack in a roasting tin and roast in the oven, basting once or twice during cooking.

To test if the meat is cooked all the way through, pierce a skewer or knife into the thickest part. The juices that run out will be clear if the meat is cooked. If not, return it to the oven and cook until it is done. Remove from the oven and wrap the meat in foil. Leave to stand for 15–20 minutes. To carve, turn the leg meat-side up, then steady the meat with a fork. Start carving from the knuckle end. When you have finished, turn over the leg and carve horizontal slices.

Using a meat thermometer

A meat thermometer is a useful device for testing whether a joint of meat is cooked thoroughly. Thorough cooking is particularly important in the case of pork, which can carry harmful bacteria and cause food poisoning if not cooked all the way through. Simply insert the thermometer into the thickest part of the meat at the start of cooking. Take care to ensure that it does not come into contact with any bone, because this could give a false reading. When the thermometer reaches the required temperature, the meat is cooked. The recommended temperatures for different meats are shown below.

Cooking temperatures

Lamb	Medium rare	75°C/167°F
	Well done	80°C/176°F
Pork	Well done	90°C/194°F
Beef	Rare	65°C/149°F
	Medium rare	70°C/158°F
	Well done	75°C/167°F

Oven temperatures and roasting times

Please note that individual oven temperatures and cooking times vary, so the following cooking times are approximate only. Remember to preheat the oven before cooking in order to ensure the best results.

Meat	Joint	Weight	Temperature	Cooking time
Lamb	Whole leg	2.5 kg/5 lb 8 oz	180°C/350°F/Gas Mark 4	2$\frac{1}{4}$ hours (medium rare) or 2$\frac{1}{2}$ hours (well done)
Lamb	Whole shoulder	2.5 kg /5 lb 8 oz	180°C/350°F/Gas Mark 4	2$\frac{1}{4}$ hours (medium rare) or 2$\frac{1}{2}$ hours (well done)
Pork	Loin (boned)	2.5 kg/5 lb 8 oz	180°C/350°F/Gas Mark 4 220°C/425°F/Gas Mark 7	3 hours at lower temperature, then 20 minutes at higher temperature (well done)
Pork	Shoulder (boned)	2.5 kg/5 lb 8 oz	180°C/350°F/Gas Mark 4 220°C/425°F/Gas Mark 7	3 hours at lower temperature, then 20 minutes at higher temperature (well done)
Beef	Sirloin	2.5 kg/5 lb 8 oz	200°C/400°F/Gas Mark 6	1$\frac{3}{4}$ hours (rare), 2$\frac{1}{4}$ hours (medium rare) or 2$\frac{1}{2}$ hours (well done)
Beef	Topside	2 kg/4 lb 8 oz	180°C/350°F/Gas Mark 4	1$\frac{1}{2}$ hours (rare), 2 hours (medium rare) or 2$\frac{1}{2}$ hours (well done)

Oven temperatures and heat descriptions

You may come across recipes that do not give a specific temperature: instead they will simply recommend cooking in a 'moderate' or 'hot' oven. Here is a list of these heat descriptions and their correct temperatures.

Oven heat description	Celsius	Fahrenheit	Gas mark
Very cool	110–120°	225–250°	$\frac{1}{4}$–$\frac{1}{2}$
Cool	140–150°	275–300°	1–2
Moderate	160–180°	325–350°	3–4
Moderately hot	190–200°	375–400°	5–6
Hot	220°	425°	7
Very hot	230°	450°	8

ROAST BEEF WITH YORKSHIRE PUDDINGS

ROAST BEEF IS PROBABLY THE MEAL FOR WHICH THE BRITISH ARE KNOWN BEST AROUND THE WORLD. OLD PAINTINGS SHOW THE FEASTS OF TUDOR TIMES, FEATURING HUGE RIBS OF BEEF SERVED AT COURT – A MAGNIFICENT HISTORICAL REMINDER OF JUST HOW BEEF OUGHT TO BE SERVED.

serves
8

preparation
15 minutes, plus
10–15 minutes'
resting time

cooking
1 hour 55
minutes–2½ hours

ingredients
- 2.7 kg/6 lb prime rib of beef
- 2 tsp English mustard powder
- 3 tbsp plain flour
- 300 ml/10 fl oz red wine
- 300 ml/10 fl oz beef stock
- 2 tsp Worcestershire sauce (optional)
- salt and pepper

YORKSHIRE PUDDINGS
- 225 g/8 oz plain flour
- 1 tsp salt
- 2 eggs, beaten
- 600 ml/1 pint milk
- 4 tbsp roast beef dripping or olive oil

cook's tip

Roast beef is the most difficult roast to get right, because, unlike other meats, you need to cook it so that it is still pink in the centre; careful timing is all. The best roast beef is a rib cooked on the bone, but this must be a good size.

1 Preheat the oven to 230°C/450°F/Gas Mark 8.

2 Season the meat with the salt and pepper and rub in the mustard and 1 tablespoon of the flour.

3 Place the meat in a roasting tin large enough to hold it comfortably and roast for 15 minutes. Reduce the heat to 190°C/375°F/Gas Mark 5 and cook for 15 minutes per 450 g/1 lb, plus 15 minutes (1 hour 45 minutes for this joint) for rare beef or 20 minutes per 450 g/1 lb, plus 20 minutes (2 hours 20 minutes) for medium beef. Baste the meat occasionally to keep it moist and if the tin becomes too dry, add a little stock or red wine.

4 Remove the meat from the oven and place on a hot serving plate, cover with foil and leave in a warm place for 10–15 minutes.

5 To make the gravy, pour off most of the fat from the tin (reserve it for the Yorkshire pudding), leaving behind the meat juices and the sediment. Place the tin on the top of the hob over a medium heat and scrape all the sediments from the base of the tin. Sprinkle in the remaining flour and quickly mix it into the juices with a small whisk.

When you have a smooth paste, gradually add the wine and most of the stock, whisking constantly. Bring to the boil, then turn down the heat to a gentle simmer and cook for 2–3 minutes. Season with salt and pepper and add the remaining stock, if needed, and a little Worcestershire sauce, if liked.

6 To make the Yorkshire puddings preheat the oven to 220°C/425°F/Gas Mark 7. Place the flour in a bowl with the salt. Make a well in the centre of the flour and add the eggs. Using a wooden spoon, gradually stir in the eggs and milk and beat until smooth. Leave to stand for 30 minutes. Heat the dripping or oil in 24 individual Yorkshire pudding tins for several minutes in the top of the oven. Remove the tins from the oven, pour in the batter and bake for 10–15 minutes until the puddings are puffed up and golden brown.

8 When ready to serve, carve the meat into slices and serve on hot plates. Pour the gravy into a warmed jug and take direct to the table and serve with the Yorkshire puddings.

BEEF BOURGUIGNON

BEEF BOURGUIGNON USES A TRADITIONAL METHOD OF PREPARATION FROM THE BURGUNDY
REGION OF FRANCE. IT CONTAINS SUCCULENT BEEF BRAISED IN RED WINE, COMPLEMENTED BY
BACON, ONIONS AND MUSHROOMS. SERVE IT WITH FRESH CRUSTY BREAD TO SOAK UP THE JUICES.

serves
6

preparation
40 minutes

cooking
3¼ hours

ingredients
- 2 tbsp olive oil
- 175 g/6 oz piece unsmoked bacon, sliced into thin strips
- 1.3 kg/3 lb stewing beef, cut into 5 cm/2 inch pieces
- 2 carrots, sliced
- 2 onions, chopped
- 2 garlic cloves, very finely chopped
- 3 tbsp plain flour
- 700 ml/1 ¼ pints red wine
- 350–450 ml/12–16 fl oz beef stock
- bouquet garni sachet
- 1 tsp salt
- ¼ tsp pepper
- 3 tbsp butter
- 350 g/12 oz pickling onions
- 350 g/12 oz button mushrooms
- 2 tbsp chopped fresh parsley, to garnish

1 Heat the oil in a large, flameproof casserole over a medium heat. Add the bacon and brown for 2–3 minutes. Remove with a slotted spoon. Add the beef in batches to the casserole and cook until browned. Drain and keep with the bacon. Add the carrots and chopped onions to the casserole and cook for 5 minutes. Add the garlic and fry until just coloured. Return the meat and bacon to the casserole. Sprinkle on the flour and cook for 1 minute, stirring. Add the wine, enough stock to cover, the bouquet garni, salt and pepper. Bring to the boil, cover and simmer gently for 3 hours.

2 Heat half the butter in a frying pan. Add the pickling onions, cover and cook until softened. Remove with a slotted spoon and keep warm. Heat the remaining butter in the frying pan. Add the mushrooms and fry briefly. Remove and keep warm.

3 Sieve the casserole liquid into a clean saucepan. Wipe the casserole with kitchen paper and tip in the meat, bacon, mushrooms and onions. Remove the surface fat from the cooking liquid, simmer for 1–2 minutes to reduce, then pour over the meat and vegetables. Serve sprinkled with chopped parsley.

BEEF STROGANOFF

BEEF STROGANOFF GETS ITS NAME FROM THE 19TH CENTURY RUSSIAN DIPLOMAT COUNT PAUL STROGANOV. THIS DELICIOUS DISH OF BEEF, ONIONS AND MUSHROOMS HAS A RICH, CREAMY SAUCE, AND THE COMBINATION OF RED WINE AND GARLIC GIVES IT AN UNFORGETTABLE FLAVOUR.

serves
4

preparation
5 minutes

cooking
12–15 minutes

ingredients
- 40 g/1 ½ oz plain flour
- 1 tsp paprika
- 700 g/1 lb 9 oz rump steak, very thinly sliced into strips
- 55 g/2 oz butter
- 1 onion, finely chopped
- 1 garlic clove, finely chopped
- 225 g/8 oz button mushrooms
- 1 tbsp lemon juice
- 2 tbsp dry red wine
- 2 tbsp tomato purée
- 350 ml/12 fl oz soured cream
- salt and pepper
- 2 tbsp snipped fresh chives, to garnish

1 Place the flour and paprika in a polythene bag and season with salt and pepper. Shake to mix, then add a few steak strips at a time and shake to coat.

2 Melt the butter in a large, heavy-based frying pan over a low heat. Add the onion and garlic and cook, stirring occasionally, for 5 minutes, or until softened. Increase the heat to high, add the steak strips and cook, stirring constantly, until browned all over. Stir in the mushrooms, lemon juice and wine, reduce the heat and simmer for 5 minutes.

3 Stir in the tomato purée and soured cream and adjust the seasoning, if necessary. Garnish with the chives and serve immediately.

cook's tip

Beef Stroganoff is traditionally served over noodles, but you can also serve it on a bed of freshly cooked rice. Use a light, fluffy long-grain rice to partner this dish.

HUNGARIAN BEEF GOULASH

THIS AUTHENTIC HUNGARIAN STEW IS MADE WITH THE TRADITIONAL INGREDIENTS OF BEEF, VEGETABLES AND PAPRIKA, AND HAS A RICH, PUNGENT FLAVOUR. IT IS CUSTOMARY TO SERVE IT ON A PLATE OF HOT, BUTTERED NOODLES, WITH GENEROUS AMOUNTS OF SOURED CREAM.

serves
4

preparation
30 minutes

cooking
3 hours

ingredients
- 2 tbsp vegetable oil
- 675 g/1 lb 8 oz stewing beef, cubed
- 3 onions, finely chopped
- 1 green pepper, deseeded and diced
- 2 garlic cloves, very finely chopped
- 2 tbsp tomato purée
- 2 tbsp plain flour
- 400 g/14 oz canned chopped tomatoes
- 250 ml/9 fl oz beef stock
- 1 bay leaf
- 3 tbsp chopped fresh parsley
- 1 tbsp paprika
- 1 tsp salt
- ¼ tsp pepper

TO SERVE
- buttered noodles
- soured cream

1 Heat the oil in a flameproof casserole over a medium–high heat. Add the meat and fry until evenly browned. Remove with a slotted spoon, transfer to a bowl and reserve until required.

2 Add the onions and pepper. Cook for 5 minutes, stirring occasionally, until softened. Add the garlic and cook until just coloured. Stir in the tomato purée and flour. Cook for 1 minute, stirring constantly.

3 Return the meat to the casserole. Add the remaining ingredients and bring to the boil. Cover and simmer over a low heat for 2½ hours, stirring occasionally. Add water or more stock if necessary.

4 Remove the lid and simmer for 15 minutes, stirring to prevent sticking, until the sauce has thickened and the meat is very tender. Serve with buttered noodles and a bowl of soured cream.

CLASSIC BEEF FAJITAS

THIS RECIPE CONTAINS SIZZLING MARINATED STRIPS OF MEAT ROLLED UP IN SOFT FLOUR TORTILLAS
WITH A TANGY SALSA. IT IS A REAL MEXICAN TREAT, AND PERFECT FOR RELAXED ENTERTAINING.
SIMPLY PASS ROUND THE INGREDIENTS AND LET YOUR GUESTS ROLL THEIR OWN FAJITAS.

serves
4–6
preparation
30 minutes,
plus 3–8 hours'
marinating
cooking
10–15 minutes

ingredients
- 700 g/1 lb 9 oz beef skirt
  steak, cut into strips
- 6 garlic cloves, chopped
- juice of 1 lime
- large pinch of mild
  chilli powder
- large pinch of paprika
- large pinch of ground cumin
- 1–2 tbsp extra virgin
  olive oil
- 12 flour tortillas
- butter, for greasing
- vegetable oil, for frying
- 1–2 avocados, stoned,
  sliced and tossed with
  lime juice
- 125 ml/4 fl oz soured cream
- salt and pepper

PICO DE GALLO SALSA
- 8 ripe tomatoes, diced
- 3 spring onions, sliced
- 1–2 fresh green chillies,
  such as jalapeño or
  serrano, deseeded
  and chopped
- 3–4 tbsp chopped fresh
  coriander
- 5–8 radishes, diced
- ground cumin

1 Combine the beef with half the
garlic, half the lime juice, the chilli
powder, paprika, cumin and olive oil.
Add salt and pepper, mix well
and leave to marinate for at least
30 minutes at room temperature,
or up to overnight in the refrigerator.

2 To make the salsa, place the
tomatoes in a bowl with the spring
onions, green chilli, coriander and
radishes. Season to taste with cumin,
salt and pepper. Reserve.

3 Heat the tortillas one by one in a
lightly greased non-stick frying pan,
wrapping each in foil as you work,
to keep warm.

4 Heat a little oil in a large, heavy-
based frying pan over a high heat.
Add the meat and stir-fry until
browned and just cooked through.

5 Serve the sizzling hot meat with
the warm tortillas, the salsa, avocado
and soured cream for each person to
make his or her own rolled-up fajitas.

cook's tip
*A lettuce and orange salad makes
a refreshing accompaniment.*

GRILLED STEAK WITH TOMATOES & GARLIC

ORIGINATING IN NAPLES, WHERE IT IS DIFFICULT TO FIND ANY DISH THAT DOES NOT FEATURE THE BRILLIANTLY COLOURED, RICH-TASTING TOMATOES OF THE REGION, THIS WAY OF SERVING STEAK IS NOW POPULAR THROUGHOUT ITALY – AND BEYOND.

serves

4

preparation

20 minutes

cooking

20–30 minutes

ingredients

- 3 tbsp olive oil, plus extra for brushing
- 700 g/1 lb 9 oz tomatoes, peeled and chopped
- 1 red pepper, deseeded and chopped
- 1 onion, chopped
- 2 garlic cloves, finely chopped
- 1 tbsp chopped fresh flat-leaf parsley
- 1 tsp dried oregano
- 1 tsp sugar
- 4 x 175 g/6 oz entrecôte (flesh from ribs) or rump steaks
- salt and pepper

1 Place the oil, tomatoes, red pepper, onion, garlic, parsley, oregano and sugar in a heavy-based saucepan and season to taste with salt and pepper. Bring to the boil, reduce the heat and simmer for 15 minutes.

2 Meanwhile, preheat the grill to high. Snip any fat around the outsides of the steaks. Season each generously with pepper (no salt) and brush with oil. Grill for 1 minute on each side, then reduce the heat to medium and cook according to taste: $1\frac{1}{2}$–2 minutes each side for rare; $2\frac{1}{2}$–3 minutes each side for medium; 3–4 minutes on each side for well done.

3 Transfer the steaks to warmed individual plates and spoon the sauce over them. Serve immediately.

MIXED GRILL

THIS MIXED GRILL IS A MEAT FEAST, AND IS IDEAL FOR AL FRESCO DINING. IT INCLUDES EVERYTHING
A MEAT-LOVER COULD WANT – SAUSAGES, BACON, STEAK AND KIDNEYS – AND THE BAY LEAVES ADD A
WONDERFUL AROMATIC FLAVOUR. SERVE IT WITH BAKED POTATOES AND A CRISP GREEN SALAD.

serves
4

preparation
20 minutes

cooking
12 minutes

ingredients
- 4 lambs' kidneys
- 6 smoked back bacon
  rashers, rinded
- 4 cherry tomatoes
- 4 small fillet steaks or
  tournedos
- 8 small pork sausages
- 4 button mushrooms
- 12 bay leaves
- salt and pepper

SPICY MARINADE
- 2 tbsp sunflower oil
- 1 large onion,
  finely chopped
- 2 garlic cloves,
  finely chopped
- 2 tbsp jerk seasoning

- 1 tbsp curry paste
- 1 tsp grated fresh
  root ginger
- 400 g/14 oz canned
  chopped tomatoes
- 4 tbsp Worcestershire sauce
- 3 tbsp light muscovado
  sugar
- salt and pepper

MUSTARD BUTTER
- 55 g/2 oz unsalted butter,
  softened
- 1½ tsp tarragon mustard
- 1 tbsp chopped fresh
  parsley
- dash of lemon juice

1 To make the marinade, heat the
oil in a heavy-based saucepan. Add
the onion and garlic and cook,
stirring occasionally, for 5 minutes,
or until softened. Stir in the jerk
seasoning, curry paste and grated
ginger and cook, stirring constantly,
for 2 minutes. Add the tomatoes,
Worcestershire sauce and sugar, then
season to taste with salt and pepper.
Bring to the boil, stirring constantly,
then reduce the heat and simmer
for 15 minutes, or until thickened.
Remove the saucepan from the heat
and leave to cool.

2 To make the mustard butter, mix
all the ingredients together in a
small bowl, beating with a fork until
well blended. Cover with clingfilm
and leave to chill in the refrigerator
until required.

3 Preheat the barbecue. Using a
sharp knife, trim the kidneys, cut in
half and, using a pair of kitchen
scissors, remove the cores. Cut the
bacon rashers in half across the
centre, then wrap a piece of bacon
around each kidney half and around
each cherry tomato.

4 Thread the kidneys, tomatoes,
steaks, sausages, mushrooms and
bay leaves alternately onto several
metal skewers. Season to taste
with salt and pepper and brush with
the marinade.

5 Cook over medium hot coals,
turning and brushing frequently
with the marinade, for 12 minutes.
Transfer the kebabs to a large
serving plate and serve immediately
with the mustard butter.

variation
*If you like, you can substitute the steak with
medallions or noisettes of other meats, such
as lamb or chicken.*

GLAZED GAMMON STEAKS

GAMMON STEAKS, WHICH ARE ALSO KNOWN AS HAM STEAKS, MAKE A TASTY DISH FOR A LUNCH OR LIGHT SUPPER. THESE STEAKS ARE DELICIOUSLY SWEET GLAZED WITH SUGAR AND MUSTARD. SIMPLY ADD A BAKED POTATO AND LIGHTLY COOKED GREEN BEANS AND YOU HAVE A PERFECT MEAL.

serves
4

preparation
5 minutes

cooking
10 minutes

ingredients
• 4 gammon steaks
• 4 tbsp dark brown sugar
• 2 tsp mustard powder
• 4 tbsp butter
• 8 slices pineapple

TO SERVE
• baked potato
• green beans

1 Preheat the griddle over a medium heat. Place the gammon steaks on it and cook for 5 minutes, turning once. If you have room for only 2 steaks at a time, cook them completely and keep warm while cooking the second pair.

2 Combine the brown sugar and mustard in a small bowl.

3 Melt the butter in a large frying pan. Add the pineapple and cook for 2 minutes to heat through, turning once. Sprinkle with the sugar and mustard mixture and continue cooking over a low heat until the sugar has melted and the pineapple is well glazed. Turn the pineapple once more so that both sides are coated with sauce. Place the gammon steaks on individual plates and arrange 2 pineapple slices either next to them or overlapping on top. Spoon over some of the sweet pan juices.

4 Serve with a baked potato and green beans.

LAMB KEBABS

LAMB AND ROSEMARY MAKE THE PERFECT PARTNERSHIP. THESE LAMB KEBABS ARE FULL OF FLAVOUR. THEY ARE ALSO RICH IN PROTEIN, AND MAKE MOUTHWATERING BARBECUE FARE. YOU CAN SERVE THEM ON THEIR OWN, OR WITH FRESHLY COOKED RICE AND A SIDE SALAD FOR A SATISFYING MEAL.

serves
4
preparation
15 minutes
cooking
10 minutes

ingredients
- 625 g/1 lb 6 oz fresh lamb mince
- 90 g/3 ¼ oz Gruyère cheese, grated
- 4 tbsp thick natural yogurt
- 2 garlic cloves, chopped
- 1 tbsp chopped fresh rosemary
- 16 button mushrooms
- 16 cherry tomatoes
- 1 tbsp olive oil
- salt and pepper
- fresh rosemary sprigs, to garnish
- freshly cooked rice, to serve

1 Preheat the grill or light a barbecue. Place the lamb, cheese, yogurt and garlic in a large bowl and mix well. Stir in the rosemary and season with salt and pepper. Using your hands, shape the mixture into small balls.

2 Thread the lamb balls onto several metal skewers, alternating them with the mushrooms and cherry tomatoes. When the skewers are full (leave a small space at either end), brush them with oil. Transfer them to the hot grill or barbecue and cook for 10 minutes, or until cooked right through, turning them frequently and brushing with more oil if necessary.

3 Remove the kebabs from the heat and serve with freshly cooked rice, garnished with rosemary sprigs.

SHEPHERD'S PIE

SHEPHERD'S PIE IS AN OLD ENGLISH DISH, AND WAS ORIGINALLY CREATED TO USE UP LEFTOVERS FROM THE SUNDAY ROAST. IT USUALLY CONTAINS MINCED LAMB OR BEEF COOKED WITH ONIONS, CARROTS, HERBS AND TOMATOES IN GRAVY, AND IS TOPPED WITH PIPED MASHED POTATOES.

serves
4–5
preparation
10 minutes
cooking
1½ hours

ingredients
- 700 g/1 lb 9 oz fresh lean lamb or beef mince
- 2 onions, chopped
- 225 g/8 oz carrots, diced
- 1–2 garlic cloves, crushed
- 1 tbsp plain flour
- 200 ml/7 fl oz beef stock
- 200 g/7 oz canned chopped tomatoes
- 1 tsp Worcestershire sauce
- 1 tsp chopped fresh sage or oregano or ½ tsp dried sage or oregano
- 750 g–1 kg/1 lb 10 oz–2 lb potatoes
- 25 g/1 oz margarine
- 3–4 tbsp skimmed milk
- 125 g/4½ oz button mushrooms, sliced (optional)
- salt and pepper

1 Preheat the oven to 200°C/400°F/Gas Mark 6. Place the meat in a heavy-based saucepan with no extra fat and cook gently until the meat begins to brown.

2 Add the onions, carrots and garlic and continue to cook gently for 10 minutes. Stir in the flour and cook for 1–2 minutes, then gradually stir in the stock and tomatoes and bring to the boil.

3 Add the Worcestershire sauce, seasoning and herbs, cover and simmer gently for 25 minutes, giving an occasional stir.

4 Cook the potatoes in boiling salted water until tender, then drain thoroughly and mash, beating in the margarine, seasoning and enough milk to give a piping consistency. Place in a piping bag fitted with a large star nozzle.

5 Stir the mushrooms (if using) into the meat and taste and adjust the seasoning if necessary. Turn into a shallow ovenproof dish.

6 Pipe the potatoes evenly over the meat. Cook in the preheated oven for 30 minutes, or until piping hot and the potatoes are golden brown.

variation

If liked, a mixture of boiled potatoes and parsnips or swede may be used for the topping.

MOUSSAKA

MOUSSAKA ORGINATED IN GREECE, BUT ITS POPULARITY IS NOW WIDESPREAD THROUGHOUT THE EASTERN MEDITERRANEAN. THERE ARE MANY VARIATIONS OF THIS DISH, BUT IT USUALLY CONTAINS SLICES OF AUBERGINE AND MINCED BEEF OR LAMB, COVERED WITH BÉCHAMEL SAUCE AND CHEESE.

serves

4

preparation

40 minutes

cooking

45 minutes

ingredients

- 2 aubergines, thinly sliced
- 450 g/1 lb fresh lean beef mince
- 2 onions, thinly sliced
- 1 tsp finely chopped garlic
- 400 g/14 oz canned tomatoes
- 2 tbsp chopped fresh parsley
- 2 eggs
- 300 ml/10 fl oz low-fat natural yogurt
- 1 tbsp freshly grated Parmesan cheese
- salt and pepper

1 Preheat the oven to 180°C/350°F/Gas Mark 4. Dry-fry the aubergine slices, in batches, in a non-stick frying pan on both sides until browned. Remove from the pan.

2 Add the beef to the frying pan and cook for 5 minutes, stirring, until browned. Stir in the onions and garlic and cook for 5 minutes, or until browned. Add the tomatoes, parsley, salt and pepper, then bring to the boil and simmer for 20 minutes, or until the meat is tender.

3 Arrange half the aubergine slices in a layer in an ovenproof dish. Add the meat mixture, then a final layer of the remaining aubergine slices.

4 Beat the eggs in a bowl, then beat in the yogurt and add salt and pepper to taste. Pour the mixture over the aubergines and sprinkle the grated cheese on top. Bake the moussaka in the oven for 45 minutes, or until golden brown. Serve straight from the dish.

cook's tip

Try experimenting with your own combinations of ingredients to vary the flavour and texture. For example, you can use minced lamb instead of the beef, and add sliced artichokes or potatoes to the aubergines.

RACK OF LAMB

IF YOU WANT A ROAST FOR TWO, A RACK OF LAMB IS IDEAL. IT IS SIMPLE TO COOK AND PROVIDES DELICIOUS MEAT, FULL OF FLAVOUR. LAMB IS BEST IN SPRING, FROM EASTER ONWARDS, WHEN IT IS AT ITS SWEETEST AND MOST SUCCULENT. FRESH MINT IS ALSO AT ITS BEST AROUND THIS TIME.

serves

2

preparation

20 minutes,
plus 3–8 hours'
marinating

cooking

30–35 minutes

ingredients

- 1 trimmed rack of lamb
  (about 250–300 g/
  9–10½ oz rack)
- 1 garlic clove, crushed
- 150 ml/5 fl oz red wine
- 1 fresh rosemary sprig,
  crushed to release
  the flavour
- 1 tbsp olive oil
- 150 ml/5 fl oz lamb stock
- 2 tbsp redcurrant jelly
- salt and pepper

MINT SAUCE

- small bunch of fresh mint
  leaves, chopped
- 2 tsp caster sugar
- 2 tbsp boiling water
- 2 tbsp white wine vinegar

1 Place the rack of lamb in a non-metallic bowl and rub all over with the garlic. Pour over the wine and place the rosemary sprig on top. Cover and leave to marinate in the refrigerator for 3 hours, or overnight if possible.

2 To make the mint sauce, combine the mint leaves with the sugar in a small bowl. Add the boiling water and stir to dissolve the sugar. Add the white wine vinegar and leave to stand for 30 minutes before serving with the lamb.

3 Preheat the oven to 220°C/425°F/Gas Mark 7.

4 Remove the lamb from the marinade, reserving the marinade, dry the meat with kitchen paper and season well with salt and pepper. Place in a small roasting tin, drizzle with the oil and roast in the oven for 15–20 minutes, depending on whether you like your meat rare or medium. Remove the lamb from the oven and leave to rest, covered with foil, in a warm place for 5 minutes.

5 Place the marinade in a small pan, bring to the boil over a medium heat and bubble away for 2–3 minutes. Add the lamb stock and redcurrant jelly and simmer until a syrupy consistency is achieved.

6 Carve the lamb into cutlets and serve on warmed plates with the stock and redcurrant jelly sauce spooned over the top. Serve the mint sauce separately.

cook's tip

Rack of lamb is an impressive dish for entertaining, too. Just double or treble the ingredients, depending on the number of guests.

PROVENÇAL BARBECUED LAMB

PROVENÇAL DISHES ARE PREPARED IN THE STYLE OF PROVENCE, A REGION IN FRANCE, AND ARE MOST OFTEN ASSOCIATED WITH GARLIC, TOMATOES AND OLIVE OIL. BE GENEROUS WITH THE FRESH HERBS AND THE AROMAS WILL TRANSPORT YOU TO THE PROVENÇAL COUNTRYSIDE!

serves
4–6
preparation
30 minutes,
plus 6–24 hours'
marinating and 10
minutes' resting
cooking
20–25 minutes

ingredients
- 1 leg of lamb, about 1.5 kg/3 lb 5 oz, boned
- olive oil, for brushing

MARINADE
- 1 bottle full-bodied red wine
- 2 large garlic cloves, chopped
- 2 tbsp extra virgin olive oil
- large handful of fresh rosemary sprigs, plus extra to garnish
- fresh thyme sprigs, plus extra to garnish

BLACK OLIVE TAPENADE
- 250 g/9 oz black Niçoise olives in brine, rinsed and stoned
- 1 large garlic clove
- 2 tbsp walnut pieces
- 4 canned anchovy fillets, drained
- 125 ml/4 fl oz extra virgin olive oil
- lemon juice, to taste
- pepper

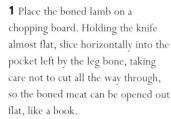

1 Place the boned lamb on a chopping board. Holding the knife almost flat, slice horizontally into the pocket left by the leg bone, taking care not to cut all the way through, so the boned meat can be opened out flat, like a book.

2 Place the lamb in a large non-metallic bowl and add all the marinade ingredients. Cover with clingfilm and leave to marinate in the refrigerator for at least 6 hours, but preferably up to 24 hours, turning the meat over several times.

3 Preheat the barbecue. To make the tapenade, place the olives, garlic, walnut pieces and anchovies in a food processor and process until blended. With the motor still running, slowly add the olive oil through the feed tube. Add lemon juice and pepper to taste. Transfer to a bowl, cover with clingfilm and chill until required.

4 When ready to cook, remove the lamb from the marinade and pat dry. Lay the lamb flat and thread 2–3 long metal skewers through the flesh, so that the meat remains flat while it cooks. Spread the tapenade all over the lamb on both sides.

5 Brush the barbecue rack with oil. Place the lamb on the rack about 10 cm/4 inches above hot coals and cook for 5 minutes. Turn the meat over, and continue cooking for a further 5 minutes. Turn twice more at 5-minute intervals, brushing with extra tapenade. Raise the rack to 15 cm/6 inches if the meat begins to look charred – it should be medium-cooked after 20–25 minutes.

6 Remove the lamb from the heat and leave to stand for 10 minutes before carving into thin slices and serving, garnished with rosemary and thyme sprigs.

LAMB SHANKS WITH ROASTED ONIONS

SLOW-ROASTED LAMB IS INFUSED WITH THE FLAVOURS OF GARLIC AND ROSEMARY AND SERVED WITH SWEET RED ONIONS AND GLAZED CARROT BATONS. YOU WON'T REQUIRE ANYTHING MORE EXCEPT A BOTTLE OF FRUITY RED WINE.

serves
4

preparation
20 minutes

cooking
2–2¼ hours

ingredients
- 4 x 350 g/12 oz lamb shanks
- 6 garlic cloves
- 2 tbsp virgin olive oil
- 1 tbsp fresh rosemary, very finely chopped
- 4 red onions
- 350 g/12 oz carrots, cut into thin batons
- 4 tbsp water
- salt and pepper

1 Preheat the oven to 180°C/ 350°F/Gas Mark 4. Trim off any excess fat from the lamb. Using a small, sharp knife, make 6 incisions in each shank. Cut the garlic cloves lengthways into 4 slices. Insert 6 garlic slices in the incisions in each lamb shank.

2 Place the lamb in a single layer in a roasting tin, drizzle with the olive oil, sprinkle with the rosemary and season with pepper. Roast in the preheated oven for 45 minutes.

3 Wrap each of the onions in a piece of foil. Remove the roasting tin from the oven and season the lamb with salt. Return to the oven and place the wrapped onions on the shelf next to it. Roast for a further 1–1¼ hours until the lamb is very tender.

4 Meanwhile, bring a large saucepan of water to the boil. Add the carrot batons and blanch for 1 minute. Drain and refresh in cold water.

5 Remove the roasting tin from the oven when the lamb is meltingly tender and transfer it to a warmed serving dish. Skim off any fat from the roasting tin and place it over a medium heat. Add the carrots and cook for 2 minutes, then add the water, bring to the boil and simmer, stirring constantly and scraping up the glazed bits from the base of the roasting tin.

6 Transfer the carrots and sauce to the serving dish. Remove the onions from the oven and unwrap. Cut off and discard about 1 cm/½ inch of the tops and add the onions to the dish. Serve immediately.

ROGAN JOSH

THIS INDIAN DISH OF CHUNKS OF LAMB BRAISED IN CREAM AND SPICES IS A KASHMIRI SPECIALITY.
THE TURMERIC GIVES IT A LOVELY GOLDEN COLOUR. IT IS DELICIOUS SERVED WITH RICE, BUT IT
CAN ALSO BE SERVED WITH NAAN BREAD TO SOAK UP THE WONDERFULLY CREAMY SAUCE.

serves
4

preparation
20 minutes,
plus 15 minutes'
cooling

cooking
50–55 minutes

ingredients
- 125 ml/4 fl oz ghee or
  vegetable oil
- 500 g/1 lb 2 oz boneless
  lamb, cut into bite-sized
  chunks
- 4 garlic cloves, chopped
- 3 fresh green chillies,
  chopped
- 2.5-cm/1-inch piece fresh
  root ginger, grated
- 1 tsp poppy seeds
- 1 cinnamon stick, ground
- 1 cardamom pod, ground
- 4 cloves, ground
- 1 tsp coriander seeds,
  ground
- 1 tsp cumin seeds, ground
- 250 ml/9 fl oz soured cream
- 1/2 tsp turmeric
- 1/2 tsp chilli powder
- 2 large tomatoes, chopped
- 1 bay leaf
- fresh coriander leaves,
  to garnish
- freshly cooked rice, to serve

1 Heat half of the ghee in a large saucepan over a high heat. Add the lamb and cook, stirring, for 5 minutes. Lift out the meat with a slotted spoon and drain on kitchen paper. Add the garlic, chillies, ginger, poppy seeds and ground spices to the saucepan and cook over a medium heat, stirring, for 4 minutes. Remove from the heat, leave to cool for a few minutes, then transfer the spice mixture to a food processor. Stir in the soured cream, turmeric and chilli powder and process the mixture until smooth.

2 Heat the remaining ghee in the saucepan over a low heat. Add the chopped tomatoes and cook, stirring, for 3 minutes. Add the soured cream mixture and cook, stirring, until the oil separates. Remove from the heat and add the lamb. Add the bay leaf, return the saucepan to the heat and cover. Simmer gently for 35–40 minutes, or until most of the liquid has been absorbed. Remove from the heat and discard the bay leaf. Garnish with coriander leaves and serve with freshly cooked rice.

POT-ROAST PORK

BEEF AND CHICKEN ARE THE MOST POPULAR CHOICES FOR POT-ROASTING, BUT A LOIN OF
PORK WORKS SUPERBLY WELL, TOO. THIS IS A RICH AND FLAVOURSOME DISH THAT IS IDEAL FOR
ENTERTAINING. SERVE IT WITH BAKED OR ROAST POTATOES AND FRESHLY COOKED PEAS.

serves
4
preparation
20 minutes
cooking
1½ hours

ingredients
- 1 tbsp sunflower oil
- 55 g/2 oz butter
- 1 kg/2 lb 4 oz boned and rolled pork loin joint
- 4 shallots, chopped
- 6 juniper berries
- 2 fresh thyme sprigs, plus extra to garnish
- 150 ml/5 fl oz dry cider
- 150 ml/5 fl oz chicken stock or water
- 8 celery sticks, chopped
- 2 tbsp plain flour
- 150 ml/5 fl oz double cream
- salt and pepper

TO SERVE
- freshly cooked peas
- boiled potatoes

1 Heat the oil with half the butter in a large, heavy-based saucepan or flameproof casserole. Add the pork and cook over a medium heat, turning frequently, for 5–10 minutes, or until browned. Transfer to a plate.

2 Add the shallots to the saucepan and cook, stirring frequently, for 5 minutes, or until softened. Add the juniper berries and thyme sprigs and return the pork to the saucepan, with any juices that have collected on the plate. Pour in the cider and stock, season to taste with salt and pepper, then cover and simmer for 30 minutes. Turn the pork over and add the celery. Re-cover the pan and cook for a further 40 minutes.

3 Meanwhile, make a beurre manié by mashing the remaining butter with the flour in a small bowl. Transfer the pork and celery to a platter with a slotted spoon and keep warm. Remove and discard the juniper berries and thyme. Whisk the beurre manié, a little at a time, into the simmering cooking liquid. Cook, stirring constantly, for 2 minutes, then stir in the cream and bring to the boil.

4 Slice the pork and spoon a little of the sauce over it. Garnish with thyme sprigs and serve immediately with the celery, freshly cooked peas and potatoes. Hand around the remaining sauce separately.

  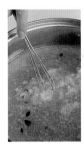

variation
Substitute 2 thinly sliced fennel bulbs for the chopped celery if you would prefer an aniseed flavour in this dish.

CITRUS PORK CHOPS

THE ADDITION OF JUNIPER AND FENNEL TO THE PORK CHOPS GIVES AN UNUSUAL AND DELICATE FLAVOUR TO THIS DISH. WHEN COMBINED WITH THE SWEET, CITRUS TASTE OF ORANGE, THE RESULT IS AN UNFORGETTABLE, MOUTHWATERING EXPERIENCE THAT WILL LEAVE YOU YEARNING FOR MORE.

serves
4

preparation
25 minutes, plus 2 hours' marinating

cooking
10–15 minutes

ingredients
- ½ fennel bulb
- 1 tbsp juniper berries, lightly crushed
- about 2 tbsp olive oil
- finely grated rind and juice of 1 orange
- 4 pork chops, about 150 g/5½ oz each

TO SERVE
- crisp salad
- fresh bread

1 Using a sharp knife, finely chop the fennel bulb, discarding the fronds and green parts.

2 Grind the juniper berries in a pestle and mortar. Mix the crushed juniper berries with the fennel flesh, oil and orange rind.

3 Using a sharp knife, score a few cuts all over each pork chop.

4 Place the pork chops in a roasting tin or an ovenproof dish. Spoon the fennel and juniper mixture over the pork chops.

5 Carefully pour the orange juice over the top of each pork chop, cover and leave to marinate in the refrigerator for 2 hours.

6 Preheat the grill to medium. Cook the pork chops under the hot grill for 10–15 minutes, depending on the thickness of the meat, until the meat is tender and cooked through, turning occasionally.

7 Transfer the pork chops to serving plates and serve with a crisp, fresh salad and plenty of fresh bread to mop up the cooking juices.

cook's tip

Juniper berries are usually associated with gin, but are often added to meat dishes in Italy for a delicate citrus flavour. They can be bought dried from health food shops.

SWEET & SOUR PORK RIBS

THIS DISH MAKES A DELICIOUS ADDITION TO ANY BARBECUE, AND THE SLICED PINEAPPLE RINGS ARE A PERFECT COMPANION TO THE RIBS. IN THIS RECIPE, THE TRADITIONAL CHINESE-STYLE SPARE RIB HAS BEEN USED, BUT BABY BACK RIBS AND LOIN RIBS ARE ALSO SUITABLE.

serves
4

preparation
15 minutes, plus 2
hours' marinating

cooking
50 minutes

ingredients
- 2 garlic cloves, crushed
- 5-cm/2-inch piece fresh root ginger, grated
- 150 ml/5 fl oz soy sauce
- 2 tbsp sugar
- 4 tbsp sweet sherry
- 4 tbsp tomato purée
- 300 g/10½ oz pineapple, cubed
- 2 kg/4 lb 8 oz pork spare ribs
- 3 tbsp clear honey
- 300 g/10½ oz pineapple rings, fresh or canned, to serve

1 Mix the garlic, ginger, soy sauce, sugar, sherry, tomato purée and cubed pineapple together in a non-porous dish.

2 Place the spare ribs in the dish and make sure that they are coated completely with the marinade.

3 Cover the dish with clingfilm. Leave the ribs to marinate at room temperature for 2 hours.

4 Preheat the barbecue. Cook the ribs over medium-hot coals for

30–40 minutes, brushing with the honey after 20–30 minutes.

5 Baste the spare ribs with the reserved marinade frequently until cooked.

6 Cook the pineapple rings over medium-hot coals for 10 minutes, turning once.

7 Transfer the cooked ribs to a serving dish and serve immediately with the barbecued pineapple rings on the side.

cook's tip

If a marinade contains soy sauce, the marinating time should be limited, usually to 2 hours. If left to marinate for too long, the meat will dry out and become tough.

BRAISED VEAL IN RED WINE

THIS IS A CLASSIC CASSEROLE OF MEAT BRAISED IN WINE WITH GARLIC, TOMATOES AND A LIBERAL AMOUNT OF HERBS. YOU CAN USE STEWING VEAL OR BEEF IN THIS RECIPE, AND THIS DISH GOES PARTICULARLY WELL WITH FRESHLY COOKED LONG-GRAIN RICE.

serves
6

preparation
25 minutes

cooking
2 hours 20
minutes–2 hours
25 minutes

ingredients
- 25 g/1 oz plain white flour
- 900 g/2 lb stewing veal or beef, cubed
- 4 tbsp olive oil
- 350 g/12 oz button onions
- 2 garlic cloves, finely chopped
- 350 g/12 oz carrots, sliced
- 300 ml/10 fl oz dry red wine
- 150 ml/5 fl oz beef or chicken stock
- 400 g/14 oz canned chopped tomatoes with herbs
- pared rind of 1 lemon
- 1 bay leaf
- 1 tbsp chopped fresh flat-leaf parsley
- 1 tbsp chopped fresh basil
- 1 tsp chopped fresh thyme
- salt and pepper
- freshly cooked rice, to serve

1 Preheat the oven to 180°C/ 350°F/Gas Mark 4. Place the flour and pepper in a polythene bag, add the meat and shake well to coat each piece. Heat the oil in a large flameproof casserole. Add the meat and fry, in batches, for 5–10 minutes, stirring constantly, until browned on all sides. Remove with a slotted spoon and reserve.

2 Add the button onions, garlic and carrots to the casserole and fry for 5 minutes until beginning to soften. Return the meat to the casserole.

3 Pour in the wine, stirring in any glazed bits from the bottom, then add the stock, the tomatoes with their juice, lemon rind, bay leaf, parsley, basil, thyme, salt and pepper. Bring to the boil then cover the casserole.

4 Cook in the preheated oven for 2 hours, or until the meat is tender. Serve hot with freshly cooked rice.

cook's tip

This is a perfect casserole for cooking in advance and then reheating. Once cooked, leave to cool and store in the refrigerator. Reheat by bringing to the boil then simmering for 15 minutes.

OSSO BUCCO WITH CITRUS RINDS

POPULAR THROUGHOUT ALL OF ITALY, YOU'LL ALSO FIND SLOW-COOKED VEAL SHINS IN MANY RESTAURANTS ALONG THE MEDITERRANEAN. THE ORANGE AND LEMON RINDS, ALONG WITH FRESH BASIL, GIVE THE DISH A REAL SOUTHERN ITALIAN FLAVOUR.

serves
6
preparation
25 minutes
cooking
1½ hours

ingredients
- 1–2 tbsp plain flour
- 6 meaty slices osso bucco (veal shins)
- 1 kg/2 lb 4 oz fresh tomatoes, peeled, deseeded and diced, or 800 g/1 lb 12 oz canned chopped tomatoes
- 1–2 tbsp olive oil
- 250 g/9 oz onions, very finely chopped
- 250 g/9 oz carrots, finely diced
- 225 ml/8 fl oz dry white wine
- 225 ml/8 fl oz veal stock
- 6 large basil leaves, torn
- 1 large garlic clove, very finely chopped
- finely grated rind of 1 large lemon
- finely grated rind of 1 orange
- 2 tbsp finely chopped fresh flat-leaf parsley
- salt and pepper
- crusty bread, to serve

1 Place the flour in a polythene bag and season with salt and pepper. Add the osso bucco, a couple of pieces at a time, and shake until well coated. Remove and shake off the excess flour. Continue until all the pieces are coated.

2 If using canned tomatoes, pass them through a sieve and leave to drain.

3 Heat 1 tablespoon of the oil in a large flameproof casserole. Add the osso bucco and fry for 10 minutes on each slide until well browned. Remove from the casserole.

4 Add 1–2 teaspoons oil to the casserole if necessary. Add the onions and fry for 5 minutes, stirring, until softened. Stir in the carrots and continue frying until they become soft.

5 Add the tomatoes, wine, stock and basil and return the osso bucco to the casserole. Bring to the boil, then reduce the heat, cover and simmer for 1 hour. Check that the meat is tender with the tip of a knife. If not, continue cooking for 10 minutes and test again.

6 When the meat is tender, sprinkle with the garlic and lemon and orange rinds, re-cover and cook for a further 10 minutes.

7 Adjust the seasoning if necessary. Sprinkle with the parsley and serve with crusty bread.

4

POULTRY
AND GAME

POULTRY IS DELICIOUS, ECONOMICAL AND VERY VERSATILE. A ROAST CHICKEN, FOR EXAMPLE, MAKES A WONDERFUL TABLE CENTREPIECE, AND WHEN YOU HAVE EATEN YOUR FILL, THERE ARE ALL KINDS OF INSPIRING DISHES YOU CAN MAKE USING THE LEFTOVERS. GAME IS ALSO DELICIOUS, AND MAKES LOVELY, IMPRESSIVE FARE FOR A DINNER PARTY.

INTRODUCTION

POULTRY IS RICH IN PROTEIN, AND QUICK AND EASY TO PREPARE AND COOK. SOME BIRDS, SUCH AS CHICKEN AND TURKEY, CAN BE A LOW-FAT CHOICE AS LONG AS THE FATTY SKIN IS REMOVED, AND THEY ARE VERY VERSATILE. DUCK IS FATTIER, BUT MAKES A GOOD DINNER PARTY CHOICE. GAME BIRDS AND ANIMALS ARE BECOMING MORE WIDELY AVAILABLE.

Buying and storing poultry and game

Always buy your poultry and game as fresh as possible and from a reputable supplier. Choose plump birds that have unblemished skin, and make sure that any wrapping or packaging is intact. As soon as you get it home, remove the packaging (if it's a fresh bird) and transfer the giblets (if any) to a separate bowl. Place the bird on a rack in a dish, then cover it and any giblets loosely with clingfilm and store in the refrigerator. Keep it well away from cooked meats to prevent any cross-contamination. Whole birds will keep for 1–2 days in the refrigerator, and giblets no longer than 1 day.

Frozen birds can be stored in the freezer in their original packaging. Thaw in the refrigerator thoroughly before cooking; you will need to allow 5 hours per 450 g/1 lb for a chicken and 6 hours per 450 g/1 lb for a turkey.

Game birds are available fresh when in season and frozen all year round. If they are truly wild birds and not farmed, they will have a lower fat content and should therefore be wrapped in bacon or pork fat during roasting. Older birds are not recommended for roasting, but are more suited to soups, casseroles and stews. Game animals, such as venison and rabbit, tend to be less tender than farmed animals because they get more exercise in the wild. They should therefore be cooked slowly until tender, but not overcooked. Braising is a good method for keeping the meat moist, or it can be roasted if wrapped first in bacon or pork fat.

Types of bird

In addition to the flavour, the choice of bird may depend on the occasion, how many people you are catering for and how much preparation you wish to do.

Chicken
There are many different varieties of chicken available, including free range, organic and corn-fed. You can buy whole birds ready prepared for the oven or frozen. You can also buy a variety of joints – wing, breast, leg, thigh or drumstick – or you can joint a whole bird yourself. Chicken is delicious roasted, steamed, poached, grilled, casseroled, barbecued, chargrilled, stir-fried, pan-fried or deep-fried.

Poussin
A poussin is a very young, small chicken. Poussins weigh up to 450 g/1 lb and you should therefore allow one whole bird per person. They are suitable for roasting, barbecuing and grilling.

Guinea fowl
This bird is related to the chicken and the partridge, and has light and dark meat and a strong flavour. It is available fresh and frozen. As guinea fowl has a low fat content, it is most suited to moist cooking methods such as casseroling. Alternatively, you can wrap it in bacon rashers or pork fat and roast it.

Turkey
These birds are much larger than chickens – some can grow to a massive 31.5 kg/70 lb – but the

Chicken

trend nowadays is for much smaller birds. This is because turkey suppliers would like to encourage their use all year round, rather than just during Christmas and other holiday periods. Turkeys have similar uses to chickens, and you can often interchange them with chickens in recipes. You can buy whole birds ready prepared for the oven or frozen. You can also buy separate joints, such as breast joints or drumsticks. Turkey is particularly suitable for roasting, casseroling, braising, stir-frying or pan-frying.

Duck

Ducks are available whole, fresh and frozen. Breast and leg joints are also available. Duck is fattier than chicken or turkey, and is therefore particularly suitable for roasting, grilling or pan-frying. Duck is often served with a tart fruit sauce, such as orange, in order to cut through any fatty aftertaste.

Goose

Geese are larger than ducks, and can be bought fresh, although they are more often bought frozen. Although they are popular during holidays and Christmas time, especially in Europe, they have become less popular year-round because of their very high fat content. Geese are best roasted, pot-roasted, braised or stewed. It is also a good idea to serve them with a tart fruit sauce in order to cut through any fatty aftertaste.

Grouse

These are small game birds, and you will need to allow one bird per person. If you are going to roast them, wrap the grouse in bacon or pork fat during cooking. You can also pot-roast, braise, casserole or stew them.

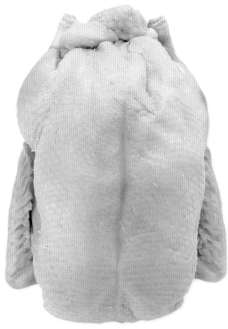

Duck

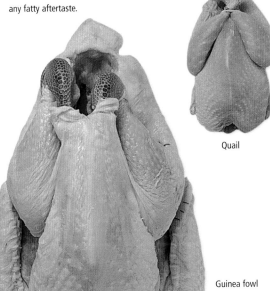

Guinea fowl

Quail

Partridge

This game bird has a dark flesh and an earthy flavour. Since its flesh can be somewhat tough, it is better braised, stewed or casseroled. However, it can also be roasted.

Pheasant

These are medium-sized game birds. The male has more brilliant plumage than the female, but the female is juicier and more tender. Young pheasants can be roasted, but older birds should be wrapped in bacon or pork fat during roasting; they can also be braised, casseroled or stewed.

Quail

These small game birds are related to the partridge. The European variety has lean, medium-dark flesh, whereas the American variety has lean but lighter flesh. Both types have a sweet flavour. Quails are suitable for roasting, pot-roasting, braising, barbecuing, casseroling or grilling. Their small eggs have a speckled brown shell and a rich flavour.

Venison

Deer is a popular game animal and the meat is available wild or farmed. It is low in cholesterol, and usually available as leg or saddle joints, or as steaks. The best meat comes from a male deer under the age of two years. Venison meat is quite dry and is therefore more suited to casseroles.

Rabbit

This game animal has fine white meat and is available fresh or frozen; you can also buy it whole or boned and cut into pieces. Tender young rabbits are suitable for grilling, frying or roasting; older rabbits should be braised, casseroled or stewed.

Preparation and cooking techniques

Preparing a bird in the right way will help to ensure that it is presented to its best advantage. It is essential to cook poultry all the way through in order to kill off any potentially harmful bacteria.

SPATCHCOCKING A SMALL BIRD

Spatchcocking helps to flatten the bird before grilling or barbecuing, ensuring quicker and more even cooking. Place the bird breast-side down (this means the legs are under the bird, and the wings are on top) on a clean chopping board. Cut along either side of the backbone and remove it (you can save it for making chicken stock or discard it). Open the bird out and turn it over. Using your palms, press down on the bird to flatten it against the chopping board.

MAKING CHICKEN STOCK

Chicken stock is ideal for soups and sauces, and you can store it, covered with clingfilm, in the refrigerator for 2–3 days. You can also freeze it for up to 6 months. Put the chicken carcass into a large saucepan with 1 chopped onion, 1 sliced carrot, 1 chopped celery stick and 1 chopped leek. Add 1 bay leaf and 1 sprig of thyme, 3 stalks of parsley and some cracked black peppercorns. Cover with water and bring to the boil, then use a slotted spoon to skim off any scum from the surface. Lower the heat, cover the pan, and leave to simmer for 2–3 hours. Strain the contents into a large bowl and discard the solids. Use the stock as required.

ROASTING A LARGE CHICKEN OR A TURKEY

First wipe the chicken or turkey inside and out with kitchen paper. If you are going to stuff it, pull back the skin around the neck cavity and insert the stuffing into the neck end only (do not overfill the bird or it will not cook through properly). If you are not stuffing the bird, simply season the cavity. Pull the skin over the top, then pull up the wings and tie with string. Pull the legs together and tie with string. Rub butter or oil over the skin of the bird, then season to taste with salt and pepper. Transfer the bird to a wire rack in a roasting tin, and roast in a preheated oven, basting occasionally, until cooked through and tender. To test, insert a sharp knife or skewer into the thickest part of the bird: if the juices run clear, the bird is cooked. If not, return it to the oven and cook until done. Alternatively, if you are using a meat thermometer, the bird is cooked when the temperature reaches 90°C/194°F. Remove from the oven and leave it to rest, covered in kitchen foil, for 15–20 minutes before carving.

CARVING A LARGE BIRD

Place the cooked bird breast-side up on a clean chopping board. Steady the bird with a carving fork, then use a carving knife to cut between one wing and the side of the breast. Remove the wing and cut thin downward slices through the breast meat. Repeat this step on the other side and reserve the wings and the breast slices. Pull out one leg and cut through the joint. Repeat with the other side. Slice the meat from the

---

Oven temperatures and roasting times

Remember that individual oven temperatures and cooking times vary, so the following cooking times are approximate only. Always preheat the oven before cooking.

Bird	Weight	Temperature	Cooking time
Chicken	3 kg/6 lb 8 oz	200°C/400°F/Gas Mark 6	2 1/4 hours
Turkey	5 kg/11 lb	180°C/350°F/Gas Mark 4	3 1/2 hours
	8 kg/18 lb	180°C/350°F/Gas Mark 4	4 3/4–5 hours
Quail	450 g/1 lb	200°C/400°F/Gas Mark 6	30 minutes
Duck	2.5 kg/5 lb 8 oz	180°C/350°F/Gas Mark 4 200°C/400°F/Gas Mark 6	50 minutes at lower temperature, then for 2 hours at higher temperature

thighs and drumsticks. Serve the wings, and the slices from the breast, thighs and drumsticks.

ROASTING AND SERVING A DUCK
Place the duck breast-side up on a clean work surface, then wipe it inside and out with kitchen paper. Duck has a high fat content, so remove any surplus fat. Season inside the tail cavity and insert a bay leaf. Transfer the bird to a wire rack in a roasting tin. Use a fork to prick holes all over it, then season with salt and freshly ground black pepper. Roast in a preheated oven until cooked through and tender (turn and baste it halfway during the cooking time). To test, insert a sharp knife or skewer into the thickest part of the bird: if the juices run clear, the bird is cooked. If not, return the bird to the oven and cook until done. Alternatively, if you are using a meat thermometer, the bird is cooked when the temperature reaches 90°C/194°F. To serve the duck, joint it by cutting it in half lengthways. Alternatively, use a sharp knife to separate the legs from the body, then cut off the wings. Remove the breast meat and slice it. Serve the legs, wings and breast slices.

Jointing a whole bird

1 To cut a large raw bird into joints, remove any string and place it on a clean chopping board, breast-side up, with the legs pointing towards you.

2 Using a sharp knife, cut the skin between one leg and the side of the breast, then use your hand to press the leg down flat to the board. Do the same with the other leg. Cut through the joint attaching one of the legs and remove the leg from the body. Do the same for the other side.

3 Turn the bird to face the other way and locate the ridge along the middle of the back. Using a knife, cut away one breast, taking a wing off with it. Do the same with the other breast.

4 To divide the legs into thighs and drumsticks, put them skin-side down on the chopping board, then cut through the line to separate the joint. Reserve the carcass for making stock.

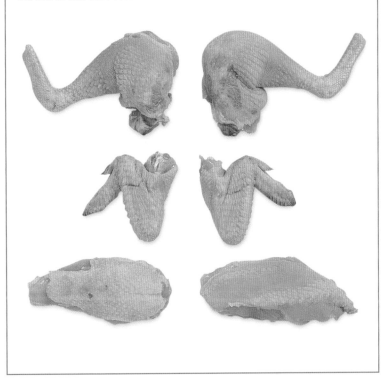

TRADITIONAL ROAST CHICKEN

ROAST CHICKEN IS A POPULAR DISH IN BRITAIN. IN THIS VERSION, A DELICIOUS MIXTURE OF GARLIC, WALNUTS AND PARSLEY IS STUFFED UNDERNEATH THE SKIN TO CREATE A WONDERFUL FLAVOUR AND TEXTURE OVER THE SURFACE OF THE BIRD. SERVE IT WITH ROAST POTATOES AND VEGETABLES.

serves
4

preparation
20 minutes,
plus 10 minutes'
resting

cooking
1 hour 50 minutes

ingredients
- 25 g/1 oz butter, softened
- 1 garlic clove,
  finely chopped
- 3 tbsp finely chopped
  toasted walnuts
- 1 tbsp chopped
  fresh parsley
- 1 oven-ready chicken,
  weighing 1.8 kg/4 lb
- 1 lime, cut into quarters
- 2 tbsp vegetable oil
- 1 tbsp cornflour
- 2 tbsp water
- salt and pepper

TO GARNISH
- lime wedges
- fresh rosemary sprigs

TO SERVE
- roast potatoes
- selection of freshly
  cooked vegetables

1 Preheat the oven to 190°C/375°F/ Gas Mark 5. Mix 1 tablespoon of the butter with the garlic, walnuts and parsley together in a small bowl. Season well with salt and pepper. Loosen the skin from the breast of the chicken without breaking it. Spread the butter mixture evenly between the skin and breast meat. Place the lime quarters inside the body cavity.

2 Pour the oil into a roasting tin. Transfer the chicken to the tin and dot the skin with the remaining butter. Roast for 1¾ hours, basting occasionally, until the chicken is

tender and the juices run clear when a skewer is inserted into the thickest part of the meat. Lift out the chicken and place on a serving platter to rest for 10 minutes.

3 Blend the cornflour with the water, then stir into the juices in the tin. Transfer to the hob. Stir over a low heat until thickened. Add more water if necessary. Garnish the chicken with lime wedges and rosemary sprigs. Serve with roast potatoes and a selection of freshly cooked vegetables and spoon over the thickened juices.

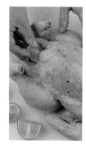

CHICKEN BIRYANI

THIS RECIPE MAY LOOK COMPLICATED, BUT IS NOT DIFFICULT TO FOLLOW. YOU CAN SUBSTITUTE
LAMB FOR THE CHICKEN, BUT IF YOU DO SO YOU WILL HAVE TO MARINATE IT OVERNIGHT FIRST.
GHEE IS A CLARIFIED BUTTER. IF IT IS UNAVAILABLE, USE ORDINARY BUTTER INSTEAD.

serves
8

preparation
15 minutes,
plus 3 hours'
marinating

cooking
1½–1¾ hours

ingredients

- 1½ tsp finely chopped fresh root ginger
- 1½ tsp crushed fresh garlic
- 1 tbsp garam masala
- 1 tsp chilli powder
- ½ tsp ground turmeric
- 2 tsp salt
- 5 green/white cardamom pods, crushed
- 300 ml/10 fl oz natural yogurt
- 1.5 kg/3 lb 5 oz chicken, skinned and cut into 8 pieces
- 150 ml/5 fl oz milk
- 1 tsp saffron strands
- 6 tbsp ghee
- 2 onions, sliced
- 450 g/1 lb basmati rice
- 2 cinnamon sticks
- 4 black peppercorns
- 1 tsp black cumin seeds
- 4 fresh green chillies
- 4 tbsp lemon juice
- 2–3 tbsp finely chopped fresh coriander leaves

1 Blend the ginger, garlic, garam masala, chilli powder, turmeric, half the salt and the cardamoms together in a bowl. Add the yogurt and chicken pieces and mix well. Cover and leave to marinate in the refrigerator for 3 hours.

2 Boil the milk in a small saucepan, pour over the saffron and reserve.

3 Heat the ghee in a saucepan. Add the onions and fry until golden. Transfer half of the onions and ghee to a bowl and reserve.

4 Place the rice, cinnamon sticks, peppercorns and black cumin seeds in a saucepan of water. Bring the rice to the boil and remove from the heat when half-cooked. Drain and place in a bowl. Mix with the remaining salt.

5 Chop the chillies and reserve. Add the chicken mixture to the saucepan containing the onions. Add half each of the chopped green chillies, lemon juice, coriander and saffron milk. Add the rice, then the rest of the ingredients, including the reserved onions and ghee. Cover tightly. Cook over a low heat for 1 hour. Check that the meat is cooked through; if it is not cooked, return to the heat and cook for a further 15 minutes. Mix well before serving.

THAI RED CHICKEN CURRY

THAI CURRY PASTE IS A PASTE OF AROMATIC HERBS, SPICES AND VEGETABLES THAT IS A POPULAR FLAVOURING IN THAI CUISINE. IT COMES IN DIFFERENT VARIETIES: RED CURRY PASTE TENDS TO VARY IN SPICINESS, WHILE GREEN CURRY PASTE IS THE HOTTEST, AND YELLOW IS THE MILDEST.

serves
4

preparation
30 minutes

cooking
40 minutes

ingredients
- 6 garlic cloves, chopped
- 2 fresh red chillies, chopped
- 2 tbsp chopped fresh lemon grass
- 1 tsp finely grated lime rind
- 1 tbsp chopped fresh kaffir lime leaves
- 1 tbsp Thai red curry paste
- 1 tbsp coriander seeds, toasted and crushed
- 1 tbsp chilli oil
- 4 skinless, boneless chicken breasts, sliced
- 300 ml/10 fl oz coconut milk
- 300 ml/10 fl oz chicken stock
- 1 tbsp soy sauce
- 55 g/2 oz shelled unsalted peanuts, toasted and ground
- 3 spring onions, sliced diagonally
- 1 red pepper, deseeded and sliced
- 3 Thai aubergines, sliced
- 2 tbsp chopped fresh Thai basil or fresh coriander
- fresh coriander, to garnish
- freshly cooked jasmine rice, to serve

1 Place the garlic, chillies, lemon grass, lime rind, lime leaves, curry paste and coriander seeds in a food processor and process until the mixture is smooth.

2 Heat the oil in a preheated wok or large frying pan over a high heat. Add the chicken and garlic mixture and stir-fry for 5 minutes. Add the coconut milk, stock and soy sauce and bring to the boil. Reduce the heat and cook, stirring, for a further 3 minutes. Stir in the ground peanuts and simmer for 20 minutes.

3 Add the spring onions, pepper and aubergines and leave to simmer, stirring occasionally, for a further 10 minutes. Remove from the heat, stir in the basil and garnish with coriander. Serve immediately with freshly cooked jasmine rice.

CHICKEN FRICASSÉE

WHILE IT IS TYPICALLY COOKED IN CREAM, THE TERM 'FRICASSÉE' SIMPLY MEANS COOKING THE
MEAT – OR SOMETIMES FISH – IN A WHITE SAUCE, WITHOUT BROWNING IT. SERVE THIS CREAM-FREE
VERSION WITH PLAIN BOILED RICE OR NEW POTATOES FOR A DELICIOUS, FILLING SUPPER.

serves
4
preparation
15 minutes
cooking
35–40 minutes

ingredients
- 1 tbsp plain flour
- 4 skinless, boneless chicken breasts, about 140 g/5 oz each, trimmed of all visible fat and cut into 2-cm/ ³/₄-inch cubes
- 1 tbsp sunflower or corn oil
- 8 baby onions
- 2 garlic cloves, crushed
- 225 ml/8 fl oz chicken stock
- 2 carrots, diced
- 2 celery sticks, diced
- 225 g/8 oz frozen peas
- 1 yellow pepper, deseeded and diced
- 115 g/4 oz button mushrooms, sliced
- 125 ml/4 fl oz low-fat natural yogurt
- 3 tbsp chopped fresh parsley
- salt and white pepper

1 Spread out the flour on a dish and season with salt and pepper. Add the chicken and, using your hands, coat in the flour. Heat the oil in a heavy-based saucepan. Add the onions and garlic and cook over a low heat, stirring occasionally, for 5 minutes. Add the chicken and cook, stirring, for 10 minutes, or until just beginning to colour.

2 Gradually stir in the stock, then add the carrots, celery and peas. Bring to the boil, then reduce the heat, cover and simmer for 5 minutes. Add the pepper and mushrooms, cover and simmer for a further 10 minutes.

3 Stir in the yogurt and chopped parsley and season to taste with salt and pepper. Cook for 1–2 minutes, or until heated through, then transfer to 4 large, warmed serving plates and serve immediately.

cook's tip
When dicing peppers, cut them in half and place them on a chopping board, shiny side downwards, to prevent the knife from slipping.

variation
You can substitute skimmed milk for the yogurt and add extra flavour with 1 teaspoon of lemon juice and a pinch of freshly grated nutmeg in Step 3.

ROAST POUSSINS

IN THIS RECIPE, POUSSINS – BABY CHICKENS – ARE STUFFED WITH LEMON GRASS, LIME LEAVES AND GINGER, COATED WITH A SPICY MARINADE, THEN ROASTED UNTIL CRISP AND GOLDEN. THE RESULT IS A DISH OF SUCCULENT GOLDEN CHICKEN, PAIRED WITH AN EXCITING FUSION OF ASIAN FLAVOURS.

serves
4
preparation
10 minutes
cooking
55 minutes

ingredients
- 4 small poussins, weighing about 350–500 g/ 12 oz–1 lb 2 oz each
- 4 blades lemon grass
- 4 fresh kaffir lime leaves
- 4 slices fresh root ginger
- about 6 tbsp coconut milk, for brushing
- a mixture of wild rice and basmati rice, to serve

MARINADE
- 4 garlic cloves, peeled
- 2 fresh coriander roots
- 1 tbsp light soy sauce
- salt and pepper

TO GARNISH
- fresh coriander leaves
- lime wedges

1 Preheat the oven to 190°C/ 375°F/Gas Mark 5. Carefully wash the poussins and pat dry on kitchen paper.

2 Place all the ingredients for the marinade in a blender and purée until smooth. Alternatively, grind to a paste in a pestle and mortar.

3 Rub the marinade mixture into the skin of the poussins, using the back of a spoon to spread it evenly over the skins.

4 Place a blade of lemon grass, a lime leaf and a piece of ginger in the cavity of each poussin.

5 Place the poussins in a roasting tin and brush lightly with the coconut milk. Roast in the preheated oven for about 30 minutes.

6 Remove from the oven, brush again with coconut milk, then return to the oven and cook for a further 15–25 minutes, or until golden and cooked through, depending upon the size of the poussin. The poussins are cooked when the juices run clear when a skewer is inserted into the thickest part of the meat.

7 Serve the poussins with the pan juices poured over. Garnish with coriander leaves and lime wedges and serve with rice.

CHICKEN & GINGER STIR-FRY

THE POMEGRANATE SEEDS ADD A SHARP CHINESE FLAVOUR TO THIS INDIAN STIR-FRY. SERVE IT IN THE SUMMER WITH A SPICY RICE SALAD OR A MIXED GREEN SALAD, OR IN THE WINTER ON A BED OF FRESHLY COOKED LONG-GRAIN RICE OR WITH SOME WARM NAAN BREAD.

serves
4
preparation
10 minutes
cooking
25 minutes

ingredients
- 3 tbsp vegetable oil
- 700 g/1 lb 9 oz lean skinless, boneless chicken breasts, cut into 5-cm/ 2-inch strips
- 3 garlic cloves, crushed
- 1 tsp pomegranate seeds, crushed
- 3.5-cm/1 1/2-inch piece fresh root ginger, cut into strips
- 1/2 tsp turmeric
- 1 tsp garam masala
- 2 fresh green chillies, sliced
- 1/2 tsp salt
- 4 tbsp lemon juice
- grated rind of 1 lemon
- 6 tbsp chopped fresh coriander, plus extra to garnish
- 125 ml/4 fl oz chicken stock
- naan bread, to serve

1 Heat the oil in a preheated wok or large frying pan. Add the chicken and stir-fry until golden brown all over. Remove from the wok and reserve.

2 Add the garlic, pomegranate seeds and ginger to the wok and stir-fry in the oil for 1 minute, taking care not to let the garlic burn.

3 Stir in the turmeric, garam masala and chillies and fry for 30 seconds.

4 Return the chicken to the wok and add the salt, lemon juice, lemon rind, coriander and stock. Stir the chicken well to make sure it is coated in the sauce.

5 Bring the mixture to the boil, then reduce the heat and simmer for 10–15 minutes, or until the chicken is thoroughly cooked. Garnish with chopped coriander and serve with warm naan bread.

DUCK BREASTS WITH CHILLI & LIME

THESE DUCK BREASTS ARE WONDERFULLY COMPLEMENTED BY THE LIME MARINADE AND PLUM JAM.
THE ACIDITY OF THE LIME CUTS THROUGH THE RICHNESS OF THE DUCK BEAUTIFULLY. DUCK IS A
VERY FATTY MEAT, SO DRAIN OFF AS MUCH EXCESS FAT AS YOU CAN DURING COOKING.

serves
4

preparation
15 minutes,
plus 3–8 hours'
marinating

cooking
10 minutes

ingredients
- 4 boneless duck breasts
- 1 tsp vegetable oil
- 125 ml/4 fl oz chicken stock
- 2 tbsp plum jam
- salt and pepper

MARINADE
- 2 garlic cloves, crushed
- 4 tsp light soft brown sugar
- 3 tbsp lime juice
- 1 tbsp soy sauce
- 1 tsp chilli sauce

TO SERVE
- mixed salad leaves
- freshly cooked rice

1 To make the marinade, mix the garlic, sugar, lime juice, and the soy and chilli sauces together.

2 Using a small sharp knife, cut deep slashes in the skin of the duck breasts to make a diamond pattern. Place the duck breasts in a wide, non-metallic dish.

3 Spoon the marinade over the duck breasts, turning well to coat them evenly in the mixture. Cover the dish with clingfilm and leave to marinate in the refrigerator for at least 3 hours, or overnight.

4 Drain the duck, reserving the marinade. Heat a large, heavy-based pan until very hot and brush with the oil. Add the duck breasts, skin-side down, and cook for 4–5 minutes until the skin is browned and crisp. Pour off the excess fat.

5 Turn the duck breasts and cook on the other side for 2–3 minutes to brown. Add the reserved marinade, stock and jam and simmer for 2 minutes. Adjust the seasoning to taste and serve hot, with the juices spooned over the meat and salad leaves and freshly cooked rice.

PEKING DUCK

NO COOKBOOK WOULD BE COMPLETE WITHOUT THIS FAMOUS DISH. IN THIS VERSION, DELICIOUS CRISPY DUCK IS SERVED WITH PANCAKES AND A TANGY SAUCE FOR A REALLY SPECIAL MEAL. IT IS AN EXCELLENT CHOICE FOR A DINNER PARTY.

serves
4

preparation
20 minutes, plus 8 hours' standing

cooking
1 hour 25 minutes–
1½ hours

ingredients
- 1.8 kg/4 lb duck
- 1.7 litres/3 pints boiling water
- 4 tbsp clear honey
- 2 tsp dark soy sauce
- carrot strips, to garnish

SAUCE
- 2 tbsp sesame oil
- 125 ml/4 fl oz hoisin sauce
- 125 g/4½ oz caster sugar
- 125 ml/4 fl oz water

TO SERVE
- Chinese pancakes
- cucumber matchsticks
- shredded spring onions

1 Place the duck on a rack set over a roasting tin and pour 1.2 litres/ 2 pints of the boiling water over it. Remove the duck and rack and discard the water. Pat dry with kitchen paper, replace the duck and rack and reserve for several hours.

2 Mix the honey, 600 ml/1 pint of boiling water and soy sauce together. Brush the mixture as a glaze over the skin and inside the duck. Reserve the remaining glaze. Set aside for 1 hour, until the glaze has dried.

3 Coat the duck with another layer of glaze. Leave to dry and repeat until all of the glaze is used.

4 Preheat the oven to 190°C/ 375°F/Gas Mark 5. To make the sauce, heat the oil and add the hoisin sauce, sugar and water. Simmer for 2–3 minutes, until thickened. Cool and chill until required.

5 Cook the duck in the preheated oven for 30 minutes. Turn the duck over and cook for 20 minutes. Turn the duck again and cook for 20–30 minutes, or until the meat is cooked through and the skin is crisp.

6 Remove the duck from the oven and leave to stand for 10 minutes. Meanwhile, heat the Chinese pancakes in a bamboo steamer for 5–7 minutes. Cut the skin and duck meat into strips and divide betweeen individual serving plates. Garnish with carrot strips and serve with the pancakes, cucumber matchsticks, shredded spring onions and sauce.

ROAST DUCK WITH APPLE

THIS DISH MAKES AN EXCELLENT SUPPER AND IS FULL OF INTERESTING FLAVOURS. THE RICHNESS OF THE DUCK MEAT IN THIS RECIPE CONTRASTS WELL WITH THE APPLES, LEMON, BAY LEAVES AND APRICOT SAUCE. IF DUCKLING PORTIONS ARE UNAVAILABLE, USE A WHOLE BIRD CUT INTO JOINTS.

serves
4

preparation
10 minutes

cooking
1½ hours

ingredients
- 4 duckling portions, about 350 g/12 oz each
- 4 tbsp dark soy sauce
- 2 tbsp light muscovado sugar
- 2 red-skinned apples
- 2 green-skinned apples
- juice of 1 lemon
- 2 tbsp clear honey
- a few bay leaves
- salt and pepper
- assorted freshly cooked vegetables, to serve

APRICOT SAUCE
- 400 g/14 oz canned apricots in fruit juice
- 4 tbsp sweet sherry

1 Preheat the oven to 190°C/ 375°F/Gas Mark 5. Wash the duck and trim away any excess fat. Place on a wire rack over a roasting tin and prick all over with a fork or a clean, sharp needle.

2 Brush the duck with the soy sauce. Sprinkle over the sugar and season with pepper. Cook in the preheated oven, basting occasionally, for 50–60 minutes, or until the meat is cooked through and the juices run clear when a skewer is inserted into the thickest part of the meat.

3 Meanwhile, core the apples and cut each into 6 wedges, then place in a small bowl and mix with the lemon juice and honey. Transfer to a small roasting tin, add a few bay leaves and season to taste with salt and pepper.

Cook alongside the duck, basting occasionally, for 20–25 minutes until tender. Discard the bay leaves.

4 To make the sauce, place the apricots in a blender or food processor with the can juices and the sherry. Process until smooth. Alternatively, mash the apricots with a fork until smooth and mix with the juice and sherry.

5 Just before serving, heat the apricot sauce in a small saucepan. Remove the skin from the duck and pat the flesh with kitchen paper to absorb any fat. Serve the duck with the apple wedges, apricot sauce and freshly cooked vegetables.

variation

Fruit complements duck perfectly. Use canned pineapple in natural juice for a delicious alternative.

ROAST TURKEY WITH BREAD SAUCE

ROAST TURKEY MAKES AN EXCELLENT TABLE CENTREPIECE FOR CHRISTMAS OR THANKSGIVING.
IN THIS RECIPE, CHESTNUTS, SAUSAGE AND SAGE COMBINE TO MAKE A WONDERFUL STUFFING FOR
THE BIRD, WHICH IS COMPLEMENTED BEAUTIFULLY BY A DELICIOUSLY SMOOTH BREAD SAUCE.

serves
8

preparation
20 minutes,
plus 10 minutes'
resting

cooking
3½ hours

ingredients
- 5 kg/11 lb turkey
- 55 g/2 oz butter
- 5 tbsp red wine
- 400 ml/14 fl oz chicken
  stock, bought fresh or made
  with a stock cube
- 1 tbsp cornflour
- 1 tsp French mustard
- 1 tsp sherry vinegar
- 2 tsp water
- roast new potatoes,
  to serve

STUFFING
- 225 g/8 oz pork
  sausagemeat
- 225 g/8 oz unsweetened
  chestnut purée
- 85 g/3 oz walnuts, chopped
- 115 g/4 oz ready-to-eat
  dried apricots, chopped
- 2 tbsp chopped fresh
  parsley
- 2 tbsp chopped fresh sage
- 2 tbsp snipped fresh chives
- 4–5 tbsp double cream
- salt and pepper

BREAD SAUCE
- 1 onion, peeled
- 4 cloves
- 600 ml/1 pint milk
- 115 g/4 oz fresh white
  breadcrumbs
- 55 g/2 oz butter

1 Preheat the oven to 220°C/
425°F/Gas Mark 7. To make the
stuffing, combine the sausagemeat
and chestnut purée in a bowl, then
stir in the walnuts, apricots and
herbs. Stir in enough cream to make
a firm, but not dry, mixture. Season
to taste with salt and pepper.

2 Spoon the stuffing into the neck
cavity of the turkey and close the
flap of skin with a skewer. Place the
bird in a large roasting tin and rub
all over with 40 g/1½ oz of the
butter. Roast for 1 hour, then reduce
the oven temperature to 180°C/
350°F/Gas Mark 4 and roast for a
further 2½ hours. You may need to
pour off the fat from the roasting
tin occasionally.

3 Meanwhile, make the bread sauce.
Stud the onion with the cloves, then
place in a saucepan with the milk,
breadcrumbs and butter. Bring just
to boiling point over a low heat, then
remove from the heat and leave to
stand in a warm place to infuse. Just
before serving, remove the onion
and reheat the sauce gently, beating
well with a wooden spoon. Season to
taste with salt and pepper.

4 Check that the turkey is cooked
by inserting a skewer or the tip of
a sharp knife into the thigh; if the
juices run clear, it is ready. Transfer
the bird to a carving board, cover
loosely with foil and leave to rest.

5 To make the gravy, skim off the
fat from the roasting tin then place
the tin on the top of the hob over a
medium heat. Add the red wine and
stir with a wooden spoon, scraping
up all the sediments from the base
of the tin. Stir in the stock. Mix the
cornflour, mustard, vinegar and the
water together in a small bowl, then
stir into the wine and stock mixture.
Bring to the boil, stirring constantly
until thickened and smooth. Stir in
the remaining butter.

6 Carve the turkey and serve with
the warm bread sauce and all the
trimmings – including stuffing, roast
potatoes and gravy.

ROAST PHEASANT WITH RED WINE & HERBS

ROAST PHEASANT IS A DELICIOUS TREAT, AND MAKES A SPLENDID DISH FOR DINNER PARTIES AND
ENTERTAINING. IN THIS RECIPE, YOU WILL NEED TO USE YOUNG PHEASANTS, BECAUSE THEIR TENDER
FLESH IS JUICY ENOUGH FOR ROASTING AND WILL NOT DRY OUT. OLDER BIRDS ARE NOT SUITABLE.

serves

4

preparation

20 minutes,
plus 15 minutes'
resting

cooking

1 hour

ingredients

- 100 g/3 1/2 oz butter,
  slightly softened
- 1 tbsp chopped fresh thyme
- 1 tbsp chopped fresh
  parsley
- 2 oven-ready young
  pheasants
- 4 tbsp vegetable oil
- 125 ml/4 fl oz red wine
- salt and pepper

TO SERVE

- roast parsnips
- sautéed potatoes
- freshly cooked Brussels
  sprouts

1 Preheat the oven to 190°C/
375°F/Gas Mark 5. Place the butter
in a small bowl and mix in the
chopped herbs. Lift the skins off
the pheasants, taking care not to
tear them, and push the herb butter
under the skins. Season to taste with
salt and pepper.

2 Pour the oil into a roasting tin,
add the pheasants and cook in the
preheated oven for 45 minutes,
basting occasionally. Remove from
the oven, pour over the red wine,
then return to the oven and cook
for a further 15 minutes, or until

cooked through. Check that each
bird is cooked by inserting a knife
between the legs and body. If the
juices run clear, they are cooked.

3 Remove the pheasants from the
oven, cover with foil and leave
to stand for 15 minutes. Divide
between individual serving plates,
and serve with roast parsnips,
sautéed potatoes and freshly cooked
Brussels sprouts.

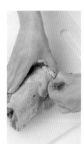

QUAILS WITH GRAPES

THIS IS A VERY POPULAR GAME DISH IN SPAIN, AND APPEARS ON MANY RESTAURANT MENUS. THE CLOVES AND BRANDY GIVE A WONDERFUL AROMATIC FLAVOUR TO THE BIRDS AND GRAPES, AND THE WEDGES OF POTATO PANCAKE PROVIDE A LOVELY CONTRAST IN TEXTURE AND FLAVOUR.

serves
4

preparation
30 minutes, plus
10–15 minutes'
cooling

cooking
1 hour

ingredients
- 4 tbsp olive oil
- 8 quails, gutted
- 280 g/10 oz green seedless grapes
- 225 ml/8 fl oz grape juice
- 2 cloves
- about 150 ml/5 fl oz water
- 2 tbsp Spanish brandy
- salt and pepper

POTATO PANCAKE
- 600 g/1 lb 5 oz unpeeled potatoes
- 35 g/1¼ oz unsalted butter or pork fat
- 1½ tbsp olive oil

1 Preheat the oven to 230°C/450°F/Gas Mark 8. For the pancake, par-boil the potatoes for 10 minutes. Drain and leave to cool completely, then peel, coarsely grate and season with salt and pepper to taste. Reserve until required.

2 Heat the 4 tablespoons of oil in a heavy-based frying pan or flameproof casserole large enough to hold the quails in a single layer over a medium heat. Add the quails and fry on all sides until they are golden brown.

3 Add the grapes, grape juice, cloves, enough water to come halfway up the side of the quails and salt and pepper to taste. Cover and simmer for 20 minutes. Transfer the quails and all the juices to a roasting tin, or casserole, and sprinkle with brandy. Roast, uncovered, in the preheated oven for 10 minutes.

4 Meanwhile, to make the potato pancake, melt the butter or pork fat with the oil in a 30-cm/12-inch non-stick frying pan over a high heat. When the fat is hot, add the grated potato and spread into an even layer. Reduce the heat and simmer for 10 minutes. Place a plate over the frying pan and, wearing oven gloves, invert them so the potato pancake drops onto the plate. Slide the potato back into the frying pan and continue cooking for 10 minutes, or until cooked through and crisp. Slide out of the frying pan and cut into 4 wedges. Keep the pancake warm until the quail is ready.

5 Place a potato pancake wedge and 2 quails on each individual serving plate. Taste the grape sauce and adjust the seasoning if necessary. Spoon the sauce over the quails and serve immediately.

CHARGRILLED VENISON STEAKS

VENISON HAS A GOOD STRONG FLAVOUR, WHICH MAKES IT AN IDEAL MEAT TO BARBECUE OR GRILL.
IN THIS RECIPE, THE VENISON STEAKS ARE FIRST MARINATED IN A DELICIOUS COMBINATION OF WINE,
OIL, SUGAR AND HERBS, AND THEN COOKED TO RELEASE ALL THEIR DELICIOUS FLAVOUR.

serves
4

preparation
15 minutes, plus 8
hours' marinating

cooking
12–24 minutes

ingredients
- 4 venison steaks
- 150 ml/5 fl oz red wine
- 2 tbsp sunflower oil
- 1 tbsp red wine vinegar
- 1 onion, chopped
- fresh parsley sprigs
- 2 fresh thyme sprigs
- 1 bay leaf
- 1 tsp caster sugar
- ½ tsp mild mustard
- salt and pepper

TO SERVE
- baked potatoes
- salad leaves
- cherry tomatoes

1 Place the venison steaks in a shallow, non-metallic dish.

2 Combine the wine, oil, wine vinegar, onion, fresh parsley, thyme, bay leaf, sugar, mustard and salt and pepper to taste in a screw-top jar and shake vigorously until well combined. Alternatively, using a fork, whisk the ingredients together in a bowl.

3 Pour the marinade mixture over the venison, cover and leave to marinate in the refrigerator overnight. Turn the steaks over in the mixture occasionally so that the meat is well coated.

4 Preheat the barbecue or grill to high. Cook the venison over hot coals, searing the meat over the hottest part of the barbecue for 2 minutes on each side. Alternatively, cook under the hot grill.

5 Move the meat to an area with slightly less intense heat, or turn down the grill to medium, and cook for a further 4–10 minutes on each side, according to taste. Test the meat by inserting the tip of a knife into the meat – the juices will range from red when the meat is still rare to clear as the meat becomes well cooked.

6 Serve the steaks immediately with baked potatoes, salad leaves and cherry tomatoes.

cook's tip

*Farmed venison is available all year round.
Look out for it in the meat section of the
supermarket or order it from an independent
butcher. Marinate overnight to tenderize.*

5

VEGETABLES AND SALADS

VEGETABLES AND SALADS ARE VERY GOOD FOR YOU AND EXTREMELY VERSATILE. YOU CAN COOK VEGETABLES IN COUNTLESS WAYS, FROM BOILING, STEAMING AND FRYING, TO BAKING, ROASTING AND STEWING. MANY OF THEM CAN BE EATEN RAW TOO. YOU CAN ALSO PRESENT THEM IN A MULTITUDE OF WAYS, FROM MASHED OR PURÉED TO JULIENNED.

INTRODUCTION

VEGETABLES ARE VERY GOOD FOR YOU: THEY ARE RICH IN VITAMINS AND MINERALS AND LOW IN FAT. THEY ARE ALSO VERY QUICK AND EASY TO PREPARE AND COOK. YOU CAN ALSO USE SURPLUS OR LEFTOVER VEGETABLES IN OTHER DISHES, SUCH AS A STOCK.

Buying and storing vegetables

Choose vegetables when they are in season because this is when they are at their best. Try to buy them in small quantities on a frequent basis to ensure a constant fresh supply – the fresher the vegetables, the better they will taste and the more nutrients they will have. Here are some of the main varieties.

ROOT VEGETABLES

Root vegetables are delicious and vary greatly in terms of flavour. They provide a colourful contrast to leafy green vegetables and are particularly good roasted or in casseroles.

Carrots

These are available all year round. Carrots should be peeled first, then you can grate them raw into salads, or slice and boil them. After boiling, you can mash them if desired. You can also steam, stir-fry or roast them.

Beetroot

These are available all year round and are excellent washed and grated raw into salads. Alternatively, you can boil or roast them whole. You can also buy beetroot ready-cooked.

Radishes

These are available in many sizes, shapes and colours all year round, the most common variety being the small red radish, which is either round or oval. Washed, trimmed and served raw, they give a peppery taste to salads and make excellent garnishes, whole or sliced.

Celeriac

This knobbly vegetable is usually available in the autumn, winter and spring. It is very good peeled and boiled, then mashed. You can also parboil and roast celariac.

Parsnips

Fresh parsnips are best during autumn and winter, although they are available all year round. They should always be cooked. You can boil and mash, or parboil and roast them. You can also steam or sauté parsnips, and they are very good in soups.

Potatoes

Available all year round and usually classified as either mealy or waxy, this versitile and popular vegetable comes in many shapes, sizes and colours including long white, round white and rounded. Potatoes range in size from small new potatoes, which are ideal for boiling and for salads, to large baking potatoes, which are excellent for baking in their skins or for making chips. Sweet potatoes are not botanically related to the potato, but they have a delicious sweet flavour and can be substituted for potatoes in many recipes. When cooking potatoes, you can either peel them first, or simply scrub them and leave unpeeled.

Potato skins are very nutritious, and delicious when cooked, so it is often a good idea to leave the skins on, unless you are making mashed potatoes, when it is better to remove them. Potatoes are excellent boiled, mashed, fried, baked and roasted. You can serve them hot or cold. After buying your potatoes, store them in a cool, dark place.

Swede

This root vegetable is available all year round and should always be peeled and cooked. You can boil and mash it or parboil and roast it. It is delicious mashed with carrots.

Turnips

Although available all year round, the peak season for turnips is in winter. Like swedes, these root vegetables are best peeled and boiled, then mashed. You can also parboil and roast them.

Parsnips

Radishes

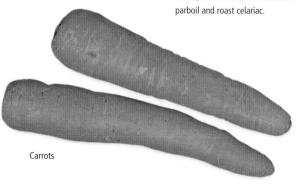

Carrots

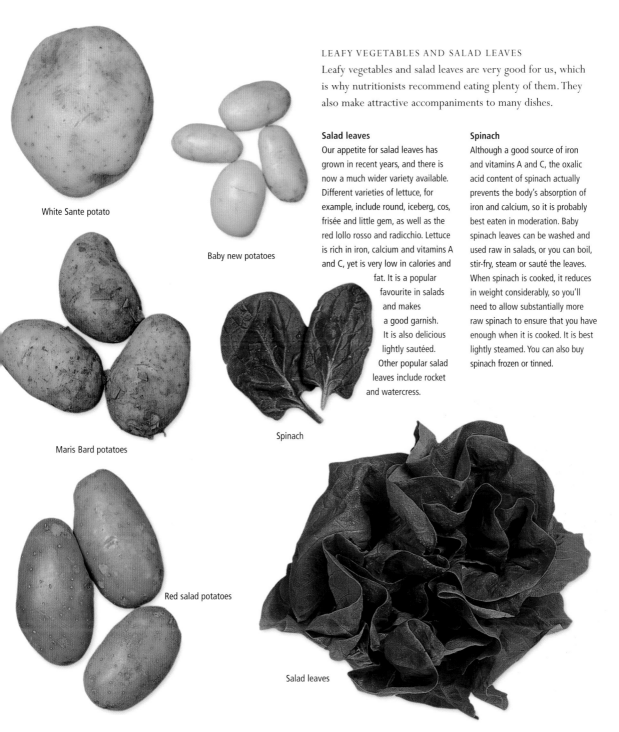

White Sante potato

Baby new potatoes

Maris Bard potatoes

Spinach

Red salad potatoes

Salad leaves

LEAFY VEGETABLES AND SALAD LEAVES
Leafy vegetables and salad leaves are very good for us, which is why nutritionists recommend eating plenty of them. They also make attractive accompaniments to many dishes.

Salad leaves
Our appetite for salad leaves has grown in recent years, and there is now a much wider variety available. Different varieties of lettuce, for example, include round, iceberg, cos, frisée and little gem, as well as the red lollo rosso and radicchio. Lettuce is rich in iron, calcium and vitamins A and C, yet is very low in calories and fat. It is a popular favourite in salads and makes a good garnish. It is also delicious lightly sautéed. Other popular salad leaves include rocket and watercress.

Spinach
Although a good source of iron and vitamins A and C, the oxalic acid content of spinach actually prevents the body's absorption of iron and calcium, so it is probably best eaten in moderation. Baby spinach leaves can be washed and used raw in salads, or you can boil, stir-fry, steam or sauté the leaves. When spinach is cooked, it reduces in weight considerably, so you'll need to allow substantially more raw spinach to ensure that you have enough when it is cooked. It is best lightly steamed. You can also buy spinach frozen or tinned.

BRASSICAS

These vegetables are excellent boiled, steamed or stir-fried. Take care not to overcook them, however – brassicas are best when tender but still slightly crisp to the bite.

Cabbages

These come in many shapes and colours, ranging from white and green to red. Look for cabbage that is crisp and fresh. You can wash and eat it raw in salads and coleslaw, or cook it in a variety of ways such as boiling, steaming or stir-frying.

Broccoli

This popular vegetable is available all year round and is very nutritious. It can be boiled, steamed, stir-fried, sautéed or baked.

Chinese leaves

These crinkly, cream-coloured leaves with green tips are available all year round. They can be used raw in salads, or sautéed, steamed, braised or baked. They are also popular in stir-fries.

Brussels sprouts

These look like tiny cabbages and are, in fact, related to the cabbage family. They are available fresh during autumn and winter, or frozen all year round. They are very good boiled or steamed, or shredded and added to stir-fries. However, due to their sulphur content, they have a strong flavour that some people dislike.

Cauliflower

Like cabbage, cauliflower comes in different colours: white, green and red, although the white variety is the most popular. You can eat it raw, or cook it by boiling, steaming, stir-frying, sautéeing or baking.

Pak choi

This is available all year round. It looks a little like celery and has crunchy white stalks and dark green leaves. It is related to Chinese leaves botanically, and is often confused with them but is not the same. However, it does have similar uses and can be used raw in salads, or stir-fried, sautéed, steamed, braised or baked.

Broccoli

Chinese leaves

Cabbage leaf

Brussels sprouts

Cauliflower

THE ONION FAMILY

These members of the onion family contain sulphuric compounds that give them their unmistakable aroma and flavour. Their taste varies from mild to pungent.

Leeks

These have a very mild onion flavour and range in size from small baby leeks to large. They can be boiled, steamed, sautéed, stir-fried or baked, and can be substituted for onions in most recipes.

Garlic

This versatile bulb was popular with the ancient Egyptians for its medicinal qualities and has many uses in modern cooking. It has an unmistakable taste, due to its sulphur content, and adds a delicious flavour to many different recipes. It can be boiled, steamed, sautéed, stir-fried, baked and roasted. When garlic is cooked with wine, it gives off a wonderful flavour and the combination is excellent in soups and sauces. It can also be used to liven up dressings.

Onions

These are available all year round in a variety of colours, from yellow and white to red. They also range in size from tiny pearl onions, to medium-sized French onions, to the large Spanish onions, and vary in flavour from mildly pungent to very strong. Once peeled and trimmed, they can be eaten raw in salads or as a garnish, or cooked in a wide variety of dishes, from stir-fries to bakes. You can also pickle onions.

Shallots

These are small onions that resemble large garlic cloves when they are peeled. Use shallots when you need a milder onion flavour. They are particularly good in stir-fries and bakes, and in kebabs.

Spring onions

These very small onions are available all year round but their peak season is during the spring and summer. They can be used raw in salads or sliced to make an attractive garnish, or they can be boiled, steamed, sautéed or baked. Spring onions are also excellent in stir-fries and soups.

Garlic

Leek

Spring onions

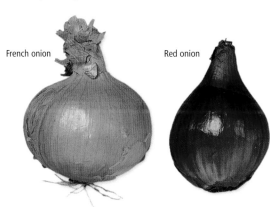

French onion

Red onion

Shallots

VEGETABLE FRUITS

The tastes of the vegetables in this category vary from the mild, creamy flavour of avocados, to the fiery heat of chillies. They are popular in a wide range of international dishes.

Aubergines

These come in different sizes and colours, but the most popular is the large, deep-purple variety. Aubergines must always be cooked, and unless you are using them in a moist recipe with lots of liquid, you should degorge them to remove bitter juices first. Simply cut the aubergine into slices about 1 cm/^{1}/$_2$ inch thick, spread them out in a large, shallow dish and sprinkle over plenty of salt. Leave the slices for 30 minutes, then transfer to a colander and rinse off the salt with plenty of cold running water. Pat dry with kitchen paper, then use in your chosen recipe.

Avocados

These are green or purplish-black vegetable fruits that are shaped like pears but have a soft, buttery interior. Look for avocados that are just beginning to yield to the touch when pressed, and have no bruises. You can use them halved as a starter, sliced in salads or mashed in dips. Avocados discolour quickly when cut, so use them straight away after cutting, or brush them with lemon juice to prevent discolouration.

Chillies

These fiery vegetable fruits usually come in red or green, and in many different sizes and shapes, from 5 mm/^{1}/$_4$ inch to 30 cm/12 inches in length. Generally, the smaller the chilli, the hotter the flavour; the small ones can be so fiery that they can burn the skin. Always wear protective gloves when handling chillies, and keep them away from your eyes. Chillies add a spicy kick to many recipes and are particularly good in sauces and stir-fries, and in dishes such as chilli con carne. Deseed chillies before use in order to reduce their fiery heat.

Peppers

When sweet peppers are young they are green, then as they ripen and get sweeter they turn red. You can also get yellow, orange, purple and brown peppers, or peppers in different shapes, such as the long pointed red Mediterranean peppers. Once sliced and deseeded, they can be used raw in salads or as crudités, or you can cook them in a variety of dishes. Roasting or grilling brings out their sweet flavour. They can also be sautéed, stir-fried, steamed, braised and baked.

Tomatoes

These are available all year round and come in many different sizes and shapes, from tiny cherry tomatoes to large beef tomatoes. Make sure your tomatoes are firm when you buy them. Tomatoes left on the vine are particularly flavourful: in order to preserve their flavour, store them on the vine until you intend to use them. You can eat tomatoes raw in salads and snacks, or cook them. They make excellent sauces, soups and pizza toppings, and are delicious sautéed, stir-fried, grilled and baked.

Peas

Mangetout

Green beans

POD VEGETABLES

Pod vegetables have a delicious flavour, and some varieties, such as sugar snap peas, are tender enough to have an edible pod, so you can eat them whole. They are very good stir-fried.

Pods

These are young vegetables that have edible pods, such as sugar snap peas, mangetout, green beans and runner beans. They have a delicious sweet flavour and can be steamed, boiled, sautéed or stir-fried.

Shelled peas and beans

These are seeds that are allowed to grow in the pod, then are served shelled. They include garden peas, petit pois (smaller peas) and broad beans, which are green and slightly kidney-shaped. All of them can be boiled or steamed.

OTHER VEGETABLES

Mushrooms and sweetcorn are delicious in salads, risottos and stir-fries, but try experimenting with more exotic varieties of vegetables too, such as Asian vegetables and seaweeds.

Exotic vegetables

There is a great variety of exotic vegetables available nowadays, and they come from all over the world. Some of the most popular include kombu, which is a dried form of kelp that is used in Japanese cooking; mooli, a long white root that is used in Asian cooking; and wakame, an edible seaweed popular in Asia.

Sweetcorn

The most popular type of sweetcorn these days is the yellow corn. The husks and silks need to be removed before cooking, then you can simply cook the corn whole on the cob, or remove the kernels and cook them on their own. Sweetcorn comes into season in the summer months, but you can also buy it frozen or canned all year round. It is delicious boiled on the cob, or the kernels can be cooked and used in soups, salads and bakes. You can also buy baby corn, which can be boiled, steamed or stir-fried.

Mushrooms

Both cultivated or wild mushrooms are available all year round. The former include the common white or chestnut, button, and large, flat field mushrooms. Wild mushrooms vary enormously in size, shape and colour, and include shiitake, porcini and pieds de moutons. They are available fresh or dried. Mushrooms can absorb a lot of water, so it is better to wipe them with a clean, damp cloth rather than wash them. They can be sautéed, stir-fried, deep-fried in batter, grilled or baked.

SQUASHES

Squashes are becoming increasingly popular these days, and we are becoming more creative with them. Small varieties can be particularly flavourful – for example, try mini-courgettes.

Courgettes

This member of the squash family is shaped like a cucumber and comes in various shades of green, sometimes with yellow stripes. It also comes in a variety of sizes, from 10 cm/4 inches to 60 cm/2 feet long (the largest are known as marrows). The smaller varieties tend to have the most flavour. Courgettes are available all year round, and are very versatile. They can be steamed, grilled, stir-fried, chargrilled, sautéed, deep-fried, baked and roasted, or you can eat them raw in salads. Courgette flowers, if you can get them, are wonderful stuffed and cooked, or battered and fried.

Cucumbers

Although best known as a salad vegetable, the cucumber is, in fact, a member of the squash family. It can be cut into crudités, with or without its skin, and served raw with dips, or lightly sautéed or stir-fried.

Pumpkins

This large squash is available in autumn and winter. The large variety is popular at Hallowe'en, when it is carved out and made into a mask or lantern. The smaller, orange variety has a sweeter flavour and is more suitable for cooking. Pumpkin pie is a particular favourite. You can also use pumpkin in soups and casseroles.

Squashes

Butternut, acorn and spaghetti squashes are classed as winter squashes. They are large and have thick skins and firm flesh. Once deseeded, they can be roasted, baked or steamed. Summer squashes, such as patty pans, are smaller and can be cooked fairly quickly by sautéeing, steaming or baking.

White mushrooms

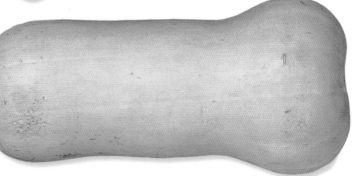

Butternut squash

Sweetcorn

BORSCHT

ANTONIN CARÊME, CHEF TO CZAR ALEXANDER I, IS CREDITED WITH INTRODUCING THIS TRADITIONAL RUSSIAN BEETROOT SOUP TO FRANCE AND SO TO THE REST OF EUROPE. THIS IS A LIGHTER, EASIER VERSION OF HIS RATHER ELABORATE RECIPE AND IS SUITABLE FOR VEGETARIANS.

serves
6
preparation
30 minutes
cooking
1¼ hours

ingredients

- 1 onion
- 55 g/2 oz butter
- 350 g/12 oz raw beetroot, cut into thin batons, and 1 raw beetroot, grated
- 1 carrot, cut into thin batons
- 3 celery sticks, thinly sliced
- 2 tomatoes, peeled, deseeded and chopped
- 1.4 litres/2 ½ pints vegetable stock

- 1 tbsp white wine vinegar
- 1 tbsp sugar
- 2 large fresh dill sprigs, snipped
- 115 g/4 oz white cabbage, shredded
- salt and pepper
- 150 ml/5 fl oz soured cream, to garnish
- rye bread, to serve (optional)

1 Slice the onion into rings. Melt the butter in a large, heavy-based saucepan over a low heat. Add the onion and cook, stirring occasionally, for 3–5 minutes, or until softened. Add the beetroot batons, carrot, celery and chopped tomatoes. Cook, stirring frequently, for 4–5 minutes.

2 Add the stock, vinegar and sugar and add a tablespoon of dill to the saucepan. Season to taste with salt and pepper. Bring to the boil, reduce the heat and simmer for 35–40 minutes, or until the vegetables are tender.

3 Stir in the cabbage, cover and simmer for 10 minutes. Stir in the grated beetroot, with any juices, and cook for a further 10 minutes. Ladle into warmed bowls. Garnish with a spoonful of soured cream and remaining snipped dill, and serve with rye bread, if liked.

variation

For a more substantial soup, add 2 diced potatoes along with the cabbage in Step 3. Cook for a further 10 minutes before adding the grated beetroot.

LEEK & POTATO SOUP

LEEK AND POTATO IS A WONDERFUL COMBINATION, ESPECIALLY WHEN TEAMED WITH HERBS AND
CREAM. IN THIS DISH, A DELICIOUS SMOKY FLAVOUR HAS BEEN INTRODUCED WITH THE ADDITION
OF THE SMOKED CHEESE. IT MAKES A SATISFYING, WARMING SOUP FOR ANY OCCASION.

serves
4

preparation
15–20 minutes,
plus 10 minutes'
cooling

cooking
35 minutes

ingredients
- 2 tbsp butter
- 2 garlic cloves, chopped
- 3 large leeks, trimmed
  and sliced
- 450 g/1 lb potatoes,
  peeled and chopped into
  bite-sized chunks
- 1 tbsp chopped
  fresh parsley
- 1 tbsp chopped
  fresh oregano
- 1 bay leaf
- 850 ml/1½ pints
  vegetable stock
- 200 ml/7 fl oz crème fraîche
- 100 g/3½ oz smoked
  firm cheese, such as
  Applewood, grated
- salt and pepper
- thick slices of fresh crusty
  bread, to serve

TO GARNISH
- fresh chives
- chopped fresh parsley

1 Melt the butter in a large saucepan
over a medium heat. Add the garlic
and cook, stirring, for 1 minute.
Add the leeks and cook, stirring,
for a further 2 minutes. Add the
potatoes, herbs and stock and season
to taste with salt and pepper. Bring
to the boil, then reduce the heat,
cover the saucepan and leave to
simmer for 25 minutes. Remove
from the heat, leave to cool for
10 minutes, then remove and discard
the bay leaf.

2 Transfer half of the soup to a food
processor and process until smooth
(you may need to do this in batches).
Return to the saucepan with the rest
of the soup, stir in the crème fraîche
and reheat gently. Season to taste
with salt and pepper.

3 Remove from the heat and stir in
the cheese. Ladle into serving bowls
and garnish with chives and chopped
fresh parsley. Serve with slices of
fresh crusty bread.

LES HALLES ONION SOUP

MORE LIKE A THICK ONION STEW THAN A SOUP, THIS TRADITIONAL RECIPE, WHICH INCLUDES A SLUG OF BRANDY, RECALLS THE DAYS WHEN THE LES HALLES DISTRICT OF PARIS WAS HOME TO THE CITY'S MEAT, SEAFOOD AND FRUIT AND VEGETABLE MARKETS, AND KNOWN AS THE 'BELLY OF PARIS'.

serves

4

preparation

20 minutes

cooking

1 hour 10 minutes–1 hour 15 minutes

ingredients

- 85 g/3 oz butter
- 2 tbsp olive oil
- 750 g/1 lb 10 oz onions, thinly sliced
- 1 tsp sugar
- ½ tsp salt
- 1½ tbsp plain flour
- 600 ml/1 pint hot beef stock
- 4 tbsp brandy
- 125 g/4½ oz Gruyère cheese, or half Gruyère and half Parmesan cheese, grated
- salt and pepper

CROÛTES

- 8 slices French bread, about 1 cm/½ inch thick
- 1 garlic clove, halved

1 Melt the butter with the oil in a large, heavy-based saucepan with a tight-fitting lid, or a flameproof casserole, over a medium–high heat. Stir in the onions, sugar and salt, then reduce the heat to low. Cover the surface with a piece of wet greaseproof paper or the lid and cook for 20–30 minutes, stirring occasionally, until the onions are a rich, dark golden brown. Uncover and stir constantly when they begin to darken, as they can burn easily.

2 Sprinkle the flour over the onions and continue cooking, stirring for 2 minutes. Stir in the hot stock and simmer, partially covered, for a further 15 minutes, skimming the surface if necessary.

3 To make the croûtes, preheat the grill to high and the oven to 200°C/400°F/Gas Mark 6. Arrange the bread slices on the grill rack and toast for 1–2 minutes, or until golden and crisp. Flip the slices over and repeat on the other side. Rub the top of each bread slice while it is still hot with the garlic halves, then reserve until required.

4 Stir the brandy into the soup and season to taste with salt and pepper. At this point, the soup can be left for up to a day, but reheat it before proceeding.

5 Divide the toasted bread between 4 heatproof soup bowls. Ladle over the soup, then top each with a quarter of the cheese. Place the bowls in the oven for 20 minutes, or until the cheese is golden and bubbling. Let the soup stand for a couple of minutes before serving.

cook's tip

The toasted croûtes are a good way to use up day-old French bread. Take care, however, not to cut the bread too thick, or it will absorb all the liquid.

RATATOUILLE

RATATOUILLE IS A WONDERFULLY VERSATILE DISH, AND IS ESPECIALLY USEFUL WHEN CATERING FOR VEGETARIANS. IT GOES WELL WITH JACKET POTATOES, PERHAPS TOPPED WITH A LITTLE SOURED CREAM, OR PILE IT ONTO A PLATTER OF FRESHLY COOKED RICE OR COUSCOUS.

serves
4

preparation
15 minutes,
plus 30 minutes'
standing

cooking
45 minutes

ingredients
- 1 aubergine, about
  250 g/9 oz
- 4 tbsp olive oil
- 2 garlic cloves, chopped
- 1 large onion, chopped
- 2 red peppers, deseeded
  and cut into bite-sized
  chunks
- 800 g/1 lb 12 oz canned
  chopped tomatoes
- 2 courgettes, sliced
- 1 celery stick, sliced
- 1 tsp sugar
- 2 tbsp chopped fresh thyme
- salt and pepper
- fresh thyme sprigs,
  to garnish

TO SERVE
- baked potatoes with butter
- fresh crusty bread

1 Trim the aubergine and cut it into bite-sized chunks, then place it in a colander. Sprinkle with salt and leave to stand for 30 minutes.

2 Heat the oil in a large saucepan over a medium heat. Add the garlic and onion and cook, stirring, for 3 minutes until softened slightly. Rinse the aubergine and drain well, then add it to the saucepan with the red peppers. Reduce the heat and cook gently, stirring frequently, for a further 10 minutes.

3 Stir in the tomatoes, courgettes, celery, sugar and thyme, and season to taste with salt and pepper. Bring to the boil, then reduce the heat, cover the saucepan, and leave to simmer gently for 30 minutes.

4 Remove the saucepan from the heat, transfer to serving plates and garnish with fresh thyme sprigs. Serve with buttered hot baked potatoes and fresh crusty bread.

variation
You can substitute the canned tomatoes with 450 g/1 lb peeled and deseeded fresh tomatoes and replace the fresh thyme with fresh basil, if you prefer.

CLASSIC ROAST POTATOES

THERE IS NOTHING QUITE LIKE LOVINGLY COOKED ROAST POTATOES, GOLDEN AND CRISP ON THE OUTSIDE, AND WONDERFULLY FLUFFY ON THE INSIDE. THESE POTATOES HAVE A LITTLE PAPRIKA FOR ADDED SPICE AND COLOUR. SIMPLY PILE THEM INTO A BOWL AND WATCH THEM DISAPPEAR.

serves
4

preparation
10 minutes

cooking
1½ hours

ingredients
- 900 g/2 lb medium–large floury potatoes, peeled
- ½ tsp salt
- paprika
- 100 ml/3½ fl oz vegetable oil
- pepper

1 Preheat the oven to 200°C/ 400°F/Gas Mark 6. Using a sharp knife, cut the potatoes in half, or into quarters if very large, then arrange in a roasting tin. Sprinkle over the salt, then season to taste with pepper and paprika.

2 Pour the oil over the potatoes, then turn them in the oil until well coated. Transfer to the preheated oven and roast, basting occasionally, for 1½ hours, or until golden brown and tender. Remove from the oven and serve immediately.

variation

To ring the changes, try adding 1 crushed garlic clove and 1 tablespoon of lemon juice to the oil before pouring over the potatoes. They will add a deliciously different flavour and the aroma will be irresistible.

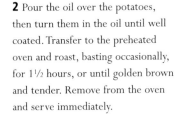

ROASTED GARLIC MASHED POTATOES

HERE ARE MASHED POTATOES WITH A DIFFERENCE. TANTALISE EVERY MEMBER OF YOUR
HOUSEHOLD WITH THESE DELICIOUS POTATOES MASHED WITH JUICY BULBS OF ROASTED GARLIC
AND GARNISHED WITH SPRIGS OF FRAGRANT, FRESH PARSLEY. AN UNFORGETTABLE COMBINATION.

serves

4

preparation

20 minutes

cooking

1 hour

ingredients

- 2 whole bulbs of garlic
- 1 tbsp olive oil
- 900 g/2 lb floury potatoes, peeled
- 125 ml/4 fl oz milk
- 55 g/2 oz butter
- salt and pepper
- fresh parsley sprigs, to garnish

1 Preheat the oven to 180°C/ 350°F/Gas Mark 4.

2 Separate the garlic cloves, place on a large piece of foil and drizzle with the oil. Wrap the garlic loosely in the foil and roast in the preheated oven for 1 hour, or until very tender. Leave to cool slightly.

3 Twenty minutes before the end of the cooking time, cut the potatoes into chunks, then cook in salted boiling water for 15 minutes, or until tender.

4 Meanwhile, squeeze the cooled garlic cloves out of their skins and push through a sieve into a saucepan. Add the milk, butter and salt and pepper to taste. Heat gently, until the butter has melted.

5 Drain the cooked potatoes, then mash in the saucepan until smooth. Pour in the garlic mixture and heat gently, stirring, until the ingredients are combined. Serve hot garnished with fresh parsley sprigs.

DAUPHINOIS POTATOES

COOKING THE HUMBLE POTATO IN THIS CLASSIC WAY ELEVATES IT TO GOURMET HEIGHTS. THIS DELICIOUS, CREAMY DISH MAKES AN EXCELLENT ACCOMPANIMENT FOR A VEGETABLE BAKE – THEY CAN BE COOKED IN THE OVEN AT THE SAME TIME AND SERVED TOGETHER.

serves
4

preparation
20 minutes

cooking
1–1½ hours

ingredients
- 25 g/1 oz butter, diced, plus extra for greasing
- 900 g/2 lb waxy potatoes, peeled and very thinly sliced
- 1 large onion, finely chopped
- 225 g/8 oz Emmenthal or Gruyère cheese, grated
- 150 ml/5 fl oz single cream
- salt and pepper

1 Preheat the oven to 190°C/375°F/Gas Mark 5. Grease a flameproof casserole with butter. Make a layer of potato slices in the base, dot with a little butter, sprinkle with onion and cheese and season to taste with salt and pepper. Pour in 2 tablespoons of the cream. Continue making layers in this way, ending with a layer of cheese. Pour over any remaining cream.

2 Cover and bake in the preheated oven for 1–1½ hours, or until the potatoes are tender.

3 Preheat the grill to medium. Remove the lid and place the casserole under the hot grill for 5 minutes, or until the top of the bake is golden brown and bubbling. Serve immediately.

variation

For Anna Potatoes, pour 225 g/8 oz of melted butter between 900 g/2 lb of seasoned, layered potato slices. Bake at 220°C/425°F/Gas Mark 7 for 1 hour.

STUFFED BAKED POTATOES

THESE WONDERFUL BAKED POTATOES MAKE AN EXCELLENT LUNCH OR SUPPER DISH. THEY ARE
SUITABLE FOR VEGETARIANS IF YOU OMIT THE HAM AND USE A CHEESE MADE WITH NON-ANIMAL
RENNET. THEY ARE EASY TO PREPARE AND ECONOMICAL FOR COOKS ON A TIGHT BUDGET.

serves
4

preparation
10 minutes

cooking
1¼ hours

ingredients
- 900 g/2 lb baking
  potatoes, washed
- 2 tbsp vegetable oil
- 1 tsp coarse sea salt
- 115 g/4 oz butter
- 1 small onion, chopped
- 115 g/4 oz grated Cheddar
  cheese or crumbled
  blue cheese
- salt and pepper
- fresh chives, to garnish

OPTIONAL INGREDIENTS
- 4 tbsp cooked ham
  or bacon, diced
- 4 tbsp sweetcorn kernels
- 4 tbsp cooked mushrooms,
  courgettes or peppers

1 Preheat the oven to 190ºC/
375ºF/Gas Mark 5. Prick the
potatoes with a fork, brush with oil,
sprinkle with the salt and bake on an
oven tray for 1 hour, or until the
skins are crispy and the inside is soft
when pierced with a fork.

2 Melt 1 tablespoon of butter in a
small frying pan. Add the onion and
cook gently for 4–5 minutes, or
until softened and golden. Reserve.

3 Remove the potatoes from the
oven and cut in half lengthways.
Scoop the insides into a large mixing

bowl and keep the shells. Increase
the oven temperature to 200ºC/
400ºF/Gas Mark 6.

4 Coarsely mash the potato and mix
in the onion and remaining butter.
Add salt and pepper and 1 or more
of the optional ingredients, if using.
Spoon the mixture back into the
empty shells. Top with cheese.

5 Return the potatoes to the oven
for 10 minutes, or until the cheese
melts and begins to brown. Garnish
with chives to serve.

ROAST SUMMER VEGETABLES

THIS APPETIZING AND COLOURFUL MIXTURE OF MEDITERRANEAN VEGETABLES MAKES A
SENSATIONAL SUMMER LUNCH FOR VEGETARIANS AND MEAT-EATERS ALIKE. ROASTING BRINGS OUT
THE FULL FLAVOUR AND SWEETNESS OF THE PEPPERS, AUBERGINES, COURGETTES AND ONIONS.

serves
4

preparation
10 minutes

cooking
20–25 minutes

ingredients
- 2 tbsp olive oil
- 1 fennel bulb
- 2 red onions
- 2 beef tomatoes
- 1 aubergine
- 2 courgettes
- 1 yellow pepper
- 1 red pepper
- 1 orange pepper
- 4 garlic cloves
- 4 fresh rosemary sprigs
- pepper
- crusty bread, to serve (optional)

1 Preheat the oven to 200°C/ 400°F/Gas Mark 6. Brush a large ovenproof dish with a little of the oil. Prepare the vegetables. Cut the fennel, red onions and tomatoes into wedges. Slice the aubergine and courgettes thickly, then deseed all the peppers and cut into chunks. Arrange the vegetables in the dish and tuck the garlic cloves and rosemary sprigs among them. Drizzle with the remaining oil and season to taste with pepper.

2 Roast the vegetables in the preheated oven for 10 minutes. Remove the dish from the oven and turn the vegetables over with a slotted spoon. Return to the oven and roast for a further 10–15 minutes until tender and beginning to turn golden brown.

3 Serve the vegetables straight from the dish, or transfer to a warmed serving plate. Serve with crusty bread, if liked.

variation

*You can substitute a herb-flavoured oil,
such as tarragon or garlic and rosemary,
for the plain olive oil, if liked.*

OVEN-DRIED TOMATOES

WHEN YOU CAN'T TAKE ADVANTAGE OF THE INTENSE MEDITERRANEAN SUN, USE THIS EASY
TECHNIQUE TO PRESERVE THE RICH FLAVOUR OF TOMATOES. MAKE SURE YOU USE ONLY RIPE,
FULL-FLAVOURED TOMATOES FOR THIS, IN ORDER TO GET THE BEST FLAVOUR POSSIBLE.

serves
4

preparation
15 minutes

cooking
2½ hours

ingredients
- 1 kg/2 lb 4 oz large, juicy full-flavoured tomatoes
- sea salt and pepper
- 500 g/1 lb 2 oz buffalo mozzarella, sliced
- basil leaves, to garnish
- extra virgin olive oil for drizzling and storing (if required)

1 Preheat the oven to 120°C/ 250°F/Gas Mark ½. Using a sharp knife, cut each of the tomatoes into quarters lengthways.

2 Using a teaspoon, scoop out the seeds and discard. If the tomatoes are large, cut each quarter in half lengthways again.

3 Sprinkle sea salt in a roasting tin and arrange the tomato slices, skin side down, on top. Roast in the preheated oven for 2½ hours, or until the edges are just beginning to look charred and the flesh is dry but still pliable. The exact roasting time and yield will depend on the size and juiciness of the tomatoes. Check the tomatoes at 30-minute intervals after 1½ hours.

4 Remove the dried tomatoes from the roasting tin and leave to cool completely. Serve with slices of buffalo mozzarella – drizzle with olive oil and sprinkle with pepper and basil leaves.

cook's tip

To preserve, place in a 250 ml/9 fl oz preserving jar and pour over enough olive oil to cover. Seal tightly and store in the refrigerator for up to 2 weeks.

CRISP NOODLE & VEGETABLE STIR-FRY

THE CHINESE CAREFULLY SELECT VEGETABLES TO ACHIEVE A HARMONIOUS BALANCE OF
CONTRASTING COLOURS AND TEXTURES. ONCE YOU HAVE CHOPPED THE VEGETABLES, THIS DISH
IS QUICK AND EASY TO PUT TOGETHER, AND MAKES AN ATTRACTIVE AND NUTRITIOUS MEAL.

serves
4
preparation
5 minutes
cooking
15–20 minutes

ingredients
- groundnut or sunflower oil, for deep-frying
- 115 g/4 oz rice vermicelli, broken into 7.5-cm/3-inch lengths
- 115 g/4 oz green beans, cut into short lengths
- 2 carrots, cut into thin batons
- 2 courgettes, cut into thin batons
- 115 g/4 oz shiitake mushrooms, sliced
- 2.5-cm/1-inch piece fresh root ginger, shredded
- ½ small head Chinese leaves, shredded
- 4 spring onions, shredded
- 85 g/3 oz beansprouts
- 2 tbsp dark soy sauce
- 2 tbsp Chinese rice wine
- large pinch of sugar
- 2 tbsp roughly chopped fresh coriander

1 Half-fill a wok or deep, heavy-based frying pan with oil. Heat to 180–190°C/350–375°F, or until a cube of bread browns in 30 seconds.

2 Add the noodles, in batches, and cook for 1½–2 minutes, or until crisp and puffed up. Remove and drain on kitchen paper. Pour off all but 2 tablespoons of oil from the wok.

3 Heat the remaining oil over a high heat. Add the green beans and stir-fry for 2 minutes.

4 Add the carrot and courgette batons, sliced mushrooms and ginger and stir-fry for a further 2 minutes.

5 Add the shredded Chinese leaves and spring onions with the beansprouts and stir-fry for a further 1 minute.

6 Add the soy sauce, rice wine and sugar and cook, stirring constantly, for 1 minute.

7 Add the noodles and chopped coriander and toss well. Serve immediately.

cook's tip
This dish also looks attractive if you serve the noodles in a small nest on top of the stir-fried vegetables, rather than tossing them with the vegetables in Step 3.

GRATIN OF MIXED VEGETABLES

THIS MIXED VEGETABLE GRATIN IS VERY EASY TO PREPARE AND MAKES AN ECONOMICAL SUPPER DISH FOR A GROUP OF PEOPLE. ONCE YOU HAVE IT ASSEMBLED IN THE DISH, IT NEEDS LITTLE ATTENTION: SIMPLY POP IT IN THE OVEN AND BRING IT OUT WHEN IT IS READY TO SERVE.

serves

6

preparation

15 minutes

cooking

1¼ hours

ingredients

- 2 parsnips, sliced
- 2 tbsp olive oil
- 1 aubergine, diced
- 1 garlic clove, finely chopped
- 2 tsp chopped fresh thyme
- 10 g/¼ oz butter
- 2 shallots, chopped

- 4 canned artichoke hearts, drained
- 4 canned celery hearts, sliced
- 55 g/2 oz Emmenthal cheese, grated
- 55 g/2 oz freshly grated pecorino cheese
- salt

1 Preheat the oven to 180°C/ 350°F/Gas Mark 4. Steam the parsnips over a saucepan of simmering water for 4 minutes, or until just tender. Drain, then leave to cool.

2 Heat the oil in a heavy-based frying pan. Add the diced aubergine and cook, stirring frequently, for 5 minutes. Add the chopped garlic and thyme, season to taste with salt and cook for 3 minutes. Transfer the aubergine mixture to a large dish with a slotted spoon. Place the butter in the frying pan. When it has melted, add the shallots and a pinch of salt and cook over a very low heat, stirring occasionally, for 7–10 minutes.

3 Mix the shallots and aubergine mixture together. Cut each artichoke heart into 8 pieces and add to the mixture with the parsnips, celery hearts, Emmenthal and half the pecorino cheese. Mix well, then sprinkle over the remaining pecorino cheese. Bake in the preheated oven for 45 minutes. Serve.

STUFFED RED PEPPERS WITH BASIL

STUFFED PEPPERS ARE POPULAR WITH VEGETARIANS AND MEAT-EATERS ALIKE. THEY ARE EASY TO PREPARE AND NUTRITIOUS: THE WALNUTS AND CHEESE ALONE ARE A RICH SOURCE OF PROTEIN. THIS DISH IS ALSO RICH IN IRON AND VITAMIN C. SERVE THESE PEPPERS FOR LUNCH OR SUPPER.

serves
4
preparation
15–20 minutes
cooking
1¼–1½ hours

ingredients
- 140 g/5 oz long-grain white or brown rice
- 4 large red peppers
- 2 tbsp olive oil
- 1 garlic clove, chopped
- 4 shallots, chopped
- 1 celery stick, chopped
- 3 tbsp chopped toasted walnuts
- 2 tomatoes, peeled and chopped
- 1 tbsp lemon juice
- 50 g/1¾ oz raisins
- 4 tbsp freshly grated Cheddar cheese
- 2 tbsp chopped fresh basil
- salt and pepper
- fresh basil sprigs, to garnish
- lemon wedges, to serve

1 Preheat the oven to 180°C/350°F/Gas Mark 4. Cook the rice in a saucepan of lightly salted boiling water for 20 minutes if using white rice, or 35 minutes if using brown. Drain, rinse under cold running water, then drain again.

2 Using a sharp knife, cut the tops off the peppers and reserve. Remove the seeds and white cores, then blanch the peppers and reserved tops in boiling water for 2 minutes. Remove from the heat and drain well. Heat half the oil in a large frying pan. Add the garlic and shallots and cook, stirring, for 3 minutes. Add the celery, walnuts, tomatoes, lemon juice and raisins and cook for a further 5 minutes. Remove from the heat and stir in the cheese, chopped basil and seasoning.

3 Stuff the peppers with the rice mixture and arrange them in a baking dish. Place the tops on the peppers, drizzle over the remaining oil, loosely cover with foil and bake in the preheated oven for 45 minutes. Remove from the oven. Garnish with basil sprigs and serve with lemon wedges.

BRAISED RED CABBAGE

BRAISED RED CABBAGE MAKES A COLOURFUL ACCOMPANIMENT TO A VARIETY OF HOT AND COLD
DISHES. TRY SERVING IT WITH FLANS AND QUICHES, AND FRESHLY BAKED PIES. THIS CABBAGE HAS
A LOVELY FLAVOUR, WITH HINTS OF AROMATIC CLOVES AND THE SWEETNESS OF RAISINS.

serves
6
preparation
15 minutes
cooking
55 minutes

ingredients
- 2 tbsp sunflower oil
- 2 onions, thinly sliced
- 2 eating apples, peeled,
  cored and thinly sliced
- 900 g/2 lb red cabbage,
  cored and shredded
- 4 tbsp red wine vinegar
- 2 tbsp sugar
- ¼ tsp ground cloves
- 55 g/2 oz raisins
- 125 ml/4 fl oz red wine
- 2 tbsp redcurrant jelly
- salt and pepper

1 Heat the oil in a large saucepan.
Add the onions and cook, stirring
occasionally, for 10 minutes, or until
softened and golden. Stir in the
apple slices and cook for 3 minutes.

2 Add the cabbage, vinegar, sugar,
cloves, raisins and red wine and
season to taste with salt and
pepper. Bring to the boil, stirring
occasionally. Reduce the heat, cover

and cook, stirring occasionally, for
40 minutes, or until the cabbage is
tender and most of the liquid has
been absorbed.

3 Stir in the redcurrant jelly,
transfer to a warmed dish and serve.

variation

*You can vary the flavour and texture of
this dish by substituting 2 tablespoons
honey for the sugar, and replacing half of
the raisins with sultanas.*

BAKED AUBERGINES

THIS DELICIOUS RECIPE IS FROM PARMA, AND CONTAINS LAYERS OF SLICED AUBERGINES BAKED
WITH TOMATO SAUCE AND MOZZARELLA CHEESE. YOU MAY NEED TO REDUCE THE TOMATO SAUCE
A LITTLE BY BOILING IT DOWN BEFORE USING, SO THAT THE END RESULT IS NOT TOO RUNNY.

serves
4

preparation
15 minutes

cooking
1¼ hours

ingredients
- 4 aubergines, trimmed
- 3 tbsp olive oil, plus extra for oiling
- 300 g/10½ oz mozzarella cheese, thinly sliced
- 4 slices Parma ham, shredded
- 1 tbsp chopped fresh marjoram
- 25 g/1 oz Parmesan cheese, grated
- fresh sage sprigs, to garnish

TOMATO SAUCE
- 4 tbsp olive oil
- 1 large onion, sliced
- 4 garlic cloves, crushed
- 400 g/14 oz canned chopped tomatoes
- 450 g/1 lb fresh tomatoes, peeled and chopped
- 4 tbsp chopped fresh parsley
- 600 ml/1 pint hot vegetable stock
- 1 tbsp sugar
- 2 tbsp lemon juice
- 150 ml/5 fl oz dry white wine
- salt and pepper

BÉCHAMEL SAUCE
- 25 g/1 oz butter
- 25 g/1 oz plain flour
- 1 tsp mustard powder
- 300 ml/10 fl oz milk
- nutmeg, freshly grated
- salt and pepper

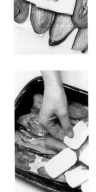

1 Preheat the oven to 190°C/375°F/Gas Mark 5. To make the tomato sauce, heat the oil in a large frying pan. Add the onion and garlic and fry until just beginning to soften. Add the canned and fresh tomatoes, parsley, stock, sugar and lemon juice. Cover and simmer for 15 minutes. Stir in the wine and season to taste with salt and pepper.

2 Slice the aubergines thinly lengthways. Bring a large saucepan of water to the boil and cook the aubergine slices for 5 minutes. Drain on kitchen paper and pat dry.

3 Pour half of the fresh tomato sauce into a large, oiled ovenproof dish. Cover with half of the cooked aubergines and drizzle with a little oil. Cover with half of the mozzarella, Parma ham and herbs. Season to taste with salt and pepper. Repeat the layers until the tomato sauce is used up.

4 To make the béchamel sauce, heat the butter in a large saucepan. When it has melted, add the flour and mustard powder. Stir until smooth and cook over a low heat for 2 minutes. Slowly beat in the milk. Simmer gently for 2 minutes. Remove from the heat and season with a large pinch of nutmeg and salt and pepper to taste.

5 Sprinkle the béchamel sauce with Parmesan cheese. Bake in the preheated oven for 35–40 minutes until golden on top. Garnish with sage sprigs and serve.

CAESAR SALAD

THIS SALAD WAS THE INVENTION OF A CHEF AT CAESAR'S, A RESTAURANT IN TIJUANA, MEXICO. IT HAS RIGHTLY EARNED AN INTERNATIONAL REPUTATION. CAESAR SALAD MAKES AN EXCELLENT LUNCH AS WELL AS AN ACCOMPANIMENT, AND IS FULL OF NUTRIENTS, ESPECIALLY PROTEIN.

serves
4
preparation
25 minutes
cooking
15–20 minutes

ingredients
- 1 large cos lettuce or 2 Little Gem lettuces
- 4 canned anchovies in oil, drained and halved lengthways
- Parmesan shavings, to garnish

DRESSING
- 2 garlic cloves, crushed
- 1½ tsp Dijon mustard
- 1 tsp Worcestershire sauce
- 4 canned anchovies in olive oil, drained and chopped
- 1 egg yolk
- 1 tbsp lemon juice
- 150 ml/5 fl oz olive oil
- 4 tbsp freshly grated Parmesan cheese
- salt and pepper

CROÛTONS
- 4 thick slices day-old bread
- 2 tbsp olive oil
- 1 garlic clove, crushed

1 Preheat the oven to 180°C/ 350°F/Gas Mark 4. To make the dressing, place the garlic, mustard, Worcestershire sauce, anchovies, egg yolk, lemon juice and seasoning in a food processor or blender and process for 30 seconds until foaming. With the machine still running, add the olive oil, drop by drop, until the mixture begins to thicken. Continue adding the oil in a steady stream until all the oil has been incorporated. Transfer to a bowl. Add a little hot water if the dressing is too thick. Stir in the grated Parmesan cheese. Season to taste with salt and pepper and chill until required.

2 For the croûtons, cut the bread into 1 cm/½ inch cubes. Toss with the oil and garlic in a bowl. Spread out on a baking sheet in a single layer. Bake in the preheated oven for 15–20 minutes, stirring occasionally, until browned and crisp. Remove from the oven and leave to cool.

3 Separate the lettuce into individual leaves and wash and spin dry in a salad spinner or pat dry on kitchen paper. (Excess moisture will dilute the dressing.) Transfer to a polythene bag and place in the refrigerator.

4 To assemble the salad, tear the lettuce into pieces and place in a large serving bowl. Add the dressing and toss well. Top with the halved anchovies, croûtons and Parmesan shavings. Serve immediately.

ROAST CHICKEN SALAD WITH ORANGE DRESSING

THIS COLOURFUL SALAD MAKES A DELICIOUS SUMMER LUNCH, AND IS AN EXCELLENT WAY OF USING UP ANY LEFTOVER ROAST CHICKEN. IT IS ALSO MOUTHWATERING FARE FOR A PICNIC. THE SUCCULENT ROAST CHICKEN AND SWEET TANG OF ORANGE MAKE A LOVELY COMBINATION.

serves
4
preparation
20 minutes
cooking
none

ingredients
- 250 g/9 oz young spinach leaves
- handful of fresh parsley leaves
- ½ cucumber, thinly sliced
- 90 g/3¼ oz walnuts, toasted and chopped
- 350 g/12 oz boneless lean roast chicken, thinly sliced
- 2 red apples
- 1 tbsp lemon juice

ORANGE DRESSING
- 2 tbsp extra virgin olive oil
- juice of 1 orange
- finely grated rind of ½ orange
- 1 tbsp crème fraîche
- fresh flat-leaf parsley sprigs, to garnish
- orange wedges, to serve

1 Wash and drain the spinach and parsley leaves, if necessary, then arrange on a large serving platter. Top with the cucumber and walnuts. Arrange the chicken slices on top of the leaves.

2 Core the apples, then cut them in half. Cut each half into slices and brush with the lemon juice to prevent discolouration. Arrange the apple slices over the salad.

3 Place all the dressing ingredients in a screw-top jar, screw on the lid tightly and shake well until thoroughly combined. Drizzle the dressing over the salad, garnish with parsley sprigs and serve immediately with orange wedges.

GREEK SALAD

WALK INTO ANY TAVERNA OR CAFÉ IN GREECE OR SOUTHERN CYPRUS AND YOU WILL SEE THIS
SALAD, OR A VARIATION OF IT, ON THE MENU. IT MAKES A DELICIOUS ACCOMPANIMENT TO OTHER
GREEK DISHES, OR A SATISFYING LUNCH IN ITS OWN RIGHT IF SERVED WITH FRESH PITTA BREAD.

serves
4
preparation
15 minutes
cooking
none

ingredients
- 4 tomatoes, cut into wedges
- 1 onion, sliced
- ½ cucumber, sliced
- 225 g/8 oz Kalamata olives, stoned
- 225 g/8 oz feta cheese, cubed (drained weight)
- 2 tbsp fresh coriander leaves
- fresh flat-leaf parsley, to garnish
- pitta bread, to serve

DRESSING
- 5 tbsp extra virgin olive oil
- 2 tbsp white wine vinegar
- 1 tbsp lemon juice
- ½ tsp sugar
- 1 tbsp chopped fresh coriander
- salt and pepper

1 To make the dressing, place the oil, vinegar, lemon juice, sugar and coriander in a large bowl. Season with salt and pepper and mix together well.

2 Add the tomatoes, onion, cucumber, olives, feta cheese and coriander. Toss all the ingredients together, then divide between individual serving bowls. Garnish with fresh parsley and serve with pitta bread.

cook's tip

For an authentic Greek salad you need to use Kalamata olives, but if they are unavailable then the same quantity of stoned green or black olives will work well in this recipe.

SPICY TOMATO SALAD

TOMATO SALAD MAKES A COLOURFUL ACCOMPANIMENT TO MANY DISHES. THIS VERSION HAS A
DELICIOUS SPICY FLAVOUR AND MAKES AN EXCELLENT SALAD FOR A PICNIC OR BUFFET. IT IS ALSO
SUITABLE FOR VEGANS AND WILL SUIT ANYONE ON A MEAT-FREE OR DAIRY-FREE DIET.

serves
4

preparation
5 minutes, plus 10
minutes' cooling

cooking
2–4 minutes

ingredients
- 4 large ripe tomatoes
- 1 small fresh red chilli
- 1 garlic clove
- 25 g/1 oz fresh basil
- 4 tbsp extra virgin olive oil
- 1 tbsp lemon juice
- 2 tbsp balsamic vinegar
- salt and pepper
- fresh crusty bread, to serve

TO GARNISH
- fresh basil sprigs
- lemon wedges

1 Bring a kettle of water to the boil.
Place the tomatoes in a heatproof
bowl, then pour over enough boiling
water to cover them. Let them soak
for 2–4 minutes, then lift out of the
water and leave to cool slightly.

2 When the tomatoes are cool
enough to handle, gently pierce the
skins with the point of a knife. The
skins should now be easy to remove.
Discard the skins, then chop the
tomatoes and place them in a large
salad bowl.

3 Deseed and finely chop the chilli,
then chop the garlic. Rinse and finely
chop the basil, then add it to the
tomatoes in the bowl with the chilli
and the garlic.

4 Mix the oil, lemon juice and
balsamic vinegar together in a
separate bowl, then season to taste
with salt and pepper. Pour the
mixture over the salad and toss
together well. Garnish with basil
sprigs and lemon wedges, and serve
immediately with fresh crusty bread.

cook's tip

*If possible, choose ripe tomatoes that
are still on the vine. Their flavour
is unmistakable, and will really
enhance the taste of the salad. If you
can't find tomatoes on the vine, then
any tomatoes will work, but try to
find some that have a good flavour.*

6

HERBS AND SPICES

HERBS AND SPICES HAVE A VERY WIDE RANGE OF WONDERFUL FLAVOURS, AND THE MEREST PINCH OF A WELL-CHOSEN HERB OR SPICE CAN ELEVATE THE TASTE OF A DISH TO AN ALTOGETHER NEW AND INSPIRING LEVEL. TAKE YOUR INSPIRATION FROM THE RECIPES FEATURED HERE, OR EXPERIMENT WITH YOUR OWN COMBINATIONS FOR NEW AND EXCITING RESULTS.

INTRODUCTION

THERE IS A WIDE RANGE OF FRESH HERBS AVAILABLE ALL YEAR ROUND IN YOUR LOCAL SUPERMARKET, AS WELL AS A TEMPTING ARRAY OF FRAGRANT AND EXOTIC SPICES. YOU CAN ALSO BUY FROZEN HERBS, WHICH ARE A GOOD SUBSTITUTE WHEN FRESH HERBS ARE UNAVAILABLE. IT IS A GOOD IDEA TO KEEP SOME POTS OF FRESH HERBS ON A WINDOWSILL AND A SELECTION OF DRIED HERBS AND SPICES IN YOUR STORECUPBOARD. NOTE THAT IF YOU ARE SUBSTITUTING A DRIED HERB FOR FRESH, YOU WILL NEED ONLY HALF THE QUANTITY.

Buying and storing herbs and spices

If you buy fresh herbs as pot plants, place them on a windowsill where they can get plenty of light, and water them regularly. Basil, in particular, needs lots of water, so make sure you do not let it dry out. Packaged fresh herbs should be stored in their wrapping in the refrigerator. If you grow herbs in your garden, after picking, keep them in a jug of clean water until you are ready to use them. Store dried herbs and ground spices in a cool, dark place – an airy storecupboard is ideal. Use all fresh herbs by their 'best before' date, and go through your storecupboard regularly and throw out any dried herbs and spices that are past their best.

Types and uses of herbs

Shown here are some of the most popular varieties of herbs and their uses. They are delicious served raw as garnishes or in salads, as well as chopped and added to cooked dishes.

Tarragon

The dark green pointed leaves of tarragon have an aromatic, aniseed-like flavour. It adds a distinctive flavour to poultry, fish, eggs, sauces, salads and dressings. It is best to use this herb on its own, since its strong flavour can overpower other herbs if mixed with them.

Basil

There are many species of this herb. It thrives in a warm, Mediterranean climate, and therefore in cold climates it will do better indoors on a windowsill with plenty of sunshine and water. It has a sweet, aromatic flavour, and is particularly good with tomatoes and mozzarella cheese. It is also delicious with poultry, fish and seafood, salads and sauces. This herb is fragile and should therefore be added to recipes towards the end of the cooking time.

Thyme

This herb comes in different varieties, and several of them are commonly used in cooking. The leaves add a pungent, aromatic flavour to meat, poultry, egg and potato dishes, and are good in soups, sauces, roasts, casseroles and stews.

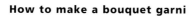

Basil

How to make a bouquet garni

You can use this combination of herbs to flavour soups and stews. Take a bay leaf, and a sprig each of parsley and thyme. Tie them together at one end with kitchen string, or enclose the herbs in a muslin bag. Add the bouquet garni to your chosen dish to flavour it during cooking, then, when the dish is cooked, remove and discard it before serving.

Thyme

Oregano

Oregano

This green herb is related to marjoram. It has a pungent flavour and should be used sparingly. It is popular in Italian cookery, particularly on pizzas, and adds an aromatic flavour to meat and poultry, eggs and cheese.

Coriander

This pungent herb has bright green leaves and is very popular in Mediterranean and Asian cooking. It adds a distinctive flavour to salads, cooked vegetables and stir-fries.

Fennel

There are two types of fennel. One has a bulbous base, which can be cooked and used like a vegetable; the other variety has no bulb. Fennel has a strong aniseed flavour. The leaves of both types can be snipped into soups and sauces, and are excellent with fish and egg dishes.

Marjoram

This ancient herb has pale green leaves and a delicate, sweet flavour. It is ideal with meat, poultry, cheese, tomatoes, eggs and dressings.

Rosemary

The silvery, needle-shaped leaves of rosemary have a strong aromatic flavour. It is used in soups, salads, roasts, stuffings, dressings and marinades, as well as on pizzas. The herb also makes delicious skewers for kebabs. It pairs particularly well with potatoes and bread, as well as meat, poultry, fish and eggs.

Bay

The leaves of this aromatic herb come from the Mediterranean laurel tree. The fresh leaves, if you can get them, have more flavour than the dried, but either type will add a good, pungent flavour to soups, sauces, stocks and casseroles. They are usually discarded once the food has absorbed their flavour.

Sage

This herb has greyish oval leaves and a pungent, slightly bitter taste. It is very common in stuffings, especially those containing onion, and is excellent with pork, poultry, beans, cheese, rice and pasta. It is also used to flavour drinks.

Chervil

The dark green, curly leaves of chervil have an aromatic flavour with a hint of aniseed. It is especially good in chicken, fish and egg dishes.

Mint

There are many species of mint, the two most well known being peppermint and spearmint. Peppermint has a more peppery flavour, while spearmint has a fresher mint taste. Mint is a hardy plant and can take over a herb garden if not carefully controlled. Use it to flavour cooked potatoes, peas, sauces, soups, meat dishes, desserts and drinks.

Dill

This herb has feathery green leaves and a mild flavour. Dill is excellent with fish, as well as in salads, cheese dishes and sauces.

Chives

These relatives of the onion family have long, hollow stems and edible purple flowers. The fresh stems are snipped into small pieces and added to salads, soups, cream cheese and egg dishes. You can also buy them frozen and dried.

Parsley

This versatile herb is rich in vitamins A and C and comes in many varieties. The two most popular types have green leaves that are either curly or flat. Curly parsley is common all year round, while flat-leaf parsley may be found only in some supermarkets and specialist delicatessens. Parsley is used in a wide range of dishes, including soups, salads, sauces, stir-fries and bakes, as well as stuffings, dressings and marinades. It adds a spicy, lingering flavour to meat, poultry, fish, eggs and vegetables, and helps to offset the sulphur aftertaste of garlic. It also makes an attractive garnish, particularly the flat-leaf variety.

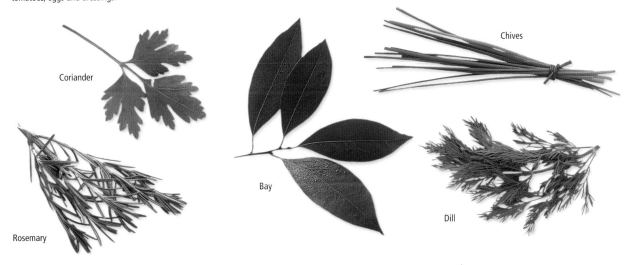

Coriander

Chives

Rosemary

Bay

Dill

Types and uses of spices

Spices used to be costly when international travel was comparatively slow and difficult – now they are both less expensive and also more widely available.

Paprika

This spice is made from ground red pepper pods and its flavour can vary from mild, sweet and pungent to fiery hot. It is excellent in salads and as a garnish. It also goes well with meat, poultry, eggs, vegetables, cream cheese, pasta, rice and beans.

Cardamom

This aromatic spice is related to ginger and has a pungent lemon flavour. You can grind and use the whole pod, or just the seeds inside. Cardamom is widely used in Asian and Middle Eastern dishes, and adds a distinctive flavour to soups, stews, curries, pastry, bread and cakes.

Allspice

This small berry comes from the West Indies and South America and has a sweet flavour of nutmeg, cinnamon and cloves. You can buy it whole or ground. It is used with meat, onions and fruit desserts, as well as cakes and bread.

Cardamom pods

Mustard

This hot, acrid spice is available in three forms: whole seeds, ground or processed into a paste. It goes well with meat, poultry, seafood, eggs, beans, potatoes, cheese, cream and butter sauces, bread, marinades, chutneys and relishes.

Chilli powder

This is a powdered mixture of spices that includes dried chillies, cumin, coriander and cloves. It has a fiery heat but you can also buy mild chilli powder. Use it to flavour soups and stews. It goes particularly well with seafood, meat, poultry, vegetables (especially potatoes), beans and eggs.

Fennel seeds

You can buy fennel seeds whole or ground. They have a sweet, mildly aniseed flavour and can be used in savoury and sweet dishes, including marinades, pizzas, stuffings, bread, cakes, biscuits and a variety of desserts and drinks. Fennel goes particularly well with meat, poultry, fish, beetroot, onions, potatoes, tomatoes, cucumber, beans, pasta, rice, cheese, eggs and fruit.

Star anise

This star-shaped brown pod comes from an Asian tree. It has a warm, aromatic, slightly bitter aniseed flavour and is available whole or ground. It is popular in Chinese cooking, and is used in marinades, stir-fries, bakes, cakes, fruit and some drinks. It goes particularly well with pork, poultry and fish.

Caraway

These seeds have a nutty, aniseed flavour and can be bought whole or ground. They are popular in German and Austrian cookery, and are used to flavour soups, stews, meat, cheese, vegetables, sauerkraut, bread, cakes and the liqueur kümmel.

Juniper

These berries are available dried and are usually crushed to release their pungent pine flavour. Use them to flavour various meats as well as pâtés, stuffings and sauces.

Mace

This sweet, fragrant spice is most often sold ground and is used to flavour a wide range of savoury and sweet dishes, including beef, chicken, fish, vegetables, pasta, beans, cheese,

chocolate, fruit, cakes, marinades, biscuits, chutneys and mulled wine.

Cayenne pepper

This type of pepper is made from tropical chillies and it has a hot, spicy flavour. Use it to add a kick to South American and Caribbean dishes. It is especially good with seafood and chutneys.

Peppercorns

The dried berries from the pepper plant come in black, white and green. Black peppercorns are the most widely used, and are available whole, cracked or ground. They deteriorate quickly when ground, so it is best to buy them whole and grind them yourself. They have an aromatic flavour and can be used in almost every savoury recipe and some sweet fruit dishes, such as balsamic strawberries.

Cinnamon

This spice comes from the bark of a tropical tree. The bark is dried and curled into quills or sticks; it can also be bought ground. Cinnamon has a sweet, aromatic smell and flavour, and is popular in Middle Eastern dishes. It is used to flavour a wide range of savoury and sweet dishes, such as stews, curries, pies, bread and cakes, and a whole host of desserts and drinks.

Chilli powder

Cinnamon sticks

Ground cinnamon

Nutmeg

Nutmeg has a sweet, fragrant flavour and is available whole or ground. It is used in a wide variety of savoury and sweet dishes, from meat, poultry, vegetables, beans, rice, cheese and eggs to chocolate, fruit, cream sauces and drinks.

Coriander

The dried seeds of the coriander plant are fragrant and lemony and can be used whole or ground. They are popular in marinades, chutneys, curries and bakes, and go particularly well with meat, poultry, fish, cheese, vegetables, beans, chocolate and jam.

Saffron

This spice has a pungent, slightly bitter flavour. It comes from the purple crocus and is available in threads or powdered. It is used to tint and flavour marinades, soups, stews, rice dishes, breads and bakes. This is the spice that gives the rice in Spanish paella its characteristic yellow colour. Saffron is expensive, so the less expensive turmeric is often used in its place.

Cloves

These come from the buds of the tropical clove tree. The dried brown buds are sold whole or powdered, and have a sweet, pungent flavour. Push whole cloves into ham, pork, onions and oranges to flavour them, or use them ground in soups, stews, bread, cakes, desserts and chutneys. You can also use them whole in drinks such as mulled wine (always remove whole cloves before serving).

Mixed spice

This blend of spices usually consists of allspice, cinnamon, cloves, ginger, coriander and nutmeg. It has a warm, sweet flavour and is delicious in fruit desserts, bread, cakes, biscuits and drinks.

Cumin

These dried seeds have a pungent, nutty flavour and are also available ground. Cumin is popular in Asian and Mexican cooking, and goes well with beef, pork, salmon, shellfish, beans, pasta, eggs, cheese and rice.

Five spice

Chinese five-spice powder is, as its name implies, a blend of five spices, usually cloves, cinnamon, fennel seeds, Szechuan peppercorns and star anise. It has a sweet, pungent flavour and is popular in Chinese and Vietnamese cooking. It is especially good in stir-fries. There is also a Tunisian version, which consists of cloves, cinnamon, nutmeg, pepper, and grains of paradise (which are also known as melegueta pepper).

Curry powder

This powder contains a mixture of spices including cardamom, chillies, cloves, coriander, fenugreek and turmeric. It is available mild or hot, and is used in curries, cream sauces and chutneys. It also goes well with beef, chicken, turkey, seafood, root vegetables, rice, eggs and cheese.

Turmeric

This spice comes from the root of a tropical plant and has a pungent, somewhat bitter flavour. The powdered variety has a bright orange-yellow colour, so is used to tint foods as well as to flavour them. Turmeric is often used as a cheaper alternative to saffron to colour food. Use this spice to colour or flavour seafood, poultry, pasta, cheese, eggs, curries, risottos, chutneys, marinades, bread and beans.

Garam masala

The blend of spices in garam masala varies, but it often includes cumin, cinnamon, cloves, cardamom, chillies, fennel, fenugreek, garlic, ginger and black pepper. It is popular in Indian cooking, especially in curries, and also goes well with vegetables, eggs, cheese and rice.

Ginger

Ginger is available fresh or dried. The fresh root has a warm, lemon flavour and can be used chopped or grated. It is especially useful in marinades, salads, soups, stews and stir-fries; it can also be preserved in syrup. Powdered ginger has a more pungent, spicy flavour, and is particularly good with chocolate, cream, fruit, gingerbread, cakes, biscuits, jams, chutneys and drinks.

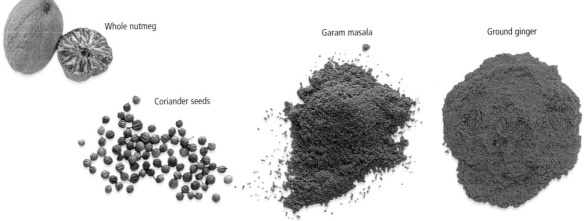

Whole nutmeg

Coriander seeds

Garam masala

Ground ginger

PEA & MINT SOUP

THE SWEETNESS OF GARDEN PEAS AND THE FRESH TASTE OF MINT PAIR TOGETHER BEAUTIFULLY IN THIS DISH, AND THE SHALLOTS AND LEEKS ADD A DELICIOUS DEPTH. THIS SOUP IS IDEAL FOR VEGETARIANS BUT ENJOYABLE FOR ALL. IT MAKES A DELICIOUS STARTER OR LIGHT LUNCH.

serves
4

preparation
15 minutes,
plus 10 minutes'
cooling

cooking
40 minutes

ingredients
- 1 tbsp butter
- 3 shallots, chopped
- 2 leeks, trimmed and finely chopped
- 1 potato, peeled and chopped
- 450 g/1 lb frozen peas
- 2 tbsp chopped fresh mint
- 850 ml/1 ½ pints vegetable stock
- salt and pepper
- fresh mint sprigs, to garnish
- slices of fresh wholemeal bread, to serve

1 Melt the butter in a large saucepan over a medium heat. Add the shallots and cook, stirring, for 2 minutes. Add the leeks and cook, stirring, for a further 2 minutes. Add the potato, peas, chopped mint and stock, and season with salt and pepper. Bring to the boil, then reduce the heat, cover the pan and simmer for 30 minutes. Remove the saucepan from the heat and leave to cool for 10 minutes.

2 Transfer the soup to a food processor and process until smooth (you may need to do this in batches).

3 Return to the saucepan, season to taste with salt and pepper and reheat gently. Remove from the heat and pour into serving bowls. Garnish with fresh mint sprigs and serve with slices of fresh wholemeal bread.

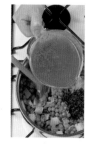

BASIL & PINE KERNEL PESTO

PESTO IS DELICIOUS STIRRED INTO PASTA, SOUPS AND SALAD DRESSINGS. IT IS AVAILABLE IN MOST SUPERMARKETS, BUT MAKING YOUR OWN GIVES A CONCENTRATED FLAVOUR. YOU CAN MAKE THIS PESTO A DAY AHEAD AND KEEP IT IN THE REFRIGERATOR UNTIL YOU ARE READY TO COOK THE PASTA.

serves
4

preparation
15 minutes

cooking
10 minutes

ingredients
- about 40 fresh basil leaves
- 3 garlic cloves, crushed
- 25 g/1 oz pine kernels
- 50 g/1¾ oz Parmesan cheese, finely grated
- 2–3 tbsp extra virgin olive oil
- 675 g/1 lb 8 oz fresh pasta or 350 g/12 oz dried pasta
- salt and pepper

1 Rinse the basil leaves and pat them dry with kitchen paper.

2 Place the basil leaves, garlic, pine kernels and grated Parmesan cheese in a food processor and process for 30 seconds, or until smooth. Alternatively, pound all of the ingredients by hand, using a pestle and mortar.

3 If you are using a food processor, keep the motor running and slowly add the olive oil. Alternatively, add the oil drop by drop while stirring briskly. Season to taste with salt and pepper.

4 Bring a large, heavy-based saucepan of water to the boil. Add the pasta, return to the boil and cook for 3–4 minutes for fresh pasta or 8–10 minutes for dried, until tender, but still firm to the bite. Drain the pasta thoroughly, then transfer to a serving plate and serve with the pesto. Toss to mix well and serve hot.

cook's tip

Only buy pine kernels in small quantities as their high oil content means they quickly turn rancid. Pine kernels are available in most large supermarkets or health food shops.

TARRAGON CHICKEN

THIS IS A CLASSIC FRENCH RECIPE AND IS SUCH A STYLISH, YET UNDERSTATED DISH THAT IT WOULD
BE AN EXCELLENT CHOICE FOR A MAIN COURSE AT AN INFORMAL DINNER PARTY. TARRAGON HAS A
POWERFUL FLAVOUR, SO USE IT SPARINGLY OR IT WILL DOMINATE THE OTHER FLAVOURS.

serves
4
preparation
5 minutes
cooking
20 minutes

ingredients
- 4 skinless, boneless chicken breasts, about 175 g/6 oz each
- 125 ml/4 fl oz dry white wine
- 225–300 ml/8–10 fl oz chicken stock
- 1 garlic clove, finely chopped
- 1 tbsp dried tarragon
- 175 ml/6 fl oz double cream
- 1 tbsp chopped fresh tarragon
- salt and pepper
- fresh tarragon sprigs, to garnish

1 Season the chicken with salt and pepper and place in a single layer in a large, heavy-based frying pan. Pour in the wine and enough chicken stock just to cover and add the garlic and dried tarragon. Bring to the boil, reduce the heat and cook gently for a further 10 minutes, or until the chicken is tender and cooked through.

2 Remove the chicken with a slotted spoon or tongs, cover and keep warm. Sieve the poaching liquid into a clean frying pan and skim off any fat from the surface. Bring to the boil and cook for 12–15 minutes, or until reduced by about two-thirds.

3 Stir in the cream, return to the boil and cook until reduced by about half. Stir in the fresh tarragon. Slice the chicken breasts and arrange on warmed plates. Spoon over the sauce, garnish with tarragon sprigs and serve immediately.

cook's tip

Tongs are the easiest way to remove the chicken breasts from the frying pan. Make sure that the chicken is completely cooked through before serving.

OMELETTES WITH FINES HERBES

FINES HERBES ARE SIMPLY A MIXTURE OF VERY FINELY CHOPPED FRESH HERBS, AND THE CLASSIC
COMBINATION IS PARSLEY, TARRAGON, CHERVIL AND CHIVES. THIS SUBTLY FLAVOURED OMELETTE
PAIRS WELL WITH A TOMATO SALAD OR MIXED SALAD LEAVES FOR A LIGHT, SUMMERY LUNCH.

serves
2
preparation
10 minutes
cooking
4 minutes

ingredients
- 6 eggs
- 4 tbsp chopped
  fresh parsley
- 4 tbsp chopped
  fresh tarragon
- 4 tbsp chopped
  fresh chervil
- 2 tbsp snipped fresh chives
- 25 g/1 oz butter
- salt and pepper
- mixed salad leaves, to serve

1 Beat the eggs with the parsley,
tarragon, chervil and chives. Season
to taste with salt and pepper.

2 Melt half the butter in an omelette
pan or small, heavy-based frying pan.
Add half the egg mixture and stir
with a fork. As the egg sets, draw
it towards the centre and tilt the
omelette pan so that the uncooked
egg runs underneath. Cook until the
underside of the omelette is golden
and set, but the top is still moist.

3 Remove the omelette pan from
the heat and slide the omelette onto
a plate, flipping the pan gently so
that the omelette folds. Keep the
omelette warm. Melt the remaining
butter and cook a second omelette
in the same way. Serve immediately
with mixed salad leaves.

cook's tip
*If you cannot find any of the four herbs
normally used to make 'fines herbes', use
marjoram, oregano or dill instead.*

SALMON COOKED WITH DILL

SALMON ALWAYS GOES DOWN WELL AT PARTIES, AND THE COMBINATION OF THE HERBS AND FENNEL, AND THE SMOKY BARBECUE TASTE, GIVES THIS DISH A MOUTHWATERING FLAVOUR THAT YOUR GUESTS WILL FIND DIFFICULT TO RESIST. SERVE IT WITH CRUSTY BREAD FOR A SATISFYING MEAL.

serves
4

preparation
5 minutes

cooking
30 minutes

ingredients
- ½ large bunch dried thyme
- 5 fresh rosemary branches, 15–20 cm/6–8 inches long
- 8 bay leaves
- 1 kg/2 lb 4 oz salmon fillet
- 1 bulb fennel, cut into 8 pieces
- 2 tbsp lemon juice
- 2 tbsp olive oil

TO SERVE
- crusty bread
- green salad

1 Preheat the barbecue. Make a base on the hot barbecue with the dried thyme, rosemary branches and bay leaves, overlapping them so that they cover a slightly bigger area than the salmon.

2 Carefully place the salmon on top of the herbs.

3 Arrange the fennel around the edge of the fish.

4 Combine the lemon juice and oil and brush the salmon with it.

5 Cover the salmon loosely with a piece of foil, to keep it moist.

6 Cook for about 20–30 minutes, basting frequently with the lemon juice mixture.

7 Remove the salmon from the barbecue, cut it into slices and serve with the fennel.

8 Serve with slices of crusty bread and a green salad.

variation

Use whatever combination of herbs you may have to hand — but avoid the stronger tasting herbs, such as sage and marjoram, which are unsuitable for fish.

TAGINE OF LAMB

THIS IS A TYPICAL MOROCCAN MIXTURE OF MEAT, VEGETABLES AND APRICOTS, FLAVOURED WITH
PLENTY OF FRESH HERBS AND SPICES. IT IS DELICIOUS – AND AUTHENTIC – IF SERVED WITH
COUSCOUS, WHICH CAN BE COOKED IN A STEAMER SET OVER THE STEW FOR 6–7 MINUTES.

serves
4
preparation
10 minutes
cooking
1 hour 40 minutes

ingredients
- 1 tbsp sunflower or corn oil
- 1 onion, chopped
- 350 g/12 oz boneless lamb, trimmed of all visible fat and cut into 2.5-cm/ 1-inch cubes
- 1 garlic clove, finely chopped
- 600 ml/1 pint vegetable stock
- grated rind and juice of 1 orange
- 1 tsp clear honey
- 1 cinnamon stick
- 1-cm/½-inch piece fresh root ginger, finely chopped
- 1 aubergine
- 4 tomatoes, peeled and chopped
- 115 g/4 oz ready-to-eat dried apricots
- 2 tbsp chopped fresh coriander
- salt and pepper
- freshly cooked couscous, to serve

1 Heat the oil in a large, heavy-based frying pan or flameproof casserole over a medium heat. Add the onion and lamb cubes and cook, stirring frequently, for 5 minutes, or until the meat is lightly browned all over. Add the garlic, stock, orange rind and juice, honey, cinnamon stick and ginger. Bring to the boil, then reduce the heat, cover and leave to simmer for 45 minutes.

2 Using a sharp knife, halve the aubergine lengthways and slice thinly. Add to the frying pan with the chopped tomatoes and apricots. Cover and cook for a further 45 minutes, or until the lamb is tender.

3 Stir in the coriander and season to taste with salt and pepper. Serve immediately, straight from the frying pan, with freshly cooked couscous.

7

RICE, PASTA, AND

THE SLOW-RELEASING CARBOHYDRATES IN PASTA, PULSES AND GRAINS MAKE THEM A GOOD SOURCE OF ENERGY. THEY ARE ALSO VERY VERSATILE AND CAN BE USED IN A WIDE VARIETY OF DISHES. SIMPLY ADD A TASTY SAUCE AND YOU HAVE A VERY SATISFYING MEAL.

PULSES GRAINS

INTRODUCTION

CARBOHYDRATES SUCH AS PASTA, NOODLES AND GRAINS PROVIDE A GOOD, INEXPENSIVE SOURCE OF ENERGY, ESPECIALLY THE WHOLEWHEAT / WHOLEGRAIN VARIETIES, AND ARE A VALUABLE SOURCE OF DIETARY FIBRE. COMBINE THEM WITH PROTEIN-RICH PULSES, AND YOU HAVE A DELICIOUS MEAL THAT IS NUTRITIOUS, SATISFYING AND HEALTHY.

Buying and storing pasta

You can buy fresh and dried pasta in a wide variety of colours, shapes and sizes. It is usually made with durum wheat or wholewheat flour. Fresh pasta usually keeps for up to 2 days in the refrigerator, and dried pasta for up to 2 years in the storecupboard, but always use them by their 'best before' date.

Buying and storing noodles

In addition to Italian pasta, there are also different types of Asian noodles. Asian noodles should be stored in a cool, dry place, and used by their 'best before' date.

How to cook pasta

Cooking pasta is quick and easy. Simply bring a large saucepan of lightly salted water to the boil, add the pasta and bring back to the boil, stirring at intervals to prevent it sticking together. Lower the heat slightly and cook until it is tender but still firm to the bite; this is known as al dente. Remove from the heat, drain and serve tossed with olive oil or accompanied by your chosen sauce or recipe.

Fine egg noodle

Medium egg noodle

Thick egg noodle

Cellophane noodles

These thread-like noodles are also known as Chinese vermicelli and are made from the starch of mung beans. Dried cellophane noodles should be soaked briefly before use, although this isn't necessary in dishes that contain a lot of liquid, such as soups.

Egg noodles

These are very popular in Asian cooking, especially in Chinese stir-fries. Check cooking instructions on the packet: some need to be soaked in hot water for about 4–5 minutes, while others can be put straight into the wok.

Ramen noodles

These noodles are deep-fried and sold packaged, often accompanied by ready-to-use broth mix.

Rice noodles

These delicate, fine, white noodles are very easy to prepare. Simply soak them in hot water for 4–5 minutes. They are very good added to soups and stir-fries, and when deep-fried they become deliciously crunchy.

Soba noodles

These thin noodles are made from wheat flour and buckwheat. They are popular in Japanese cooking.

Pasta names

Anelli Very small rings

Cannelloni Large, hollow tubes

Conchiglie Ridged shells

Farfalle Bows

Fettucine Long, narrow ribbons

Fusilli Spirals

Lasagne Large, flat rectangular sheets

Linguine Long, narrow ribbons with flattened edges

Lumaconi Snail shapes

Macaroni Long or short narrow tubes, often curved

Penne Hollow quills

Ravioli Square cushions

Spaghetti Long, narrow strings

Tagliatelle Long ribbons, a little wider than fettucine

Vermicelli Long, very fine, hair-like strings

Udon noodles

These thick Japanese noodles are like spaghetti, except that they can be square as well as round. They are made from cornflour or wheat flour, and are available fresh or dried.

Making your own fresh pasta

You can buy good-quality fresh pasta nowadays, but if you prefer to make your own, the process is simple. You might also like to invest in a pasta machine in order to create perfect pasta shapes of your choice.

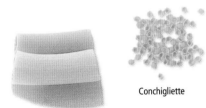

Conchigliette

Cannelloni

Home-made pasta

Serves 6

280 g/10 oz plain flour, plus extra for dusting
1 tsp salt
2 eggs, lightly beaten
3 tbsp tomato purée (optional – use if you want a red, tomato-flavoured pasta)

Lightly dust a clean work surface with flour. Sift the flour and salt into a mound on the work surface. ❶ Make

a well in the centre of the flour, add the beaten eggs and tomato purée, if using, and mix to a stiff dough. If necessary, stir in a few tablespoons of water.

❷ Knead the dough vigorously for about 8 minutes, then wrap it in clingfilm and leave it to rest for 30 minutes, or for up to 2 days if not required straight away.

Roll out the dough to the desired thickness, then use a sharp knife to cut it into pieces of the required shape and size. ❸ Alternatively, use a pasta machine to cut the dough. The pasta is now ready to be cooked.

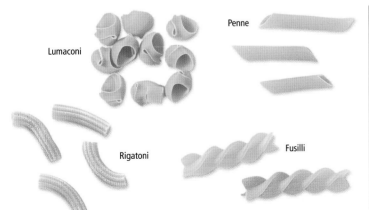

Lumaconi

Penne

Rigatoni

Fusilli

Pasta cooking times

Use a large saucepan for cooking pasta and bring lightly salted water to the boil. Add 1 tablespoon olive oil and the pasta and bring back to the boil. When the pasta is tender, but still firm to the bite, drain and use as soon as possible.

Type of pasta	Unfilled/filled	Cooking time
Fresh	Unfilled	3 minutes
Fresh	Filled	10 minutes
Dried	Unfilled	10 minutes
Dried	Filled	15–20 minutes

Buying and storing pulses

Beans, lentils and peas all fall into the category of pulses. You can buy these protein-rich foods dried, or ready to use in cans if you are short of time. When buying dried pulses, store them in airtight containers in a cool, dry place and use by the 'best before' date, or, if there is no date on the package, within 1 year for best results. Do not mix old and new beans because they will take different lengths of time to cook. Once cooked, refrigerate leftover beans and use within 3 days, or freeze them in an airtight container and use within 6 months.

Preparing and cooking pulses

Most pulses need soaking for at least 8 hours, then boiling rapidly for 10 minutes, followed by further cooking for at least 45 minutes or until they are tender. The main exceptions are soya beans, which need 12 hours to soak and 4 hours to cook, and chickpeas, which need 8 hours to soak and 2 hours to cook. Haricot beans need to soak overnight and need up to 1½ hours to cook. Lentils and split peas usually need no soaking and can be cooked in around 25–30 minutes.

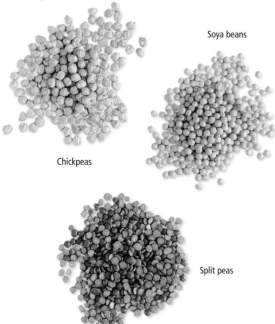

Soya beans

Chickpeas

Split peas

Black-eyed beans

Chickpeas
These round and cream-coloured peas have a nutty flavour, and are excellent in soups, salads, dips and stews, as well as pasta or grain dishes. Chickpeas can also be roasted for snacks, and are used in falafel, a Middle Eastern dish in which the mashed beans are formed into balls and deep-fried. Soak chickpeas for at least 8 hours before use. After soaking, drain and rinse them, then cover with fresh water and bring to the boil. Lower the heat and simmer for 2 hours until they are thoroughly cooked.

Soya beans
The most common colour of soya beans is pale yellow. These beans are good in soups and other savoury dishes, such as curries. Remember that they need to be soaked for at least 12 hours. After soaking, drain and rinse them, then cover with fresh water and bring to the boil. Boil them for the first hour of cooking, then simmer for another 3 hours until they are thoroughly cooked.

Aduki beans
These small red beans are good in soups and salads.

Cannellini beans
Add these long creamy-white beans to soups and salads.

Split peas
These small peas are disc-shaped like lentils, but they are split along a natural seam. Split peas are yellow or green. They can be cooked and puréed, and used in soups, bakes and other savoury dishes.

Lentils
These are small, disc-shaped pulses. Use red or orange lentils puréed and in soups and sauces; green or brown lentils are best in salads, sauces, stews and other savoury dishes.

Red kidney beans
These red kidney-shaped beans can be added to soups, salads and stews, and other savoury dishes such as chilli con carne.

Haricot beans
These white beans can be used in a wide variety of savoury dishes, including soups, salads, stews and casseroles. They are used as baked beans with tomato sauce.

Butter beans
These white kidney-shaped beans are excellent in soups and salads.

Flageolet beans
These small green beans are excellent in salads and also make a delicious accompaniment to meat dishes.

Borlotti beans
These oval beans vary in colour from pale pink to maroon-streaked skin. Use them in soups, dips and other savoury dishes.

Black-eyed beans
These beans are small and beige and have a circular black 'eye'. Use them in sauces, stir-fries and soups.

Long-grain rice

Pudding rice

Buying and storing rice

There are many different varieties of rice available. Store rice in airtight containers for up to 3 years in a cool, dry place, or use by the 'best before' date if sooner.

Short-grain rice
This rice has short, fat grains that are more starchy and moist than medium- and long-grain rice. Varieties of short-grain rice include arborio and carnaroli rice, which are used in risottos.

Medium-grain rice
These grains are a little shorter than long-grain rice. They are more moist and therefore tend to clump together when cooked. Medium-grain rice is used in savoury dishes.

Long-grain rice
Both white and brown long-grain rice are excellent for savoury dishes because the grains stay dry and separate when cooked.

Basmati rice
This Himalayan long-grain rice has a nutty flavour and is excellent in savoury dishes. It is available in white or brown and the grains stay dry and separate when cooked.

Jasmine rice
This tender rice has a delicate, fragrant, aromatic flavour. It is popular in both Vietnamese and Thai cooking.

Arborio rice
This starchy, short-grain creamy rice is ideal in risottos.

Carnaroli rice
This short-grain rice has often been called 'the king of Italian rice'. It has a high starch content and makes a lovely creamy risotto.

Pudding rice
This rice has a high starch content and becomes very sticky and creamy when cooked. It is popular in desserts, especially rice pudding.

Easy-cook rice
These rice grains are polished and partly boiled so that they are quick to cook. They stay fluffy and separate when cooked, but have less flavour than white or brown rice.

Red rice
This rice is grown in the Camargue region of France and in China. It has a pale red colour and a nutty flavour that is similar to brown rice.

Wild rice
This rice is in fact a marsh grass, not a rice. The grains are long and black, with a nutty flavour. It is often mixed with brown long-grain rice for reasons of economy.

How to cook long-grain and basmati rice

To cook rice for four people, put 300 g/10½ oz rice into a sieve and rinse under cold running water. Transfer to a large saucepan and pour in 600 ml/1 pint cold water. Add a large pinch of salt, then bring to the boil. Lower the heat, stir briefly, then cover the pan and simmer gently until the rice is tender and all the liquid has been absorbed (but do not let the rice burn). As a rough guide, white rice will need 15 minutes, and brown rice will need 25–30 minutes. Remove from the heat and leave to stand for 5 minutes with the lid on. Fluff the grains with a fork and serve.

Other grains

It is always worthwhile experimenting with other types of grain. Try using them in salads, soups and stews, or piling them on a platter and topping them with tasty cooked vegetables.

Barley
The polished variety of barley, known as pearl barley, is the kind most widely available. You can also buy pot barley, which is unpolished, from specialist stores and health-food shops. Barley is excellent in soups, casseroles and stews.

Millet
This protein-rich grain is a staple in Africa and Asia, and is boiled in a similar way to rice.

Couscous
This is not a true grain, but pieces of semolina. Steam it in accordance with the instructions on the packet. It makes an excellent bed of grains on which to pile meats and vegetables.

Polenta
This yellow grain is made from cornmeal and features widely in Italian cooking. Follow the cooking instructions on the packet because methods and cooking times vary. To serve cold, once the mixture pulls away from the pan, pour it into a baking tray, let cool, then cut it into squares and serve. To serve hot, at the same stage stir in a generous knob of butter, then remove from the heat and stir vigorously until the polenta stays firm.

Bulgar wheat
This comprises wheat kernels that have been precooked. It is a golden-brown grain with a nutty flavour. Since it has already been cooked, you simply need to soak it in plenty of cold water for 20–30 minutes, then strain it in a sieve, pressing out as much water as possible. This grain is excellent in salads, especially the Middle Eastern dish known as tabbouleh. It is also good in pilaus.

SPAGHETTI BOLOGNESE

THE CLASSIC MEAT SAUCE IN THIS RECIPE IS MOST OFTEN PARTNERED WITH SPAGHETTI, AS SHOWN HERE. HOWEVER, IT ALSO GOES WELL WITH LASAGNE, CANNELLONI OR ANY OTHER BAKED PASTA DISHES. YOU CAN ALSO SERVE IT WITH A BAKED POTATO FOR A TASTY LUNCH OR SUPPER.

serves
4

preparation
15 minutes

cooking
1¼ hours

ingredients
- 3 tbsp olive oil
- 2 garlic cloves, crushed
- 1 large onion, finely chopped
- 1 carrot, diced
- 225 g/8 oz fresh lean beef or chicken mince
- 85 g/3 oz chicken livers, finely chopped
- 100 g/3½ oz lean Parma ham, diced
- 150 ml/5 fl oz Marsala wine
- 280 g/10 oz canned chopped plum tomatoes
- 1 tbsp chopped fresh basil leaves
- 2 tbsp tomato purée
- 450 g/1 lb dried spaghetti
- salt and pepper

1 Heat 2 tablespoons of the oil in a large saucepan. Add the garlic, onion and carrot and fry for 6 minutes.

2 Add the mince, chicken livers and Parma ham to the saucepan and cook over a medium heat for 12 minutes, or until well browned.

3 Stir in the Marsala, tomatoes, basil and tomato purée and cook for 4 minutes. Season to taste with salt and pepper. Cover and leave to simmer for 30 minutes.

4 Remove the lid from the saucepan, stir and leave to simmer for a further 15 minutes.

5 Meanwhile, bring a large saucepan of lightly salted water to the boil. Add the spaghetti and the remaining oil, return to the boil and cook for 12 minutes, or until tender, but still firm to the bite. Drain and transfer to a serving dish. Pour the sauce over the pasta, toss and serve hot.

variation

Chicken livers are considered an essential ingredient in a classic Bolognese sauce, adding richness. However, you can substitute them with the same quantity of beef or chicken mince, if you prefer.

VEGETABLE LASAGNE

THIS COLOURFUL AND TASTY LASAGNE HAS LAYERS OF DICED AND SLICED VEGETABLES IN TOMATO SAUCE, ALL TOPPED WITH A RICH CHEESE SAUCE. IN THIS RECIPE, VERDI (GREEN) SHEETS OF PASTA HAVE BEEN USED, BUT IF YOU PREFER YOU COULD USE NO PRE-COOK WHITE PASTA SHEETS INSTEAD.

serves

4

preparation

15 minutes,
plus 20 minutes'
standing

cooking

55 minutes

ingredients

- 1 aubergine, sliced
- 3 tbsp olive oil
- 2 garlic cloves, crushed
- 1 red onion, halved and sliced
- 3 mixed peppers, deseeded and diced
- 225 g/8 oz mixed mushrooms, sliced
- 2 celery sticks, sliced
- 1 courgette, diced
- 1/2 tsp chilli powder
- 1/2 tsp ground cumin
- 2 tomatoes, chopped
- 300 ml/10 fl oz passata
- 2 tbsp chopped fresh basil

- 8 no pre-cook lasagne verdi sheets
- salt and pepper

CHEESE SAUCE
- 2 tbsp butter or margarine
- 1 tbsp flour
- 150 ml/5 fl oz vegetable stock
- 300 ml/10 fl oz milk
- 75 g/2³/4 oz grated Cheddar cheese
- 1 tsp Dijon mustard
- 1 tbsp chopped fresh basil
- 1 egg, beaten

1 Place the aubergine slices in a colander, sprinkle with salt and leave for 20 minutes. Rinse under cold water, drain and reserve.

2 Preheat the oven to 180°C/350°F/Gas Mark 4. Heat the oil in a saucepan. Add the garlic and onion and sauté for 1–2 minutes. Add the peppers, mushrooms, celery and courgette and cook, stirring constantly, for 3–4 minutes.

3 Stir in the spices and cook for 1 minute. Mix in the tomatoes, passata and basil and season to taste with salt and pepper.

4 For the sauce, melt the butter in a saucepan. Stir in the flour and cook for 1 minute. Remove from the heat, stir in the stock and milk, return to the heat and add half the cheese and the mustard. Boil, stirring, until thickened. Stir in the basil. Remove from the heat and stir in the egg.

5 Place half the lasagne in an ovenproof dish. Top with half the vegetables, half the tomato sauce, then half the aubergines. Repeat and then spoon the cheese sauce on top. Sprinkle with the remaining cheese and bake in the oven for 40 minutes, or until golden brown and bubbling.

GNOCCHI WITH QUICK TOMATO SAUCE

THE WORD 'GNOCCHI' IS ITALIAN FOR 'DUMPLINGS', AND IS USED TO DESCRIBE SMALL BALLS OR
CONCAVE OVAL DISCS MADE FROM A DOUGH OF POTATOES AND/OR FLOUR. THEY ARE USUALLY
BOILED OR BAKED, AND SERVED WITH A SAUCE OR JUST SOME PARMESAN CHEESE.

serves
4

preparation
25 minutes

cooking
20 minutes

ingredients
- 900 g/2 lb floury potatoes
- 1 tbsp olive oil
- 225–280 g/8–10 oz plain
  flour, plus extra for dusting
- 1 tsp salt
- 1 tsp baking powder
- 1 egg, beaten
- freshly grated Parmesan
  cheese, to serve

TOMATO SAUCE
- 2 tbsp vegetable oil
- 1 large onion, chopped
- 2 garlic cloves, chopped
- 400 g/14 oz canned
  chopped tomatoes
- ½ vegetable stock
  cube dissolved in 100 ml/
  3½ fl oz boiling water
- 2 tbsp fresh basil, shredded

1 Peel the potatoes and cut into
chunks. Cook in lightly salted boiling
water for 15 minutes, or until
tender. Drain well, then push
through a sieve into a large bowl.
Mix in the oil.

2 Stir the flour, 1 teaspoon of salt
and the baking powder together.
Add half to the potatoes, with the
egg, and mix together. Gradually
knead in the remaining flour to form
a smooth, slightly sticky dough.

3 For the tomato sauce, heat the
oil in a pan. Add the onions and
garlic and cook for 3–4 minutes.
Add the tomatoes and stock and
cook, uncovered, for 10 minutes.
Season with salt and pepper
to taste.

4 Shape the dough on a floured
surface into 2.5-cm/1-inch thick
rolls, then cut into 2-cm/¾-inch
pieces. Using the tines of a fork,
roll each piece towards you to curl
in the sides and mark the top.

5 Bring a large saucepan of water
to the boil, then reduce to a simmer.
Add about 30 gnocchi and cook for
1–2 minutes until they float to the
surface. Repeat until all the gnocchi
are cooked.

6 Stir the basil into the tomato sauce
and pour over the gnocchi. Season
with pepper to taste. Sprinkle with
grated Parmesan and serve
immediately.

GOLDEN POLENTA, ITALIAN-STYLE

POLENTA IS MADE FROM CORNMEAL AND IS A POPULAR FOOD IN NORTHERN ITALY. ONCE COOKED, IT CAN BE EATEN HOT OR COLD. THIS RECIPE MAKES A DELICIOUS STARTER OR TASTY ACCOMPANIMENT TO A MAIN MEAL. IT ALSO MAKES A SATISFYING BREAKFAST.

serves
4
preparation
20 minutes, plus
2½ hours' cooling
and standing
cooking
1 hour

ingredients
- 1.5 litres/2¾ pints water
- 1½ tsp salt
- 300 g/10½ oz polenta or cornmeal flour
- vegetable oil, for frying and oiling
- 2 beaten eggs (optional)
- 125 g/4½ oz fresh fine white breadcrumbs (optional)

TOMATO SAUCE
- 2 tbsp olive oil
- 1 small onion, chopped
- 1 garlic clove, chopped
- 400 g/14 oz canned chopped tomatoes
- 2 tbsp chopped fresh parsley
- 1 tsp dried oregano
- 2 bay leaves
- 2 tbsp tomato purée
- 1 tsp sugar
- salt and pepper

1 Bring the water and salt to the boil in a large saucepan and gradually sprinkle in the polenta, stirring constantly to prevent lumps forming. Simmer gently, stirring frequently, for 30 minutes, or until the polenta becomes very thick and begins to draw away from the sides of the pan.

2 Thoroughly oil a 28 x 18-cm/11 x 7-inch shallow tin, then spoon in the polenta. Spread out evenly, using a wet wooden spoon or spatula. Let cool, then leave to stand for 2 hours at room temperature, if possible.

3 Cut the polenta into 30–36 squares. Heat the oil in a frying pan. Add the pieces and fry until golden brown all over, turning several times, for about 5 minutes. Alternatively, dip each piece of polenta in beaten egg and coat in breadcrumbs before frying in the hot oil. Keep warm.

4 For the tomato sauce, heat the oil in a pan over a medium heat. Add the onion and fry for 2 minutes until translucent. Add the garlic and fry for 1 minute. Stir in the chopped tomatoes, herbs, tomato purée, sugar and salt and pepper to taste. Bring to the boil, then simmer, uncovered, for 20 minutes, or until the sauce has reduced by half. Discard the bay leaf.

5 Serve the polenta pieces with the hot tomato sauce.

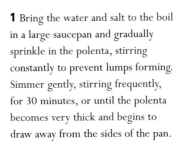

CHINESE FRIED RICE

THIS IS A DELICIOUS ADAPTATION OF A POPULAR CHINESE RECIPE. THE STRIPS OF BACON ARE A MOUTHWATERING ADDITION AND GIVE AN IRRESISTIBLE FLAVOUR TO THE RICE. TO MAKE THIS DISH WORK REALLY WELL, MAKE SURE YOU USE COLD, DRY RICE WITH GRAINS THAT ARE WELL SEPARATED.

serves
4

preparation
5 minutes, plus 20 minutes' cooling

cooking
30 minutes

ingredients
- 700 ml/1¼ pints water
- ½ tsp salt
- 300 g/10½ oz long-grain rice
- 2 eggs
- 4 tsp cold water
- 3 tbsp sunflower oil
- 4 spring onions, sliced diagonally
- 1 red, green or yellow pepper, cored, deseeded and thinly sliced
- 3–4 lean bacon rashers, rinded and cut into strips
- 200 g/7 oz fresh beansprouts
- 125 g/4½ oz frozen peas, thawed
- 2 tbsp soy sauce (optional)
- salt and pepper

1 Pour the water into the wok with the salt and bring to the boil. Rinse the rice in a sieve under cold running water until the water runs clear, drain thoroughly and add to the boiling water. Stir well, then cover the wok tightly with the lid, and simmer gently for 12–13 minutes. (Do not remove the lid during cooking or the steam will escape and the rice will not be cooked.)

2 Remove the lid, give the rice a good stir and spread out on a large plate or baking tray to cool and dry.

3 Meanwhile, beat each egg separately with salt and pepper and 2 teaspoons of cold water. Heat 1 tablespoon of oil in a preheated wok, pour in the first egg, swirl it around and leave to cook

undisturbed until set. Transfer to a chopping board and cook the second egg. Cut the omelettes into thin slices.

4 Add the remaining oil to the wok and when really hot add the spring onions and pepper and stir-fry for 1–2 minutes. Add the bacon and continue to stir-fry for a further 2 minutes. Add the beansprouts and peas and toss together thoroughly. Stir in the soy sauce, if using.

5 Add the rice and salt and pepper to taste and stir-fry for 1 minute, then add the strips of omelette and continue to stir-fry for 2 minutes, or until the rice is piping hot. Serve immediately.

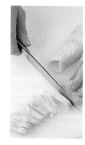

RISOTTO MILANESE

RISOTTO IS A DELICIOUS ITALIAN DISH AND VERY EASY TO MAKE, BUT IT DOES REQUIRE CONSTANT ATTENTION AND STIRRING WHILE COOKING. MAKE SURE YOU USE A STARCHY, SHORT-GRAIN RICE SUCH AS ARBORIO OR CARNAROLI, BECAUSE THIS WILL GIVE A LOVELY CREAMY CONSISTENCY.

serves
4

preparation
5 minutes

cooking
20 minutes

ingredients
- 1 litre/1¾ pints chicken stock
- 1 litre/1¾ pints white wine
- 1 tsp saffron strands
- 1 tbsp olive oil
- 3 tbsp butter
- 1 small onion, finely chopped
- 400 g/1 lb arborio rice
- 55 g/2 oz freshly grated Parmesan cheese
- salt and pepper

1 Bring the stock and white wine to the boil, then reduce the heat and simmer. Infuse the saffron strands in the stock and continue to simmer while preparing the risotto.

2 Heat the oil with 2 tablespoons of butter in a deep saucepan over a medium heat until the butter has melted. Stir in the onion and cook gently until soft and beginning to turn golden but not brown.

3 Add the rice and mix to coat in oil and butter. Cook, stirring, for 2–3 minutes, or until the grains are translucent.

4 Gradually add the stock and saffron mixture, a ladleful at a time. Stir constantly, adding more liquid as the rice absorbs it. Increase the heat slightly so that the liquid bubbles. Cook for 20 minutes, or until all the liquid is absorbed.

5 Remove the risotto from the heat. Add the remaining butter, mix well, then stir in the Parmesan cheese. Season to taste with salt and pepper and serve immediately.

BROWN RICE VEGETABLE PILAF

PILAFS ARE POPULAR AROUND THE EASTERN MEDITERRANEAN AND IN ASIA. THE COOKING METHOD INVOLVES SAUTÉEING THE RICE IN HOT BUTTER OR OIL, THEN POURING IN THE STOCK AND SIMMERING. PILAF INGREDIENTS VARY – THEY CAN CONTAIN VEGETABLES, MEATS, POULTRY OR FISH.

serves
4

preparation
30 minutes

cooking
15 minutes

ingredients
- 4 tbsp vegetable oil
- 1 red onion, finely chopped
- 2 tender celery sticks, leaves included, quartered lengthways and diced
- 2 carrots, coarsely grated
- 1 fresh green chilli, deseeded and finely chopped
- 3 spring onions, green part included, finely chopped
- 40 g/1½ oz whole almonds, sliced lengthways
- 350 g/12 oz cooked brown basmati rice
- 150 g/5½ oz cooked split red lentils
- 175 ml/6 fl oz chicken or vegetable stock
- 5 tbsp fresh orange juice
- salt and pepper
- fresh celery leaves, to garnish

1 Heat 2 tablespoons of the oil in a high-sided frying pan with a lid over a medium heat. Add the onion. Cook for 5 minutes, or until softened.

2 Add the celery, carrots, chilli, spring onions and almonds. Stir-fry for 2 minutes, or until the vegetables are al dente but still brightly coloured. Transfer to a bowl and reserve until required.

3 Add the remaining oil to the frying pan. Stir in the rice and lentils. Cook over a medium–high heat, stirring, for 1–2 minutes, or until heated through. Reduce the heat. Stir in the stock and orange juice. Season to taste with salt and pepper.

4 Return the vegetables to the frying pan. Toss with the rice for a few minutes until heated through. Transfer to a warmed dish, garnish with celery leaves and serve.

VEGETABLE COUSCOUS

COUSCOUS IS A SEMOLINA GRAIN THAT IS WIDELY EATEN IN NORTH AFRICA. IT IS VERY QUICK AND EASY TO COOK, AND MAKES A PLEASANT CHANGE FROM RICE OR PASTA. IT CAN ALSO BE COOKED WITH MILK TO MAKE A PORRIDGE, OR MIXED WITH FRUITS AND SERVED AS A DESSERT.

SERVES
4

preparation
20 minutes

cooking
40 minutes

ingredients

- 2 tbsp vegetable oil
- 1 large onion, roughly chopped
- 1 carrot, chopped
- 1 turnip, chopped
- 600 ml/1 pint vegetable stock
- 175 g/6 oz couscous
- 2 tomatoes, peeled and quartered
- 2 courgettes, chopped
- 1 red pepper, deseeded and chopped
- 125 g/4½ oz French beans, chopped
- grated rind of 1 lemon
- pinch of turmeric (optional)
- 1 tbsp finely chopped fresh coriander or parsley
- salt and pepper
- fresh flat-leaf parsley sprigs, to garnish

1 Heat the oil in a large saucepan. Add the onion, carrot and turnip and fry for 3–4 minutes. Add the stock, bring to the boil, cover and leave to simmer for 20 minutes.

2 Meanwhile, place the couscous in a bowl and moisten with a little boiling water, stirring, until the grains have swollen and separated.

3 Add the tomatoes, courgettes, pepper and French beans to the saucepan and stir.

4 Stir the lemon rind into the couscous and add the turmeric, if using, and mix thoroughly. Place the couscous in a steamer and position it over the saucepan of vegetables. Simmer the vegetables so that the couscous steams for 8–10 minutes.

5 Pile the couscous onto warmed serving plates. Ladle the vegetables and some of the liquid over the top. Scatter over the coriander and serve immediately, garnished with parsley sprigs.

TABBOULEH

THIS MIDDLE EASTERN SALAD IS BECOMING INCREASINGLY FASHIONABLE IN OTHER PARTS OF THE
WORLD. IT IS A CLASSIC ACCOMPANIMENT TO LAMB, BUT IT ALSO GOES WELL WITH MOST GRILLED
MEATS. ALTERNATIVELY, SERVE IT WITH HUMMUS AND PITTA BREAD FOR A VEGETARIAN LUNCH.

serves

4

preparation

10 minutes,
plus 1½ hours'
marinating and
standing

cooking

ingredients

- 175 g/6 oz bulgar wheat
- 3 tbsp extra virgin olive oil
- 4 tbsp lemon juice
- 4 spring onions
- 1 green pepper,
  deseeded and sliced
- 4 tomatoes, chopped
- 2 tbsp chopped
  fresh parsley
- 2 tbsp chopped fresh mint
- 8 black olives, stoned
- salt and pepper
- fresh mint sprigs, to garnish

1 Place the bulgar wheat in a large
bowl and add enough cold water to
cover. Leave to stand for 30 minutes,
or until the wheat has doubled in
size. Drain well and press out as
much liquid as possible. Spread out
the wheat on kitchen paper to dry.

2 Place the wheat in a serving bowl.
Mix the olive oil and lemon juice
together in a jug and season to taste
with salt and pepper. Pour the lemon
mixture over the wheat and leave to
marinate for 1 hour.

3 Using a sharp knife, finely chop the
spring onions, then add to the salad
with the green pepper, tomatoes,
parsley and mint and toss lightly to
mix. Top the salad with the olives and
garnish with fresh mint sprigs, then
serve immediately.

cook's tip

*The bulgar wheat grains have been cracked
by boiling and so are already partially
cooked, meaning it just needs to be
rehydrated. Don't make this salad too far
in advance as it may go soggy.*

CASSOULET

A STICK-TO-THE-RIBS WINTER WARMER, THIS TRADITIONAL GASCONY BEAN FEAST HAS SO MANY VARIATIONS THAT IT IS ALMOST IMPOSSIBLE TO GIVE A DEFINITIVE RECIPE. WHAT IS IMPORTANT, HOWEVER, IS TO USE SMALL, WHITE KIDNEY BEANS THAT HOLD THEIR SHAPE DURING COOKING.

serves
6–8
preparation
30 minutes,
plus 5–8 hours'
soaking
cooking
5½ hours

ingredients
- 325 g/11½ oz dried white kidney beans, soaked for at least 5 hours or according to the packet instructions
- 140 g/5 oz plain or smoked belly of pork, rind removed, cut into thick pieces
- 4 large garlic cloves, chopped
- 1 large bouquet garni of 4 fresh parsley sprigs, 6 fresh thyme sprigs, and 1 bay leaf
- large pinch of quatre épices
- 8 Toulouse sausages
- 4 pieces of goose or duck confit, about 400 g/14 oz
- 400 g/14 oz boneless shoulder of pork, cut into 5-cm/2-inch chunks
- 200 g/7 oz day-old French bread, made into fine breadcrumbs
- 8 tbsp finely chopped fresh flat-leaf parsley
- chicken or vegetable stock, if needed
- salt and pepper

1 Rinse the beans, then place them in a large, heavy-based saucepan with water to cover, over a high heat. Bring to the boil, boil rapidly for 10 minutes, then drain. Return the beans to the wiped-out pan with 5 cm/2 inches of water to cover and bring to the boil. Reduce the heat to a simmer and skim the surface until the grey foam stops rising.

2 Add the belly of pork, garlic, bouquet garni, quatre épices and pepper to taste. Adjust the heat so that bubbles just appear around the edge, then partially cover the saucepan and leave the beans to simmer for 1–1½ hours, or according to the packet instructions, until the beans are just slightly less than tender. The older the beans are, the longer they will take to cook. Do not let them boil or the skins will split.

3 Meanwhile, preheat the grill to high. Grill the sausages, turning them frequently, just until the casings are browned, then reserve.

4 Heat 2 tablespoons of fat from the confit in a frying pan over medium–high heat. Add the pork chunks and sauté until brown on each side. Reserve.

5 Preheat the oven to 150°C/ 300°F/Gas Mark 2. When the beans are almost tender, place a large sieve over a large bowl and strain the beans, discarding the bouquet garni but reserving the cooking liquid.

6 Place half the beans in a large flameproof casserole. Add the sausages, confit and pork chunks. Season to taste with salt and pepper, then cover with the remaining beans.

7 Pour in enough of the reserved cooking liquid to cover all the ingredients, topping up with stock if necessary. Mix the breadcrumbs and parsley together, then spread half thickly over the surface.

8 Bake, uncovered, for 4 hours. After 1 hour, use the back of a spoon to lightly push the breadcrumbs into the liquid, repeating this twice more at hourly intervals.

9 After 4 hours, sprinkle the top with the remaining breadcrumbs but do not press into the liquid. Return the casserole to the oven and continue baking for 1 hour, or until the top is golden and crisp. If the liquid appears to evaporate too quickly, pour in a little extra stock at the edges. Serve from the casserole.

CHILLI CON CARNE

THIS TEX-MEX FAVOURITE IS OFTEN SERVED WITH RICE, BUT IT IS JUST AS DELICIOUS EATEN WITH A
BAKED POTATO, THICK SLICES OF FRESH CRUSTY BREAD, OR TORTILLAS. YOU CAN BUY READY-MADE
SOFT FLOUR TORTILLAS AND HEAT THEM THROUGH BRIEFLY IN A DRY FRYING PAN BEFORE SERVING.

serves
4
preparation
15 minutes
cooking
30–35 minutes

ingredients
- 2 tbsp sunflower oil
- 500 g/1 lb 2 oz fresh
  beef mince
- 1 large onion, chopped
- 1 garlic clove, finely
  chopped
- 1 green pepper,
  deseeded and diced
- 1 tsp chilli powder
- 800 g/1 lb 12 oz canned
  chopped tomatoes
- 800 g/1 lb 12 oz canned
  red kidney beans, drained
  and rinsed
- 450 ml/16 fl oz beef stock
- salt
- handful of fresh coriander
  sprigs, plus a few to garnish
- 2 tbsp soured cream,
  to serve

1 Heat the oil in a large, heavy-based
saucepan or flameproof casserole.
Add the beef and cook over a
medium heat, stirring frequently,
for 5 minutes, or until broken up
and browned.

2 Reduce the heat, add the onion,
garlic and pepper and cook, stirring
frequently, for 10 minutes.

3 Stir in the chilli powder, tomatoes
with their juices and kidney beans.
Pour in the stock and season to
taste with salt. Bring to the boil,
reduce the heat and simmer, stirring
frequently, for 15–20 minutes,
or until the meat is tender.

4 Chop the coriander sprigs,
reserving a few for a garnish, and
stir into the chilli. Adjust the
seasoning, if necessary. Either garnish
with coriander sprigs and serve
immediately with a splash of soured
cream or leave to cool, then store
in the refrigerator overnight.
Reheating it the next day makes
the dish even more flavoursome.

variation

*Substitute 1–2 finely chopped, deseeded
fresh chillies for the chilli powder in Step 3.
Anaheim (mild) or jalapeño (hot) chillies
are both classic Tex-Mex varieties.*

CHINESE NOODLES

THIS DISH IS USUALLY SERVED AS A SNACK OR LIGHT MEAL, BUT IT MAY ALSO BE SERVED AS AN ACCOMPANIMENT TO PLAIN MEAT AND FISH DISHES. STIR-FRYING IS QUICK, EASY AND INEXPENSIVE. IT IS ALSO A HEALTHY WAY TO COOK BECAUSE IT USES A MINIMUM OF FAT.

serves
4

preparation
5 minutes

cooking
15 minutes

ingredients
- 350 g/12 oz egg noodles
- 3 tbsp vegetable oil
- 675 g/1 lb 8 oz lean beef steak, cut into thin strips
- 125 g/4½ oz green cabbage, shredded
- 75 g/2¾ oz bamboo shoots
- 6 spring onions, sliced
- 25 g/1 oz green beans, halved
- 1 tbsp dark soy sauce
- 2 tbsp beef stock
- 1 tbsp dry sherry
- 1 tbsp light brown sugar
- 2 tbsp fresh chopped parsley, to garnish

1 Cook the noodles in a saucepan of boiling water for 2–3 minutes. Drain well, rinse under cold running water and drain thoroughly again.

2 Heat 1 tablespoon of the oil in a preheated wok or large frying pan, swirling it around until it begins to smoke.

3 Add the noodles and stir-fry for 1–2 minutes. Drain the noodles and reserve until required.

4 Heat the remaining oil in the wok. Add the beef and stir-fry for 2–3 minutes. Add the cabbage, bamboo shoots, spring onions and beans to the wok and stir-fry for 1–2 minutes.

5 Add the soy sauce, stock, dry sherry and sugar to the wok, stirring to mix well. Stir the noodles into the mixture in the wok, tossing to mix well. Transfer to serving bowls, garnish with chopped parsley and serve immediately.

8

FRUIT

FRUIT IS DELICIOUS. IT CAN BE EATEN RAW OUT OF YOUR HAND OR COOKED IN A MULTITUDE OF WAYS, BOTH SAVOURY AND SWEET. IN THE FOLLOWING PAGES YOU WILL FIND AN INSPIRING COLLECTION OF RECIPES TO WHET YOUR APPETITE, WHETHER YOU ARE LOOKING FOR A LOW-FAT DESSERT FOR A SLIMMER OR A SUMPTUOUS CREATION FOR ENTERTAINING.

INTRODUCTION

FRUIT IS A HEALTHY CHOICE BECAUSE IT IS FULL OF VITAMINS AND VERY LOW IN FAT. IT IS ALSO VERY VERSATILE – DELICIOUS IN SAVOURY DISHES AND CHUTNEYS, AND DELIGHTFUL IN A WIDE RANGE OF DESSERTS AND CAKES.

Buying and storing fruit

Some fruits, such as apples and pears, are available fresh all year round, whereas others, such as cherries, have a limited season. Always buy your fruit as fresh as possible from a reputable supplier. Avoid any fruits that are bruised or damaged, or that are showing signs of mould. Choose fruits that are plump and free from blemishes: they should feel firm to the touch and not too soft. Many fruits, such as apples, pears and oranges, can be stored for around a week at room temperature, or even longer in the refrigerator. Other fruits, such as blueberries, have a short shelf life and should be kept in the refrigerator and eaten by the 'best before' date, but usually within a couple of days.

You can also freeze a wide range of fruits, such as bananas and mangoes (peel and slice them first) – even grapes are excellent frozen whole and used instead of ice cubes in drinks.

Orchard fruits

Orchard fruits, such as apples, pears and peaches, are delicious and very versatile. They can be eaten raw on their own and in fruit salads, or in cooked dishes such as fruit tarts and pies.

Apples

There are countless different varieties of apple in existence, in a range of colours from pale yellow to deep red. Some have a sweet flavour, while others are more acidic. Some apples, such as Golden Delicious and Braeburn, are excellent eaten raw as a snack or in salads. They also pair very well with cheese. Other varieties of apple are excellent for cooking, such as Bramley's Seedling, Cox's Orange Pippin and Granny Smith. They make excellent desserts, and are delicious stuffed and baked, or made into pie fillings. They can also be used in some savoury dishes, such as curries, and make very good sauces and purées.

Pears

Like apples, there are thousands of different types of pear, although we see only a selection of these in our shops. Pears bruise easily, so buy them while they are still hard and let them ripen at home. Many varieties, such as Comice or Conference pears, are delicious eaten as a snack, and they are excellent in salads and with cheese. Some types, such as Williams, are also very good for cooking. They can be stuffed and baked like apples, and are excellent peeled and poached in red wine.

Nectarines

These fruits are usually available in summer and autumn. Their smooth skins should be yellow with patches of red, with no green areas and no bruises. They will keep in the refrigerator for 5–6 days. You can eat nectarines raw as a snack or sliced in desserts. You can also poach or bake them. If they need further ripening, leave them out at room temperature for 1–2 days. If they

Braeburn apple

Golden Delicious apple

Pear

Nectarine

Apricot

Plum

do not soften during this time, they will not be suitable for eating raw, so cook them instead.

Peaches
These fruits are similar to nectarines except that they have downy instead of soft skin. Store and use them in the same way as nectarines.

Cherries
There are two main varieties of cherry: the larger sweet cherries, which are delicious eaten raw, and the smaller sour cherries, which are too tart to eat raw but can be cooked and made into excellent desserts and jams. Cherries are usually available during late spring and early summer, and should be stored in the refrigerator before use.

Apricots
These fruits are usually yellow or orange and have a large central stone. Some varieties are sweet enough to eat raw as a snack, while others need to be cooked. Cooked apricots make excellent desserts and jams, and can also be used in some

savoury dishes. Dried apricots are also very popular. The deep orange varieties have been treated with sulphur dioxide in order to preserve their colour. Untreated dried apricots are dark brown, so some people may find them less attractive, but they have just as much, if not more, flavour and goodness.

Plums
Hundreds of varieties of plum exist, and all tend to have a large, central stone. Their colour varies from yellow or green to red or purple, and they can grow to up to 7.5 cm/3 inches in diameter. They are in season through the summer months until early autumn, and will keep at room temperature for several days, or a little longer if stored in the refrigerator. Ripe plums are deliciously sweet and juicy and can be eaten raw as a snack or in a salad. They can also be cooked. Plum crumble is a popular baked dessert, and consists of a dish of plums covered with a crunchy topping. Plums also make excellent jam.

Citrus fruits
The fragrance and juicy tang of a ripe citrus fruit is irresistible, and wonderful in a whole host of chilled and cooked desserts. These fruits are also rich sources of vitamin C.

Oranges
These citrus fruits are available all through the year and come in many different varieties, such as the sweet oranges that can be eaten as a snack and sliced in salads and desserts. A variation of these is the blood orange, which is just as sweet and juicy, but which has redder flesh. Some oranges are seedless, while others have many seeds. You can also buy bitter oranges, such as Seville oranges: they are too sour to eat but they make excellent marmalade. Oranges will keep at room temperature for up to a week, but are better stored in the refrigerator to preserve their Vitamin C content. They will keep in the refrigerator for up to 2 weeks. Oranges make excellent garnishes, and are popular in a wide range of savoury and sweet dishes.

Grapefruits
Grapefruits can be seeded or seedless, and vary in colour from yellow to pink to red. They are available all year round, and are usually eaten raw. However, they can also be sprinkled with sugar and lightly grilled.

Lemons
These oval, yellow fruits have a tart flavour but a wide range of uses. They are available all year round and will keep at room temperature for around a week, and in the refrigerator for up to 3 weeks (but less time if cut). Lemons make an excellent flavouring and a good garnish or decoration for a wide range of savoury and sweet dishes. You can use the juice, grated zest or the flesh.

Limes
These green citrus fruits are smaller than lemons and have a milder flavour, but can replace lemons in many savoury and sweet dishes. They will keep whole in the refrigerator for up to 10 days.

Mandarin orange family
These small, round, orange fruits include mandarins, clementines, satsumas and tangerines. They are generally available in the winter months. Mandarins and tangerines have thick skins that are easy to peel. Clementines have thinner skins, and no seeds. Satsumas are also easy to peel, and are seedless. They are delicious eaten raw as a snack and in salads, and they all pair well with cream cheese.

Lemon

Orange

Grapefruit

Lime

Soft fruits

Juicy berries are delicious in desserts such as sorbets, ice creams, puddings, fruit crumbles and pies, but they can also be used in savoury dishes, such as chicken with blackberries.

Strawberries

These juicy red berries are available all year round, but peak season for strawberries is spring and early summer. Fresh strawberries will keep for up to 3 days in the refrigerator, and are delicious eaten raw, perhaps with whipped cream or marinated in balsamic vinegar. They also make excellent jams and syrups, and are very popular in a range of desserts. Dried strawberries have a deliciously tangy flavour and are wonderful in muesli.

Gooseberries

These large berries are usually green, but can also come in white and yellow. They are available in the summer months and are usually cooked before eating. Gooseberries make excellent jams and fillings for sweet pies. They will keep in the refrigerator for up to 4 days.

Blackberries

Blackberries are also known as 'brambles', and they grow wild on bushes. They are also cultivated. Blackberries come into season in the summer months. Use them straight away, or refrigerate them for up to 2 days. You can eat blackberries raw or cooked in sweet pies and desserts. They are often paired with apples. Blackberries also make good jam.

Raspberries

The most common colour of raspberry is red. These fruits are very popular with dieters, since they are very low in calories and fat, and yet have a delicious flavour. They will keep in the refrigerator for up to 3 days, and are delicious raw in a wide range of desserts. They can also be cooked, and make good coulis and fillings for puddings, as well as excellent jam.

Blueberries

These small, round dark-blue berries are sweet and can be eaten raw or cooked in sweet pies and other desserts. Like most berries, they make excellent jam. They are available during the summer and early autumn, and will keep in the refrigerator for 4–5 days.

Cranberries

These small, shiny red berries are available in late autumn and will keep in the refrigerator for 6–8 weeks and in the freezer for around 9 months. They have a tart flavour and therefore are usually mixed with sweeter fruits, such as apple – cranberry and apple juice is very popular. Cranberries can also be cooked and make an excellent sauce. They can be used in sweet pies and other cooked desserts.

Currants

Fresh currants are tiny berries that can be white, red or black. White- and redcurrants can be eaten raw and make excellent decorations for sweet dishes. Blackcurrants are quite tart and are better cooked and made into syrup or jam. Fresh currants are available in summer and will keep in the refrigerator for 3–4 days. They should not be confused with dried currants, which are like dark raisins.

Grapes

Other fruits

Other well-known fruits, such as bananas, grapes and melons, are widely available. They are very popular as snacks in their own right, and are also used in a wide range of desserts and cakes.

Grapes

These small oval fruits range in colour from yellowish-green to purplish-black, and can be seeded or seedless. The eating varieties are sweet and juicy, and are delicious eaten raw as a snack or added to salads. They also make excellent decorations and are wonderful paired with cheese. Other varieties of grapes are made into grape juice, wine, jam or raisins.

Bananas

These long fruits start off green, but turn yellow when they have ripened. Contrary to popular opinion, very fresh bananas can be stored in the refrigerator: the skins will turn brown but the flesh will be unaffected. If you prefer your bananas to stay yellow, store them at room temperature for a day or two. Bananas are delicious peeled and eaten as they are or added to a wide range of desserts. They can also be lightly grilled or baked.

Strawberries

Raspberries

Rhubarb

Rhubarb has edible red stalks, and comes into season in spring. The stalks will keep in the refrigerator for up to 3 days. Rhubarb has a tart flavour but, once cooked and sweetened, will make a good jam, sweet pie filling or other dessert. It also pairs well with ginger.

Melons

These fruit come in many sizes and colours. The popular edible types include galia, charentais, watermelon and cantaloupe. They are delicious eaten fresh on their own, or as a starter, perhaps combined with figs and ham, or alternatively port wine. They are also good in fruit salads.

Pineapples

This golden oval fruit has a tough, prickly exterior and spearlike leaves. Large pineapples are the most common, but baby pineapples are also available. The flesh is juicy with a tangy flavour, and is delicious

sliced and eaten on its own or added to fruit salads or other desserts. It is also good when cooked. It can be lightly grilled, or baked in a cake. Fresh pineapple will keep in the refrigerator for up to 3 days. You can also buy it canned.

Exotic fruits

There is a wonderfully wide range of exotic fruits available nowadays, from physalis to dragon fruit. Here is a small selection of some of the popular ones – there are many more.

Mango

These large oval fruits vary in colour from yellow to red. Eat them raw, perhaps in a fruit salad, or frozen in a sorbet.

Star fruit

These star-shaped yellow fruits make beautiful decorations when cut across in slices.

Dates

These oval fruits are available fresh or dried. Chopped dried dates are delicious in muesli and desserts.

Kiwi fruit

These oval fruits have brown 'hairy' skin and soft green flesh. Eat the flesh with a teaspoon. Alternatively, peel and slice them and add them to fruit salads and other desserts.

Lychees

These small fruits are available fresh or canned. They have a rough, pink, inedible skin, but the flesh inside is juicy and fragrant. You can eat them raw or lightly poached.

Figs

These soft, pear-shaped fruits are delicious eaten raw or poached. Dried figs are also good.

Passion fruit

Cut these brown-skinned, wrinkly fruits in half and eat the pulp by scooping it out with a teaspoon.

Pawpaw

This large, pear-shaped fruit is cooked when green and unripe, or eaten raw when it is ripe and golden-yellow. Pawpaw is good in salads.

Lychees

Pineapple

Star fruit

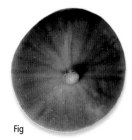

Fig

Banana

BERRY YOGURT ICE

THIS REFRESHING ICE MAKES A WONDERFUL SUMMER DESSERT AFTER A FILLING MEAL, AS IT IS LIGHT AND COOLING WITHOUT THE RICHNESS – OR FAT – OF ICE CREAM. SERVE WITH A SELECTION OF FRESH SUMMER BERRIES.

serves
4

preparation
15 minutes,
plus 4 hours'
freezing

cooking
5 minutes

ingredients
- 125 g/4½ oz raspberries
- 125 g/4½ oz blackberries
- 125 g/4½ oz strawberries
- 1 large egg
- 175 ml/6 fl oz Greek yogurt
- 125 ml/4 fl oz red wine
- 2¼ tsp powdered gelatine
- fresh berries, to decorate

1 Place the raspberries, blackberries and strawberries in a blender or food processor and process until a smooth purée forms. Rub the purée through a sieve into a bowl to remove the seeds.

2 Break the egg and separate the yolk and white into separate bowls. Stir the egg yolk and yogurt into the berry purée and set the egg white aside.

3 Pour the wine into a heatproof bowl set over a saucepan of water. Sprinkle the gelatine on the surface of the wine and leave to stand for 5 minutes to soften. Heat the pan of water and simmer until the gelatine has dissolved. Pour the mixture into the berry purée in a steady stream, whisking constantly. Transfer the mixture to a freezerproof container and freeze for 2 hours, or until slushy.

4 Whisk the egg white in a spotlessly clean, grease-free bowl until very stiff. Remove the berry mixture from the freezer and fold in the egg white. Return to the freezer and freeze for 2 hours, or until firm. To serve, scoop the berry yogurt ice into glass dishes and decorate with fresh berries of your choice.

cook's tip

Vegetarians can use a vegetarian gelatine, which is available in health food shops, to make this ice. Follow the instructions on the packet and proceed as in the main recipe.

ORANGE SORBET

SORBETS HELP TO CLEANSE THE PALATE AFTER A MEAL, AND ARE DELICIOUSLY REFRESHING IN HOT WEATHER. THEY ARE ALSO INVALUABLE TO THE HEALTH-CONSCIOUS OR AS PART OF A SLIMMING DIET BECAUSE THEY ARE VIRTUALLY FAT-FREE. THE LIQUEUR IN THIS SORBET IS AN ADDED TREAT.

serves
4

preparation
20 minutes, plus
4 hours' chilling
and freezing

cooking
4 minutes

ingredients
- 500 ml/18 fl oz water
- 200 g/7 oz caster sugar
- 4 large oranges
- 2 tbsp orange liqueur,
  such as Cointreau
- 4 scooped-out oranges,
  to serve

1 Heat the water and sugar in a saucepan over a low heat, stirring, until dissolved. Boil without stirring for 2 minutes. Pour into a heatproof bowl. Cool to room temperature.

2 Grate the rind from 2 oranges and extract the juice. Extract the juice from 2 more oranges. Mix the juice and rind in a bowl, cover with clingfilm and reserve. Discard the squeezed oranges. Stir the orange juice, grated rind and orange liqueur into the cooled syrup. Cover with clingfilm and leave to chill for 1 hour. Transfer to an ice cream machine and churn for 15 minutes.

3 If you do not have an ice cream machine, place the mixture in a freezerproof container. Freeze for 1 hour, then transfer to a bowl. Beat to break up the crystals, then return it to the freezerproof container and freeze for 30 minutes. Repeat twice more, freezing for 30 minutes and whisking each time.

4 Divide the frozen sorbet between the scooped-out orange cups and serve immediately.

TROPICAL FRUIT SALAD

A TROPICAL FRUIT SALAD IS DELIGHTFULLY REFRESHING DURING HOT SUMMER DAYS OR SULTRY EVENINGS. THIS ONE CONTAINS A LITTLE MIXED SPICE FOR A TANTALIZING HINT OF AROMATIC SWEETNESS. YOU CAN ALSO SERVE THIS WITH HALF-FAT CRÈME FRAÎCHE, IF YOU PREFER.

serves
6

preparation
20 minutes, plus
1 hour's chilling

cooking
3 minutes

ingredients
- 6 tbsp caster sugar
- 400 ml/14 fl oz water
- ½ tsp mixed spice
- grated rind of ½ lemon
- 1 pawpaw
- 1 mango
- 1 pineapple
- 4 oranges, peeled and cut into segments
- 125 g/4½ oz strawberries, hulled and quartered
- single or double cream, to serve (optional)

1 Place the sugar, water, mixed spice and lemon rind in a saucepan. Bring to the boil, stirring constantly, then continue to boil for 1 minute. Remove from the heat and leave to cool to room temperature.

2 Transfer to a jug or bowl, cover with clingfilm and chill in the refrigerator for at least 1 hour.

3 Peel and halve the pawpaw and remove the seeds. Cut the flesh into small chunks or slices, and place in a large bowl.

4 Cut the mango twice lengthways, close to the stone. Remove and discard the stone. Peel and cut the flesh into small chunks or slices, and add to the bowl.

5 Cut off the top and bottom of the pineapple and remove the hard skin. Cut the pineapple in half lengthways, then into quarters and remove the tough core. Cut the remaining flesh into small pieces and add to the bowl.

6 Add the orange segments and strawberries. Pour over the chilled syrup, cover with clingfilm and chill until required. Serve with cream, if liked.

TRADITIONAL APPLE PIE

THIS SWEET APPLE PIE HAS A DELICIOUS DOUBLE CRUST. IT IS A SUBSTANTIAL DESSERT AND MAKES
AN IMPRESSIVE FINISH TO ANY MEAL. IT CAN BE SERVED EITHER HOT OR COLD, ON ITS OWN OR
WITH CREAM OR CUSTARD. YOU CAN ADJUST THE AMOUNT OF SUGAR ACCORDING TO YOUR TASTE.

serves
6

preparation
25 minutes,
plus 30 minutes'
chilling

cooking
50 minutes

ingredients
- 750 g–1 kg/1 lb 10 oz–2 lb
  4 oz cooking apples,
  peeled, cored and sliced
- about 125 g/4½ oz
  brown or white sugar,
  plus extra for sprinkling
- ½–1 tsp ground cinnamon,
  mixed spice or ground
  ginger
- 1–2 tbsp water

SHORTCRUST PASTRY
- 350 g/12 oz plain flour, plus
  extra for dusting
- pinch of salt
- 85 g/3 oz butter or
  margarine

- 85 g/3 oz white
  vegetable fat
- about 6 tbsp cold water
- milk or beaten egg,
  to glaze

1 To make the pastry, sift the flour
and salt into a large bowl. Add the
butter and fat and rub it in with
your fingertips until the mixture
resembles fine breadcrumbs. Add
enough water to mix to a dough.
Wrap the dough in clingfilm and
leave to chill for 30 minutes.

2 Preheat the oven to 220°C/
425°F/Gas Mark 7. Roll out almost
two-thirds of the pastry thinly on a
lightly floured surface and use to line
a 20–23-cm/8–9-inch deep pie plate
or shallow pie tin.

3 Mix the apples with the sugar and
spices and pack into the pastry case;
the filling can come up above the
rim. If the apples are a dry variety
add a little water to moisten.

4 Roll out the remaining pastry to
form a lid. Dampen the edges of
the pie rim with water and position
the lid, pressing the edges firmly
together. Trim and crimp the edges.

5 Use the pastry trimmings to
cut out leaves or other shapes to
decorate the top of the pie. Dampen
the shapes and attach. Glaze the top
of the pie with milk or beaten egg,
make 1–2 slits in the top and put the
pie on a baking sheet.

6 Bake in the oven for 20 minutes,
then reduce the oven temperature to
180°C/350°F/Gas Mark 4 and cook
for 30 minutes, or until the pastry is
a light golden brown. Serve hot or
cold, sprinkled with sugar.

STUFFED BAKED APPLES

BAKED APPLES ARE A TRADITIONAL FAMILY FAVOURITE AND ARE USUALLY STUFFED WITH A TASTY COMBINATION OF SULTANAS, RAISINS, BROWN SUGAR AND SWEET SPICES. THIS GINGER-FLAVOURED FLAPJACK STUFFING IS MORE UNUSUAL, AND MAKES A WELCOME CHANGE.

serves
4
preparation
10 minutes
cooking
45 minutes

ingredients
- 25 g/1 oz blanched almonds
- 55 g/2 oz ready-to-eat dried apricots
- 1 piece stem ginger, drained
- 1 tbsp clear honey
- 1 tbsp syrup from the stem ginger jar
- 4 tbsp rolled oats
- 4 large cooking apples

1 Preheat the oven to 180°C/ 350°F/Gas Mark 4. Using a sharp knife, chop the almonds very finely. Chop the apricots and stem ginger very finely. Reserve.

2 Place the honey and syrup in a saucepan and heat until the honey has melted. Stir in the oats and cook gently over a low heat for 2 minutes. Remove the saucepan from the heat and stir in the almonds, apricots and stem ginger.

3 Core the apples, widen the tops slightly and score around the circumference of each to prevent the skins bursting during cooking. Place the apples in an ovenproof dish and fill the cavities with the stuffing. Pour just enough water into the dish to come about one-third of the way up the apples. Bake in the preheated oven for 40 minutes, or until tender. Serve immediately.

variation

Use an extra tablespoon of honey instead of the stem ginger and syrup, replace the almonds with walnuts and add ½ teaspoon of ground cinnamon.

TARTE AU CITRON

FEW DESSERTS CAN BE MORE APPEALING TO ROUND OFF A MEAL ON A HOT EVENING THAN THIS DELICIOUSLY TANGY TART. IT LOOKS WONDERFULLY INVITING AND SERVES UP BEAUTIFULLY, MAKING IT THE IDEAL DESSERT TO TEMPT YOUR DINNER GUESTS OR MEMBERS OF YOUR HOUSEHOLD.

serves
6–8

preparation
25 minutes, plus
1 hour's chilling

cooking
35 minutes

ingredients
- grated rind of 2–3 large lemons
- 150 ml/5 fl oz lemon juice
- 100 g/3 ½ oz caster sugar
- 125 ml/4 fl oz double cream or crème fraîche, plus extra to serve
- 3 large eggs
- 3 large egg yolks
- icing sugar, for dusting

PASTRY
- 175 g/6 oz plain flour, plus extra for dusting
- ½ tsp salt
- 115 g/4 oz cold unsalted butter, diced
- 1 egg yolk beaten with 2 tbsp ice-cold water

TO SERVE
- candied citrus peel
- fresh strawberry halves

1 To make the pastry, sift the flour and salt into a large bowl. Add the butter and rub it in with your fingertips until the mixture resembles fine breadcrumbs. Add the egg yolk and water and stir to mix to a dough.

2 Gather the dough into a ball, wrap in clingfilm and leave to chill for at least 1 hour.

3 Preheat the oven to 200°C/400°F/Gas Mark 6. Roll the dough out on a lightly floured work surface and use to line a 23–25-cm/9–10-inch fluted tart tin with a removable base. Prick the base all over with a fork and line with baking paper and baking beans.

4 Bake in the preheated oven for 15 minutes until the pastry looks set. Remove the paper and beans. Reduce the oven temperature to 190°C/375°F/Gas Mark 5.

5 Beat the lemon rind, lemon juice and sugar together until blended. Slowly beat in the cream, then beat in the eggs and yolks, one by one.

6 Set the pastry case on a baking sheet and pour in the filling. Transfer to the preheated oven and bake for 20 minutes until the filling is set.

7 Leave to cool completely on a wire rack. Dust with icing sugar. Serve with a spoonful of cream, candied citrus peel and halved strawberries.

GOLDEN BAKED APPLE PUDDING

THIS IS A WARM AND SATISFYING DESSERT DURING COLD WEATHER, YET IT IS SURPRISINGLY LOW IN FAT, MAKING IT THE IDEAL CHOICE FOR SLIMMERS AND THE HEALTH-CONSCIOUS. YOU CAN ADJUST THE AMOUNT OF SUGAR ACCORDING TO YOUR TASTE. TRY SERVING IT WITH LOW-FAT CUSTARD.

serves
4

preparation
15 minutes

cooking
30–35 minutes

ingredients
- 450 g/1 lb cooking apples
- 1 tsp ground cinnamon
- 2 tbsp sultanas
- 115 g/4 oz wholemeal bread
- 125 g/4½ oz low fat cottage cheese
- 4 tbsp soft light brown sugar
- 250 ml/9 fl oz semi-skimmed milk

1 Preheat the oven to 220°C/425°F/Gas Mark 7. Peel and core the apples and chop the flesh into 1 cm/½-inch pieces. Place in a bowl and toss with the cinnamon and sultanas.

2 Remove the crusts and cut the bread into 1-cm/½-inch cubes. Add to the apples with the cottage cheese and 3 tablespoons of the brown sugar and mix together. Stir in the milk.

3 Turn the mixture into an ovenproof dish and sprinkle with the remaining sugar. Bake in the preheated oven for 30–35 minutes, or until golden brown. Serve hot.

variation

Replace the cottage cheese with either cream cheese or ricotta and the sultanas with raisins, if liked.

TROPICAL FRUIT DESSERT

FRUIT FOOLS ARE ALWAYS POPULAR, AND THIS LIGHTLY TANGY VERSION WILL BE NO EXCEPTION.
YOU CAN VARY THIS RECIPE BY USING YOUR FAVOURITE COMBINATIONS OF FRUITS IF YOU PREFER.
FOR EXAMPLE, TRY USING PAWPAW INSTEAD OF THE MANGO, AND MELON INSTEAD OF THE KIWI FRUIT.

serves

4

preparation

20 minutes,
plus 20 minutes'
chilling

cooking

ingredients

- 1 ripe mango
- 2 kiwi fruit
- 1 banana
- 2 tbsp lime juice
- ½ tsp finely grated lime
  rind, plus extra to decorate
- 2 egg whites
- 425 g/15 oz canned custard
- ½ tsp vanilla essence
- 2 passion fruits

1 Peel the mango and slice either
side of the smooth, flat central stone.
Roughly chop the flesh and process
the fruit in a food processor or
blender until smooth. Alternatively,
mash with a fork.

2 Peel the kiwi fruit, chop the flesh
into small pieces and place in a bowl.
Peel and chop the banana and add to
the bowl. Toss all of the fruit in the
lime juice and rind and mix well.

3 Whisk the egg whites in a grease-
free bowl until stiff then gently fold
in the custard and vanilla essence
until thoroughly mixed.

4 Alternately layer the chopped
fruit, mango purée and custard
mixture, finishing with a layer of
custard in 4 tall glasses. Leave to chill
in the refrigerator for 20 minutes.

5 Halve the passion fruits, scoop out
the seeds and spoon the passion fruit
over the fruit fools. Decorate each
serving with the extra lime rind and
serve immediately.

variation

*Other tropical fruits to try include pawpaw
purée, with chopped pineapple and dates,
and pomegranate seeds to decorate.
Alternatively, make a summer fruit fool
by using strawberry purée, topped with
blackberries, with cherries to finish.*

APPLE STRUDEL WITH WARM CIDER SAUCE

STRUDELS ARE POPULAR IN GERMANY AND AUSTRIA, AND ARE STUFFED WITH SAVOURY OR SWEET FILLINGS. APPLE IS THE MOST FAMOUS SWEET STRUDEL, AND THIS VERSION HAS AN ADDED ADVANTAGE IN THAT IT IS EXTREMELY LOW IN FAT AND SUITABLE FOR THOSE WITH LOW-FAT DIETS.

serves
2–4

preparation
25 minutes

cooking
15–20 minutes

ingredients
- 8 crisp eating apples
- 1 tbsp lemon juice
- 85 g/3 oz sultanas
- 1 tsp ground cinnamon
- ½ tsp grated nutmeg
- 1 tbsp soft light brown sugar
- 6 sheets filo pastry
- vegetable oil spray
- icing sugar, to serve

CIDER SAUCE
- 1 tbsp cornflour
- 450 ml/16 fl oz cider

1 Preheat the oven to 190°C/375°F/Gas Mark 5. Line a baking sheet with non-stick paper. Peel and core the apples and chop them into 1-cm/½-inch dice. Toss the pieces in a bowl, with the lemon juice, sultanas, cinnamon, nutmeg and sugar.

2 Lay out a sheet of filo pastry, spray with vegetable oil and lay a second sheet on top. Repeat with a third sheet. Spread over half the apple mixture and roll up lengthways,

tucking in the ends to enclose the filling. Repeat to make a second strudel. Slide onto the baking sheet, spray with oil and bake in the oven for 15–20 minutes.

3 For the sauce, blend the cornflour in a saucepan with a little cider until smooth. Add the remaining cider and heat gently, stirring constantly, until the mixture boils and thickens. Serve the strudel warm or cold, dredged with icing sugar and accompanied by the cider sauce.

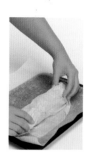

DATE & APRICOT TART

THIS DRIED FRUIT TART IS RICH IN PROTEIN AND DIETARY FIBRE, AND THEREFORE MAKES A
HEALTHY CHOICE FOR A DESSERT. THERE IS NO NEED TO ADD ANY EXTRA SUGAR TO THIS FILLING
BECAUSE THE DRIED FRUIT IS NATURALLY SWEET. THE TART CAN BE SERVED HOT OR COLD.

serves
8

preparation
15 minutes,
plus 30 minutes'
chilling

cooking
50 minutes

ingredients
- 225 g/8 oz plain wholemeal flour, plus extra for dusting
- 55 g/2 oz mixed nuts, ground
- 100 g/3½ oz margarine, cut into small pieces
- 4 tbsp water
- 225 g/8 oz dried apricots, chopped
- 225 g/8 oz chopped stoned dates
- 425 ml/15 fl oz apple juice
- 1 tsp ground cinnamon
- grated rind of 1 lemon
- custard, to serve (optional)

1 Place the flour and ground nuts in a large bowl. Add the margarine and rub it in with your fingertips until the mixture resembles fine breadcrumbs. Stir in the water and mix to a dough. Wrap the dough in clingfilm and leave to chill in the refrigerator for 30 minutes.

2 Meanwhile, place the apricots and dates in a saucepan, with the apple juice, cinnamon and lemon rind. Bring to the boil, cover and simmer over a low heat for 15 minutes until the fruit softens. Mash to a purée.

3 Preheat the oven to 200ºC/400ºF/Gas Mark 6. Reserve a small ball of pastry for making lattice strips. Roll out the rest of the dough on a lightly floured work surface to form a round and use to line a 23-cm/9-inch loose-based quiche tin.

4 Spread the fruit filling evenly over the base of the pastry case. Roll out the reserved pastry and cut into strips 1 cm/½ inch wide. Cut the strips to fit the tart and twist them across the top of the fruit to form a decorative lattice pattern. Moisten the edges of the strips with a little water and seal them firmly around the rim of the tart.

5 Bake for 25–30 minutes until golden brown. Cut into slices and serve with custard, if liked.

9

BAKING

THERE IS NOTHING LIKE THE SMELL OF FRESHLY HOME-
BAKED BREAD AND PASTRIES TO GET EVERY MEMBER OF
THE HOUSEHOLD HOVERING AROUND THE KITCHEN.
IN THIS CHAPTER YOU WILL ENCOUNTER SOME TRULY
INSPIRITIONAL BREAD RECIPES, AND A WONDERFUL
SELECTION OF OTHER BAKED TREATS, INCLUDING
SAVOURY PASTRIES AND SWEET, STICKY BUNS.

INTRODUCTION

THERE IS NOTHING LIKE THE AROMA OF FRESHLY BAKED BREAD, PASTRY, CAKES AND BISCUITS TO STIMULATE THE APPETITE. BAKING THESE ITEMS FOR YOURSELF IS VERY SATISFYING, AND THE MOUTHWATERING AROMAS WILL PROVE TO BE AN IRRESISTIBLE TEMPTATION FOR YOUR FAMILY AND FRIENDS.

Making bread at home

Making your own bread does not have to be difficult – anyone can make delicious loaves and rolls with the minimum of effort. The key to making perfect bread is to use the right ingredients at the right temperature. Always use strong bread flour rather than ordinary flour: bread flour has a higher gluten content than ordinary flour, which increases the elasticity of the dough. You can use any of the different kinds of yeast, but each has a different method for breadmaking. You will also need to use the correct quantities: 15 g/½ oz fresh yeast or 1 tbsp dried yeast is enough to make 750 g/1 lb 10 oz strong bread flour rise. When you add water, make sure it is tepid, because if it is too hot, it will kill the yeast.

Fresh yeast
Crush this in a jug with a little warm water, then cover and leave it to stand until the surface starts to bubble.

Dried yeast
Sprinkle the dried yeast over a little warm water in a jug, then stir in a pinch of sugar. Cover and leave to stand until it froths.

Easy-blend yeast
Mix this yeast straight into the flour before the warm water is added.

Yeast

Key techniques for making dough

Making the perfect dough can be straightforward, but it is important to follow a certain procedure to achieve good results every time.

MIXING

❶ To mix the dough, sift the flour and salt into a mixing bowl. Make a well in the centre, then add the yeast. Pour in hand-hot water, then gradually pull in the flour from the edges and mix together, adding more hand-hot water as necessary in order to form a soft dough.

KNEADING

❷ This process is necessary in order to make the dough smooth and increase its elasticity. To knead the dough, push your hand into it, then stretch it away from you. Pick up the furthest end of the dough and pull it back to the top, then turn the dough 45° and repeat the kneading action away from you. Keep turning the dough 45° and repeating the kneading action. The kneading process usually takes about 5 minutes. To save time and effort, you could use a standing mixer or food processor with a dough hook

Bread

to mix and knead the dough for you.
Kneading will take about 3 minutes if
you do it this way.

RISING

❸ After the dough has been kneaded,
place it in an oiled bowl, cover it with
clingfilm and put it in a warm place,
such as an airing cupboard. Leave it
to rise to about double its original size.

KNOCKING BACK

This process is also known as 'punching
down'. Simply punch your fist into the
risen dough so that it collapses and
releases the air. Then turn the dough out
onto a floured work surface (some of it
may need scraping out) and knead
it for about 1 minute until it has lost its
cold feel and has an even temperature.

PROVING

This stage literally means proving that
the yeast is still active. To do this, after
knocking back the dough, divide and
shape it as required (see below). Cover
as before and leave it to rise for a second
(but shorter) time, until the dough has
doubled in size.

SHAPING

❹ To shape the dough correctly for a
loaf tin, use your hands to form the
dough into an oval, then bring over the
two short sides to the centre, turn the
dough over and transfer, seam-side
down, to a greased loaf tin. To make
rolls, simply use your hands to roll even-
sized pieces of the dough into balls, and
place on a greased baking sheet.

Baking and storing bread

The dough will keep, covered, in the
refrigerator for up to a day before
baking. To bake the bread, you will need
a hot oven, so make sure you preheat
it beforehand. Underbaked bread has
a moist, doughlike consistency and
flavour, so it is always better to overbake
if necessary. To test if the bread is
properly baked, remove it from the
oven, turn it out of its tin, and use your
knuckles to give it a sharp tap on the
bottom. If it sounds hollow, the bread
is done. It it does not, return it to the
oven and bake for another 5 minutes or
until the bread is properly baked. When
it is done, remove from the oven and
leave to cool on a wire rack. If you want
a soft crust, cover the loaf with a clean
tea towel while it is cooling. Freshly
baked bread will keep, covered, for 2–3
days at room temperature, but no longer
because it has no added preservatives.
You can also keep it wrapped in the
refrigerator for up to a week, or wrap
it in a freezer bag and freeze it for up
to a month.

Making pastry

Pastry is very versatile and lends a professional finish to a wide range of savoury and sweet dishes. Choose your pastry to match the occasion: shortcrust pastry for savoury or sweet pies, flans and tartlets; choux pastry for profiteroles and eclairs; paper-thin filo pastry for savoury pancake rolls or sweet apple strudel; or puff pastry for sausage rolls and a wide range of desserts.

Shortcrust pastry

This recipe will make enough pastry to line a 20-cm/8-inch flan tin.

175 g/6 oz plain flour
90 g/3¼ oz butter, diced
2–3 tbsp cold water

❶ To make the pastry, sift the plain flour. ❷ Use your fingertips to rub in the butter until the mixture resembles fine breadcrumbs. Gradually mix in enough water to make a soft dough. ❸ Use your hands to shape the dough into a ball. Cover with clingfilm and refrigerate before use. When you are ready to use it, turn it out onto a clean work surface lightly dusted with flour. ❹ Use a rolling pin to roll it out to the desired thickness.

Variation: To make a sweet shortcrust pastry, stir 1 tablespoon of caster sugar into the flour after sifting, and replace half the water with 2 beaten egg yolks.

Choux pastry

This quantity will make about 24 round choux buns.

185 ml/6½ fl oz water
75 g/2¾ oz butter
115 g/4 oz plain flour
½ tsp salt
½ tsp icing sugar
3 eggs, plus a little beaten egg to glaze

Preheat the oven to 200°C/400°F/ Gas Mark 6. Pour the water into a saucepan and add the butter. Gently bring to the boil. Sift the flour and salt into a bowl, then mix in the icing sugar. In a separate bowl, beat the eggs.

When the butter is just beginning to boil, remove from the heat and stir in the flour mixture. Continue to stir until smooth, then return to the heat and stir until the mixture begins to pull away from the sides of the saucepan. Remove from the heat and gradually beat in the eggs until the mixture forms a thick, glossy paste.

Put 24 rounded spoonfuls of the mixture onto greased baking sheets and brush the tops with a little beaten egg. Bake in the preheated oven for 20 minutes, or until golden. Remove from the oven and cool.

Serving suggestion: Split the cooled buns in half horizontally and sandwich with whipped cream. You can also brush melted chocolate over the tops and leave to cool, or serve with a chocolate sauce.

Making cakes and biscuits

You can make cakes of varying densities depending on the ingredients you use and the method of mixing. For cakes and biscuits there are four basic methods of mixing, as follows:

CREAMING

This is a good method for making light sponge cakes. Simply beat the butter and sugar together until light, then beat in the eggs and fold in the flour. Use softened butter or margarine for this method.

ALL-IN-ONE

This method saves time and effort when making light sponge cakes, and can be done manually or in a machine. Put all the ingredients into a mixing bowl and beat well until smooth. Alternatively, put the ingredients into a free-standing mixer or food processor and beat on slow speed for 2–3 minutes until smooth.

RUBBING IN

This method is ideal for scones and teabreads. Use your fingertips to rub the butter into the flour until it resembles fine breadcrumbs. Then mix in the sugar, egg and any other liquid ingredients. Stir in the flour from the sides of the bowl.

MELTING

Use this method for moist cakes and biscuits. Melt the butter in a saucepan along with the sugar and any other dissolvable ingredients. Remove from the heat and allow to cool slightly. Meanwhile, sift the flour into a bowl and make a well in the centre. Beat together the eggs and milk and pour into the well, then add the egg mixture. Stir in the flour from the sides of the bowl.

Basic sponge mixture

This recipe will make enough for two 20-cm/8-inch greased and lined sandwich tins.

225 g/8 oz unsalted butter, softened, or soft margarine suitable for baking
225 g/8 oz caster sugar
4 eggs
225 g/8 oz self-raising flour, sifted
2 tsp baking powder
pinch of salt

Preheat the oven to 190°C/375°F/ Gas Mark 5. Grease and line the sandwich tins. Put the butter or margarine in a large bowl, then add the sugar and use a wooden spoon to beat together until the mixture is smooth and light. Gradually beat in the eggs, making sure that the mixture stays smooth throughout.

In a separate bowl, sift together the flour, baking powder and salt, then fold into the egg mixture in a figure-of-eight movement. Divide the mixture between the sandwich tins and bake for about 25 minutes until golden and risen. Remove from the oven and leave to cool in the tins for about 5 minutes before turning out on a wire rack to cool completely.

Variation: To make a chocolate version of this sponge, replace 1 tablespoon of the self-raising flour with 1 tablespoon of unsweetened cocoa powder.

Butter shortbread

This recipe makes 8 large pieces of shortbread or 16 smaller pieces.

125 g/4½ oz unsalted butter, softened, plus extra for greasing
175 g/6 oz plain flour
40 g/1½ oz rice flour
50 g/1¾ oz caster sugar, plus extra for sprinkling

Preheat the oven to 160°C/325°F/ Gas Mark 3. Grease a 20-cm/8-inch loose-bottomed flan tin. Sift the plain and rice flours into a large bowl.

In a separate bowl, cream together the butter and caster sugar, then stir in the sifted flours. Put the mixture into the prepared flan tin and smooth the surface. Lightly sprinkle over some caster sugar, then prick all over the surface with a fork. Using a sharp knife, score the surface into 8 wedges (or 16 smaller wedges, if preferred), then bake in the preheated oven for 30 minutes, or until lightly golden.

Remove from the oven and leave to cool in the tin for 5 minutes. Slide the shortbread out of the tin, then use a sharp knife to cut along the score marks and divide the shortbread into wedges. Cool on a wire rack, then serve immediately or store in an airtight container for up to a week.

CRUSTY WHITE BREAD

THERE IS A LOT OF MYSTIQUE THAT STILL SURROUNDS BREADMAKING, BUT IN REALITY ANYONE CAN BAKE THEIR OWN BREAD AT HOME. THIS RECIPE IS EASY TO DO, AND WILL MAKE YOU WANT TO BAKE YOUR OWN BREAD AGAIN AND AGAIN.

makes
1 medium loaf
preparation
30 minutes, plus
1½ hours' rising
cooking
30 minutes

ingredients
- 1 egg
- 1 egg yolk
- hand-hot water, as required
- 500 g/1 lb 2 oz strong white bread flour, plus extra for dusting
- 1½ tsp salt
- 2 tsp sugar
- 1 tsp easy-blend dried yeast
- 25 g /1 oz butter, diced

1 Place the egg and egg yolk in a jug and beat lightly to mix. Add enough hand-hot water to make up to 300 ml/10 fl oz. Stir well.

2 Place the flour, salt, sugar and yeast in a large bowl. Add the butter and rub it in with your fingertips until the mixture resembles breadcrumbs. Make a well in the centre, add the egg mixture and work to a smooth dough.

3 Turn the dough out onto a lightly floured work surface and knead for 10 minutes, or until the dough is smooth and elastic. Place the dough in an oiled bowl, cover with clingfilm and leave in a warm place to rise for 1 hour, or until it has doubled in size.

4 Oil a loaf tin. Turn the dough out onto a lightly floured surface and knead for 1 minute until smooth. Shape the dough the length of the tin and three times the width. Fold the dough into three lengthways and place it in the tin with the join underneath. Cover and leave in a warm place for 30 minutes until it has risen above the tin.

5 Preheat the oven to 220°C/ 425°F/Gas Mark 7. Bake in the oven for 30 minutes, or until firm and golden brown. Test that the loaf is cooked by tapping it on the bottom – it should sound hollow. Transfer to a wire rack to cool completely before serving.

WHOLEMEAL HARVEST BREAD

THIS WHOLEMEAL LOAF IS FULL OF HEALTHY FIBRE AND NATURAL GOODNESS. IT NEEDS VERY LITTLE PREPARATION AND IS VERY EASY TO MAKE. SIMPLY FOLLOW THE INSTRUCTIONS GIVEN HERE, POP THE DOUGH IN THE OVEN, AND WAIT FOR THE DELICIOUS AROMA TO PERVADE YOUR KITCHEN.

makes
1 small loaf

preparation
30 minutes, plus
1½ hours' rising

cooking
30 minutes

ingredients
- 225 g/8 oz strong wholemeal bread flour
- 1 tbsp skimmed milk powder
- 1 tsp salt
- 2 tbsp soft brown sugar
- 1 tsp easy-blend dried yeast
- 1½ tbsp sunflower oil
- 175 ml/6 fl oz hand-hot water

1 Place the flour, milk, salt, sugar and yeast in a large bowl. Pour in the oil and and add the water then mix well to make a smooth dough.

2 Turn the dough out onto a lightly floured work surface and knead for 10 minutes, or until the dough is smooth. Place the dough in an oiled bowl, cover with clingfilm and leave in a warm place to rise for 1 hour, or until it has doubled in size.

3 Oil a 900-g/2-lb loaf tin. Turn the dough out onto a lightly floured surface and knead for 1 minute until smooth. Shape the dough the length of the tin and three times the width. Fold the dough into three lengthways and place it in the tin with the join underneath. Cover and leave in a warm place for 30 minutes until it has risen above the tin.

4 Preheat the oven to 220°C/ 425°F/Gas Mark 7. Bake in the oven for 30 minutes, or until firm and golden brown. Test that the loaf is cooked by tapping it on the bottom – it should sound hollow. Transfer to a wire rack to cool completely before serving.

MIXED SEED BREAD

THIS SEEDED BREAD IS DELICIOUSLY AROMATIC AND TASTES WONDERFUL. IT IS RICHER IN CALCIUM AND PROTEIN THAN PLAIN LOAVES OF BREAD. IT IS ALSO RICH IN OMEGA-3 ESSENTIAL FATTY ACIDS, WHICH NUTRITIONISTS SAY CONTRIBUTE TO GOOD HEALTH AND OVERALL WELLBEING.

makes
1 medium loaf
preparation
30 minutes, plus
1½ hours' rising
cooking
30 minutes

ingredients
- 375 g/13 oz strong white bread flour
- 125 g/4½ oz rye flour
- 1½ tbsp skimmed milk powder
- 1½ tsp salt
- 1 tbsp light brown sugar
- 1 tsp easy-blend dried yeast
- 1½ tbsp sunflower oil
- 2 tsp lemon juice
- 300 ml/10 fl oz hand-hot water
- 1 tsp caraway seeds
- ½ tsp poppy seeds
- ½ tsp sesame seeds

TOPPING
- 1 egg white
- 1 tbsp water
- 1 tbsp sunflower or pumpkin seeds

1 Place the flours, milk, salt, sugar and yeast in a large bowl. Pour in the oil and add the lemon juice and water. Stir in the seeds and mix well to make a smooth dough.

2 Turn the dough out onto a lightly floured work surface and knead for 10 minutes, or until the dough is smooth and elastic. Place the dough in an oiled bowl, cover with clingfilm and leave in a warm place to rise for 1 hour, or until it has doubled in size.

3 Oil a 900-g/2-lb loaf tin. Turn the dough out onto a lightly floured surface and knead for 1 minute until smooth. Shape the dough the length of the tin and three times the width. Fold the dough into three lengthways and place it in the tin with the join underneath. Cover and leave in a warm place for 30 minutes until it has risen above the tin.

4 Preheat the oven to 220°C/425°F/Gas Mark 7. For the topping, lightly beat the egg white with the water to make a glaze. Just before baking, brush the glaze over the loaf, then gently press the sunflower or pumpkin seeds all over the top.

5 Bake in the oven for 30 minutes, or until firm and golden brown. Test that the loaf is cooked by tapping it on the bottom – it should sound hollow. Transfer to a wire rack to cool completely before serving.

OLIVE & SUN-DRIED TOMATO BREAD

THIS DELICIOUS BREAD CONJURES UP AROMAS AND FLAVOURS OF THE WARM MEDITERRANEAN, WITH PLUMP, JUICY OLIVES AND RIPE, FLAVOURFUL TOMATOES DRIED IN THE HOT MIDDAY SUN. THE TASTE IS IRRESISTIBLE – IT WILL LEAVE YOUR HOUSEHOLD AND YOUR GUESTS LONGING FOR MORE.

serves
4

preparation
20 minutes, plus
2¼ hours' rising

cooking
40 minutes

ingredients

- 400 g/14 oz plain flour, plus extra for dusting
- 1 tsp salt
- 1 sachet easy-blend dried yeast
- 1 tsp brown sugar
- 1 tbsp chopped fresh thyme
- 200 ml/7 fl oz warm water (heated to 50°C/122°F)
- 4 tbsp olive oil, plus extra for oiling
- 50 g/1¾ oz black olives, stoned and sliced
- 50 g/1¾ oz green olives, stoned and sliced
- 100 g/3½ oz sun-dried tomatoes in oil, drained and sliced
- 1 egg yolk, beaten

1 Place the flour, salt and yeast in a bowl and mix together, then stir in the sugar and thyme. Make a well in the centre. Slowly stir in enough water and oil to make a dough. Mix in the olives and sun-dried tomatoes. Knead the dough for 5 minutes, then form it into a ball. Brush a bowl with oil, add the dough and cover with clingfilm. Leave to rise in a warm place for about 1½ hours, or until it has doubled in size.

2 Dust a baking sheet with flour. Knead the dough lightly, then cut into halves and shape each half into ovals or rounds. Place them on the baking sheet, cover with clingfilm and leave to rise again in a warm place for 45 minutes, or until they have again doubled in size.

3 Preheat the oven to 200°C/400°F/Gas Mark 6. Make 3 shallow diagonal cuts on the top of each piece of dough. Brush with the egg. Bake for 40 minutes, or until cooked through – they should be golden on top and sound hollow when tapped on the bottom. Transfer to wire racks to cool. Store in an airtight container for up to 3 days.

BANANA & ORANGE BREAD

THE SWEETNESS OF THE BANANA AND THE CITRUS TANG OF THE ORANGE MAKE A WONDERFUL COMBINATION IN THIS BREAD. IT IS DELICIOUS SPREAD WITH CREAMY UNSALTED BUTTER, BUT YOU CAN ALSO USE A LOWER-FAT MARGARINE TO KEEP THE FAT CONTENT LOW.

makes
1 medium loaf

preparation
30 minutes, plus
1½ hours' rising

cooking
30 minutes

ingredients
- 500 g/1 lb 2 oz strong white bread flour, plus an extra 1–2 tbsp for sticky dough
- 1 tsp salt
- 1 tsp easy-blend dried yeast
- 40 g/1½ oz butter, diced
- 2 medium ripe bananas or 1 large ripe banana, peeled and mashed
- 4 tbsp orange juice
- 200 ml/7 fl oz hand-hot buttermilk or water
- 1½ tbsp skimmed milk powder (if using water)
- 3 tbsp clear honey
- milk, to glaze (optional)

1 Place the flour, salt, sugar and yeast in a large bowl. Rub in the butter and add the mashed bananas and honey. Make a well in the centre and gradually work in the the orange juice and buttermilk or water to make a smooth dough. If using water, add the skimmed milk powder to the mixture.

2 Turn the dough out onto a lightly floured work surface and knead for 5–7 minutes, or until the dough is smooth and elastic. If the dough looks very sticky, add a further 1–2 tablespoons of white bread flour. (The stickiness depends on the ripeness and size of the bananas.) Place the dough in an oiled bowl, cover with clingfilm and leave in a warm place to rise for 1 hour, or until it has doubled in size.

3 Oil a 900-g/2-lb loaf tin. Turn the dough out onto a lightly floured surface and knead for 1 minute until smooth. Shape the dough the length of the tin and three times the width. Fold the dough into three lengthways and place it in the tin with the join underneath. Cover and leave in a warm place for 30 minutes until it has risen above the tin.

4 Preheat the oven to 220°C/425°F/Gas Mark 7. Just before baking, brush the milk over the loaf to glaze, if desired.

5 Bake in the oven for 30 minutes, or until firm and golden brown. Test that the loaf is cooked by tapping it on the bottom – it should sound hollow. Transfer to a wire rack to cool completely before serving.

FRESH CROISSANTS

PREPARE THIS RECIPE THE NIGHT BEFORE. MAKE THE DOUGH AND ROLL INTO CROISSANT SHAPES, THEN BRUSH WITH THE GLAZE, COVER WITH CLINGFILM AND REFRIGERATE OVERNIGHT. THE NEXT MORNING, LEAVE TO RISE FOR 30–45 MINUTES, THEN PLACE ON A BAKING TRAY AS PER THE RECIPE.

makes

12 croissants

preparation

40 minutes, plus
2 hours' rising
and chilling

cooking

15–20 minutes

ingredients

- 500 g/1 lb 2 oz strong white bread flour, plus extra for dusting
- 40 g/1 ½ oz caster sugar
- 1 tsp salt
- 2 tsp easy-blend dried yeast
- 300 ml/10 fl oz milk, heated until just warm to the touch
- 300 g/10½ oz butter, softened, plus extra for greasing
- 1 egg, lightly beaten with 1 tbsp milk, to glaze
- jam, to serve (optional)

1 Stir the dry ingredients into a large bowl, make a well in the centre and add the milk. Mix to a soft dough, adding more milk if too dry. Knead on a lightly floured work surface for 5–10 minutes, or until smooth and elastic. Leave to rise in a large, greased bowl, covered, in a warm place until doubled in size. Meanwhile, flatten the butter with a rolling pin between 2 sheets of greaseproof paper to form a rectangle 5-mm/¼-inch thick, then leave to chill.

2 Knead the dough for 1 minute. Remove the butter from the refrigerator and leave to soften slightly. Roll out the dough on a well-floured work surface to 46 x 15 cm/18 x 6 inches. Place the butter in the centre, folding up the sides and squeezing the edges together gently. With the short end of the dough towards you, fold the top third down towards the centre, then fold the bottom third up. Rotate 45° clockwise so that the fold is to your left and the top flap towards your right. Roll out to a rectangle and fold again. If the butter feels soft, wrap the dough in clingfilm and chill. Repeat the rolling process twice more. Cut the dough in half. Roll out one half into a triangle 5 mm/¼ inch thick (keep the other half refrigerated). Use a cardboard triangular template, base 18 cm/7 inches and sides 20 cm/8 inches, to cut out the croissants.

3 Brush the triangles lightly with the glaze. Roll into croissant shapes, starting at the base and tucking the point underneath to prevent unrolling while cooking. Brush again with the glaze. Place on an ungreased baking tray and leave to double in size. Preheat the oven to 200°C/400°F/Gas Mark 6. Bake for 15–20 minutes until golden brown. Serve with jam, if liked.

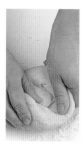

CHELSEA BUNS

SWEET AND STICKY CHELSEA BUNS, WITH A HINT OF SPICE, ARE AN IRRESISTIBLE ADDITION TO A
TRADITIONAL AFTERNOON TEA, OR AN EXCELLENT SNACK AT ANY TIME OF DAY. THEY ARE ALSO
WONDERFULLY PORTABLE. WHY NOT TAKE A FEW ALONG TO FINISH A PICNIC IN STYLE?

makes
9
preparation
30 minutes, plus
1¾ hours' rising
cooking
30 minutes

ingredients
- 25 g/1 oz butter, plus
  extra for greasing
- 225 g/8 oz strong white
  bread flour, plus extra
  for dusting
- ½ tsp salt
- 2 tsp easy-blend dried yeast
- 1 tsp golden caster sugar
- 125 ml/4 fl oz tepid milk
- 1 egg, beaten
- vegetable oil, for brushing
- 85 g/3 oz icing sugar,
  to glaze

FILLING
- 55 g/2 oz light
  muscovado sugar
- 115 g/4 oz luxury mixed
  dried fruits
- 1 tsp ground mixed spice
- 55 g/2 oz butter, softened

1 Grease an 18-cm/7-inch square
cake tin. Sift the flour and salt into a
warmed bowl, stir in the yeast and
sugar and rub in the butter. Make a
well in the centre. Mix the milk and
egg together in a separate bowl and
pour into the dry ingredients. Beat to
make a soft dough.

2 Turn out onto a floured work
surface and knead for 5–10 minutes,
or until smooth. Brush a clean bowl
with oil, place the dough in the
bowl, cover with oiled clingfilm and
leave in a warm place for 1 hour, or
until doubled in size.

3 Turn the dough out onto a floured
work surface and knead lightly for
1 minute. Roll out into a 30 x
23-cm/12 x 9-inch rectangle.

4 To make the filling, place the
muscovado sugar, fruit and spice in
a bowl and mix. Spread the dough
with the softened butter and sprinkle
the fruit mixture on top. Roll up
from a long side, then cut into
9 pieces. Place in the prepared tin,
cut-side up. Cover with oiled
clingfilm and leave in a warm place
for 45 minutes, or until well risen.

5 Preheat the oven to 190°C/
375°F/Gas Mark 5. Bake the buns
in the oven for 30 minutes, or until
golden. Leave to cool in the tin for
10 minutes, then transfer, in one
piece, to a wire rack to cool. Sift the
icing sugar into a bowl and stir in
enough water to make a thin glaze.
Brush over the buns and leave to
set. Pull the buns apart to serve.

cook's tip

*When you place the buns in the prepared
cake tin, place them close to each other in
three rows, so that they join up into one
single piece as they expand during cooking.*

BLINIS

BLINIS COME FROM RUSSIA. TRADITIONALLY THESE SMALL YEAST PANCAKES ARE MADE WITH BUCKWHEAT FLOUR, WHICH GIVES THEM A TASTY AND UNUSUAL FLAVOUR. THIS RECIPE PRESERVES THAT TRADITION. YOU CAN ALSO SERVE THESE PANCAKES WITH CAVIAR.

makes
8

preparation
20 minutes, plus
1 hour's standing

cooking
20 minutes

ingredients
- 115 g/4 oz buckwheat flour
- 115 g/4 oz strong white bread flour
- 7-g/⅙-oz sachet easy-blend dried yeast
- 1 tsp salt
- 375 ml/13 fl oz tepid milk
- 2 eggs, 1 whole and 1 separated
- vegetable oil, for brushing

TO SERVE
- soured cream
- smoked salmon

1 Sift both flours into a large, warmed bowl. Stir in the yeast and salt. Beat in the milk, whole egg and egg yolk until smooth. Cover the bowl and leave to stand in a warm place for 1 hour.

2 Place the egg white in a spotlessly clean bowl and whisk until soft peaks form. Fold into the batter. Brush a heavy-based frying pan with oil and set over a medium–high heat. When the frying pan is hot, pour enough of the batter onto the surface to make a blini about the size of a saucer.

3 When bubbles rise, turn the blini over with a palette knife and cook the other side until light brown. Wrap in a clean tea towel to keep warm while cooking the remainder. Serve the warm blinis with soured cream and smoked salmon.

variation
If buckwheat flour is unavailable, use wholemeal bread flour instead.

LEEK & ONION TARTLETS

THESE FLAVOURSOME TARTLETS ARE RATHER LIKE MINI QUICHES. THEY ARE RICH IN PROTEIN AND
VERY VERSATILE. YOU CAN SERVE THEM WARM OR COLD, AND THEY MAKE AN EXCELLENT CHOICE
FOR A LUNCH BOX OR A PICNIC, ACCOMPANIED BY A CRISP SALAD.

serves
6
preparation
30 minutes, plus
1 hour's chilling
and cooling
cooking
40 minutes

ingredients
- butter, for greasing
- 225 g/8 oz ready-made
  shortcrust pastry
- plain flour, for dusting

FILLING
- 25 g/1 oz unsalted butter
- 1 onion, thinly sliced
- 450 g/1 lb leeks,
  thinly sliced
- 2 tsp chopped fresh thyme
- 55 g/2 oz Gruyère
  cheese, grated
- 3 eggs
- 300 ml/10 fl oz
  double cream
- salt and pepper

1 Lightly grease 6 x 10-cm/4-inch
tartlet tins with butter. Roll out the
dough on a lightly floured work
surface and stamp out 6 rounds with
a 13-cm/5-inch cutter. Ease the
dough into the tins, prick the bases
and leave to chill for 30 minutes.

2 Preheat the oven to 190°C/
375°F/Gas Mark 5. Line the pastry
cases with foil and baking beans, then
place on a baking sheet and bake for
8 minutes. Remove the foil and beans
and bake for a further 2 minutes.
Transfer the tins to a wire rack to
cool. Reduce the oven temperature
to 180°C/350°F/Gas Mark 4.

3 Meanwhile, make the filling. Melt
the butter in a large, heavy-based
frying pan. Add the onion and cook,
stirring constantly, for 5 minutes, or
until softened. Add the leeks and
thyme and cook, stirring, for
10 minutes, or until softened. Divide
the leek mixture between the tartlet
cases. Sprinkle with Gruyère cheese.

4 Lightly beat the eggs with the
cream and season to taste with salt
and pepper. Place the tartlet tins on a
baking sheet and divide the egg
mixture between them. Bake in the
preheated oven for 15 minutes, or
until the filling is set and golden
brown. Transfer to a wire rack to
cool slightly before removing from
the tins and serving.

variation

*For a slightly milder version of these
tartlets, substitute 450 g/1 lb of sliced
courgettes for the leeks.*

STEAK & KIDNEY PUDDING

STEAK AND KIDNEY STEAMED IN A SUET CRUST PASTRY, FLAVOURED WITH MUSHROOMS AND
PARSLEY, MUST BE THE MOST BRITISH OF BRITISH MEAT DISHES. ALSO GOING BY THE AFFECTIONATE
COCKNEY NAME OF 'KATE & SYDNEY', THIS PUDDING IS TRADITIONAL ALL OVER THE BRITISH ISLES.

serves
4

preparation
40 minutes

cooking
4–5 hours

ingredients
- butter, for greasing
- 450 g/1 lb braising steak,
  trimmed and cut into
  2.5-cm/1-inch pieces
- 2 lamb's kidneys, cored
  and cut into 2.5-cm/
  1-inch pieces
- 55 g/2 oz plain flour
- 1 onion, finely chopped
- 115 g/4 oz large field
  mushrooms, sliced
  (optional)
- 1 tbsp chopped
  fresh parsley
- about 300 ml/10 fl oz
  stock, or a mixture of beer
  and water
- salt and pepper

SUET PASTRY
- 350 g/12 oz
  self-raising flour
- 175 g/6 oz suet
- 225 ml/8 fl oz cold water
- salt and pepper

1 Lightly grease a 1.2-litre/2-pint pudding basin with butter.

2 Place the prepared meat with the flour and salt and pepper in a large polythene bag and shake well until all the meat is well coated. Add the onion, mushrooms, if using, and the parsley and shake again.

3 Make the suet pastry by mixing the flour, suet and a little salt and pepper together. Add enough of the cold water to make a soft dough.

4 Keep a quarter of the dough to one side and roll the remainder out to form a round large enough to line the pudding basin. Line the basin, making sure that there is a good 1 cm/¹⁄₂ inch hanging over the edge.

5 Place the meat mixture in the basin and pour in enough of the stock to cover the meat.

6 Roll out the remaining pastry to make a lid. Fold in the edges of the pastry, dampen them and place the lid on top. Seal firmly in place.

7 Cover with a piece of greaseproof paper and then foil, with a pleat to allow for expansion during cooking, and seal well. Place in a steamer or large saucepan half-filled with boiling water. Simmer the pudding for 4–5 hours, topping up the water occasionally.

8 Remove the basin from the steamer and take off the coverings. Wrap a clean cloth around the basin and serve at the table.

MUSHROOM & SPINACH PUFF PASTRY

THESE PUFF-PASTRY PARCELS HAVE A MOUTHWATERING FILLING OF GARLIC, MUSHROOMS AND SPINACH. THEY ARE EASY TO MAKE AND DELICIOUS TO EAT, AND MAKE A SUPERB SNACK, LUNCH OR SUPPER. SERVE THEM HOT, OR LET THEM COOL AND POP THEM INTO LUNCH BOXES FOR A PICNIC.

serves
4

preparation
20 minutes

cooking
30–35 minutes

ingredients
- 2 tbsp butter
- 1 red onion, halved and sliced
- 2 garlic cloves, crushed
- 225 g/8 oz open-cap mushrooms, sliced
- 175 g/6 oz baby spinach
- pinch of nutmeg
- 4 tbsp double cream
- 225 g/8 oz prepared puff pastry
- plain flour, for dusting
- 1 egg, beaten
- 2 tsp poppy seeds
- salt and pepper

1 Preheat the oven to 200°C/400°F/Gas Mark 6. Melt the butter in a frying pan. Add the onion and garlic and sauté for 3–4 minutes until the onion has softened.

2 Add the mushrooms, spinach and nutmeg and cook for a further 2–3 minutes. Stir in the cream, mixing well. Season to taste with salt and pepper and remove the frying pan from the heat.

3 Roll the pastry out on a lightly floured surface and cut into 4 x 15-cm/6-inch rounds. Spoon a quarter of the filling onto one half of each round and fold the pastry over to encase the filling. Press down to seal the edges of the pastry and brush with the beaten egg. Sprinkle with the poppy seeds.

4 Place the parcels onto a dampened baking tray and cook in the preheated oven for 20 minutes until risen and golden brown.

5 Transfer the mushroom and spinach puff pastry parcels to serving plates and serve immediately.

cook's tip

The baking tray is dampened so that steam forms with the heat of the oven and helps the pastry to rise and set.

VEGETABLE JALOUSIE

A JALOUSIE IS A SMALL FRENCH LATTICED CAKE MADE WITH PUFF PASTRY AND AN ALMOND AND JAM FILLING. THIS JALOUSIE IS A SAVOURY VERSION. IT LOOKS IMPRESSIVE, BUT IS REALLY VERY EASY TO MAKE. THE MIXTURE OF VEGETABLES GIVES IT A WONDERFUL COLOUR AND FLAVOUR.

serves
4

preparation
30 minutes

cooking
45–50 minutes

ingredients
- 450 g/1 lb prepared puff pastry
- plain flour, for dusting
- 1 egg, beaten, to glaze

FILLING
- 2 tbsp butter or margarine
- 1 leek, shredded
- 2 garlic cloves, crushed
- 1 red pepper, sliced
- 1 yellow pepper, sliced
- 50 g/1 ¾ oz mushrooms, sliced
- 75 g/2 ¾ oz small asparagus spears
- 2 tbsp plain flour
- 6 tbsp vegetable stock
- 6 tbsp milk
- 4 tbsp dry white wine
- 1 tbsp chopped oregano
- salt and pepper

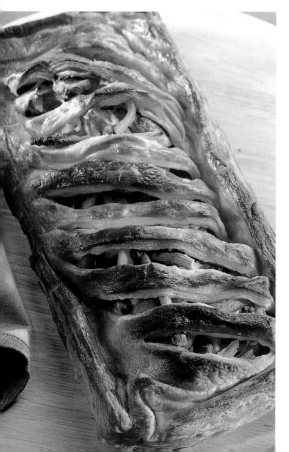

1 Preheat the oven to 200°C/400°F/Gas Mark 6. For the filling, melt the butter in a saucepan. Add the leek and garlic and sauté for 2 minutes. Add the remaining vegetables and cook, stirring, for 3–4 minutes.

2 Add the flour and cook for 1 minute. Remove the saucepan from the heat and stir in the stock, milk and white wine. Return the pan to the heat and bring to the boil, stirring, until thickened. Stir in the oregano and season to taste with salt and pepper.

3 Roll half of the pastry out on a lightly floured work surface to form a rectangle 38 x 15 cm/15 x 6 inches.

4 Roll out the other half of the pastry to the same shape, but a little larger. Place the smaller rectangle on a baking tray lined with dampened baking paper.

5 Spoon the filling on top of the smaller rectangle, leaving a 1-cm/½-inch clean edge. Cut parallel slits across the larger rectangle to within 2.5 cm/1 inch of each edge.

6 Brush the edge of the smaller rectangle with egg and place the larger rectangle on top, sealing the edges well.

7 Brush the whole jalousie with egg and cook in the preheated oven for 30–35 minutes until risen and golden. Serve immediately.

POTATO, BEEF & LEEK PASTIES

THESE DELICIOUS PASTIES ARE FILLED WITH POTATOES, SUCCULENT CUBES OF BEEF, CARROTS AND LEEKS. THEY MAKE A SATISFYING MEAL AT ANY TIME OF DAY. SINCE YOU CAN SERVE THEM COLD AS WELL AS HOT, THEY ARE IDEAL FARE FOR LUNCH BOXES AND PICNICS.

makes
4
preparation
35 minutes
cooking
50 minutes

ingredients
- butter, for greasing
- 225 g/8 oz waxy potatoes, diced
- 1 small carrot, diced
- 225 g/8 oz beef steak, cubed
- 1 leek, sliced
- 225 g/8 oz ready-made shortcrust pastry
- plain flour, for dusting
- 15 g/½ oz butter
- 1 egg, beaten
- salt and pepper
- green salad or onion gravy, to serve

1 Preheat the oven to 200°C/ 400°F/Gas Mark 6. Lightly grease a baking sheet with butter. Mix the potatoes, carrots, beef and leek together in a large bowl. Season well with salt and pepper.

2 Divide the pastry into 4 equal portions. Roll each portion out on a lightly floured work surface into a 20-cm/8-inch round.

3 Spoon the potato mixture onto one half of each round, to within 1 cm/½ inch of the edge. Top the potato mixture with the butter, dividing it equally between the rounds. Brush the pastry edge with a little of the beaten egg.

4 Fold the pastry over to encase the filling and crimp the edges together. Transfer the pasties to the prepared baking sheet and brush them with the beaten egg.

5 Cook in the preheated oven for 20 minutes. Reduce the oven temperature to 160°C/325°F/ Gas Mark 3 and cook the pasties for a further 30 minutes until cooked through. Serve the pasties with a crisp salad or onion gravy.

variation

Use other types of meat, such as pork or chicken, in the pasties and add chunks of apple in Step 2, if preferred.

PROFITEROLES

WHO CAN RESIST THE RICH, BUTTERY TASTE OF PROFITEROLES, WITH THEIR SUMPTUOUS CREAMY CENTRES? THESE PROFITEROLES HAVE A LUXURIOUS CHOCOLATE AND BRANDY SAUCE POURED OVER THEM – THE ULTIMATE EXPERIENCE FOR THE HOPELESSLY INFATUATED CHOCOLATE LOVER.

serves
4
preparation
25 minutes
cooking
35 minutes

ingredients

CHOUX PASTRY
- 5 tbsp butter, plus extra for greasing
- 200 ml/7 fl oz water
- 100 g/3 ½ oz plain flour
- 3 eggs, beaten

CREAM FILLING
- 300 ml/10 fl oz double cream
- 3 tbsp caster sugar
- 1 tsp vanilla essence

CHOCOLATE & BRANDY SAUCE
- 125 g/4 ½ oz plain dark chocolate, broken into small pieces
- 2 ½ tbsp butter
- 6 tbsp water
- 2 tbsp brandy

1 Preheat the oven to 200°C/ 400°F/Gas Mark 6. Grease a large baking sheet with butter.

2 To make the pastry, place the water and butter in a saucepan and bring to the boil. Meanwhile, sift the flour into a bowl. Turn off the heat and beat in the flour until smooth. Cool for 5 minutes.

3 Beat in enough of the eggs to give the mixture a soft, dropping consistency. Transfer to a piping bag fitted with a 1-cm/½-inch plain nozzle. Pipe small balls onto the baking sheet. Bake for 25 minutes.

4 Remove from the oven. Pierce each ball with a skewer to let the steam escape.

5 To make the filling, whip the cream, sugar and vanilla essence together. Cut the pastry balls across the middle, then fill with cream.

6 To make the sauce, gently melt the chocolate, butter and water together in a small saucepan, stirring constantly, until smooth. Stir in the brandy. Pile the profiteroles onto individual serving dishes or into a pyramid on a raised cake stand. Pour over the sauce and serve.

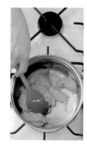
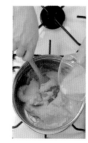

CHERRY SCONES

THESE ARE AN APPEALING ALTERNATIVE TO TRADITIONAL SCONES, USING SWEET GLACÉ CHERRIES, WHICH NOT ONLY CREATE COLOUR BUT ADD A DISTINCT AND PLEASURABLE FLAVOUR, AS WELL AS ADDED CHEWINESS. THESE ARE SURE TO PLEASE THE MOST DISCERNING PALATE.

makes
8
preparation
10 minutes
cooking
30 minutes

ingredients
- 6 tbsp butter, cut into small pieces, plus extra for greasing
- 225 g/8 oz self-raising flour, plus extra for dusting
- 15 g/½ oz caster sugar
- pinch of salt
- 40 g/1½ oz glacé cherries, chopped
- 40 g/1½ oz sultanas
- 1 egg, beaten
- 50 ml/2 fl oz milk

1 Preheat the oven to 220°C/425°F/ Gas Mark 7. Lightly grease a baking tray with a little butter.

2 Sieve the flour, sugar and salt into a mixing bowl. Add the butter and rub it in with your fingertips until the mixture resembles breadcrumbs.

3 Stir in the glacé cherries and sultanas. Add the egg.

4 Reserve 1 tablespoon of the milk for glazing, then add the remainder to the mixture. Mix well together to form a soft dough.

5 Roll out the dough on a lightly floured work surface to a thickness of 2 cm/¾ inch and cut out 8 scones, using a 5-cm/2-inch cutter.

6 Place the scones on the prepared baking tray and brush the tops with the reserved milk.

7 Bake in the preheated oven for 8–10 minutes, or until the scones are golden brown.

8 Leave to cool on a wire rack, then serve split and buttered.

cook's tip

These scones will freeze very successfully but they are best thawed within 1 month and eaten immediately.

297

TREACLE TART

THIS IS A TRADITIONAL DESSERT THAT NEVER SEEMS TO GO OUT OF FASHION: IT STILL DELIGHTS PEOPLE TIME AFTER TIME. IT IS ALSO VERY QUICK TO MAKE IF YOU USE READY-MADE PASTRY, WHICH YOU CAN BUY FROZEN FROM MOST SUPERMARKETS. SIMPLY DEFROST IT AND IT IS READY TO USE.

serves
8

preparation
25 minutes,
plus 30 minutes'
chilling

cooking
35–40 minutes

ingredients
- 250 g/ 9 oz fresh ready-made shortcrust pastry
- plain flour, for dusting
- 350 g/12 oz golden syrup
- 125 g/4½ oz fresh white breadcrumbs
- 125 ml/4 fl oz double cream
- finely grated rind of ½ lemon or orange
- 2 tbsp lemon or orange juice
- custard, to serve

1 Preheat the oven to 190ºC/375ºF/ Gas Mark 5. Roll out the pastry on a lightly floured work surface and use to line a 20-cm/8-inch loose-based quiche/flan tin, reserving the pastry trimmings. Prick the base of the pastry with a fork and leave to chill in the refrigerator.

2 Cut out small shapes from the reserved pastry trimmings, such as leaves, stars or hearts, to decorate the top of the tart.

3 Mix the golden syrup, breadcrumbs, double cream and grated lemon rind and lemon juice together in a small bowl.

4 Pour the mixture into the pastry case and decorate the edges of the tart with the pastry cut-outs.

5 Bake in the preheated oven for 35–40 minutes, or until the filling is just set.

6 Leave the tart to cool slightly in the tin before turning out and serving with custard.

variation
Use the pastry trimmings to create a lattice pattern on top of the tart, if preferred.

RICH FRUIT CAKE

THIS MOIST, FRUIT-LADEN CAKE LOOKS VERY IMPRESSIVE, YET IT IS DECEPTIVELY SIMPLE TO MAKE.
SERVE IT FOR A SPECIAL OCCASION – IT WOULD MAKE AN EXCELLENT TREAT FOR CHRISTMAS OR
THANKSGIVING, OR A MEMORABLE BIRTHDAY CAKE IF YOU ADD A FEW SMALL CANDLES.

serves
4

preparation
25 minutes,
plus 40 minutes'
cooling

cooking
1³/4 hours

ingredients
- butter, for greasing
- 175 g/6 oz stoned unsweetened dates
- 125 g/4 ½ oz no-soak dried prunes
- 200 ml/7 fl oz unsweetened orange juice
- 2 tbsp black treacle
- 1 tsp finely grated lemon rind
- 1 tsp finely grated orange rind
- 225 g/8 oz wholemeal self-raising flour

- 1 tsp mixed spice
- 125 g/4 ½ oz seedless raisins
- 125 g/4 ½ oz golden sultanas
- 125 g/4 ½ oz currants
- 125 g/4 ½ oz dried cranberries
- 3 large eggs, separated
- 1 tbsp apricot jam, warmed

ICING
- 125 g/4 ½ oz icing sugar
- 1–2 tsp water
- 1 tsp vanilla essence
- icing sugar, for dusting
- orange rind strips, to decorate
- lemon rind strips, to decorate

1 Preheat the oven to 160°C/325°F/
Gas Mark 3. Grease and line a deep
20-cm/8-inch round cake tin. Chop
the dates and prunes and place in a
saucepan. Pour over the orange juice
and simmer for 10 minutes. Remove
the saucepan from the heat and beat
the fruit mixture until puréed. Add
the treacle and citrus rinds and cool.

2 Sift the flour and spice into a bowl,
adding any bran that remains in the
sieve. Add the dried fruits. When
the date and prune mixture is cool,
whisk in the egg yolks. Whisk the egg
whites in a separate clean bowl until
stiff. Spoon the fruit mixture into the
dry ingredients and mix together.

3 Gently fold in the egg whites.
Transfer to the prepared tin and bake
in the preheated oven for 1 ½ hours.
Leave to cool in the tin.

4 Remove the cake from the tin and
brush the top with jam. To make the
icing, sift the sugar into a bowl and
mix with enough water and the
vanilla essence to form a soft icing.
Lay the icing over the top of the cake
and trim the edges. Decorate with
orange and lemon rind.

CHOCOLATE & ALMOND LAYER CAKE

THIS CAKE IS UTTERLY IRRESISTIBLE. IT BOASTS THIN LAYERS OF DELICIOUS LIGHT CHOCOLATE CAKE SANDWICHED TOGETHER WITH A RICH CHOCOLATE ICING. IT SHOULD CARRY A WARNING, BECAUSE IT WILL SERIOUSLY AFFECT THE RESTRAINT OF THE MOST STRONG-WILLED IN YOUR HOUSEHOLD.

serves
10–12

preparation
40 minutes,
plus 40 minutes'
cooling

cooking
30–35 minutes

ingredients
- butter, for greasing
- 7 eggs
- 200 g/7 oz caster sugar
- 150 g/5 1/2 oz plain flour
- 50 g/1 3/4 oz cocoa powder
- 50 g/1 3/4 oz butter, melted

FILLING
- 200 g/7 oz plain dark chocolate
- 125 g/4 1/2 oz butter
- 50 g/1 3/4 oz icing sugar

TO DECORATE
- 75 g/2 3/4 oz toasted flaked almonds, lightly crushed
- small chocolate curls or grated chocolate

1 Preheat the oven to 180°C/350°F/ Gas Mark 4. Grease a deep 23-cm/ 9-inch square cake tin and line the base with baking paper.

2 Whisk the eggs and caster sugar together in a mixing bowl with an electric whisk for 10 minutes, or until the mixture is very light and foamy and the whisk leaves a trail that lasts a few seconds when lifted.

3 Sieve the flour and cocoa together and fold half into the mixture. Drizzle over the melted butter and fold in the rest of the flour and cocoa. Pour into the prepared tin and bake in the preheated oven for 30–35 minutes, or until springy to

the touch. Leave to cool slightly, then remove from the tin and cool completely on a wire rack. Wash and dry the tin and return the cake to it.

4 To make the filling, melt the chocolate and butter together, then remove from the heat. Stir in the icing sugar, leave to cool, then beat until thick enough to spread.

5 Halve the cake lengthways and cut each half into 3 layers. Sandwich the layers together with three-quarters of the chocolate filling. Spread the remainder over the cake and mark a wavy pattern on the top. Press the almonds on to the sides. Decorate with chocolate curls or grated chocolate before slicing and serving.

JEWEL-TOPPED MADEIRA CAKE

BRIGHTLY COLOURED CRYSTALLIZED FRUITS MAKE A STUNNING AND UNUSUAL TOPPING FOR THIS
CLASSIC MADEIRA CAKE. IT WILL GO DOWN A TREAT WITH TEA, COFFEE OR A GLASS OF SHERRY, OR
WHY NOT BRING IT OUT AS A SPECTACULAR FINALE TO A DINNER PARTY?

serves

8

preparation

25 minutes, plus
30 minutes'
cooling

cooking

1¼–1½ hours

ingredients

- 225 g/8 oz butter, softened,
  plus extra for greasing
- 225 g/8 oz golden
  caster sugar
- finely grated rind of
  1 lemon
- 4 eggs, beaten
- 280 g/10 oz self-raising
  flour, sifted
- 2–3 tbsp milk

FRUIT TOPPING

- 2½ tbsp clear honey
- 225 g/8 oz crystallized fruit

1 Preheat the oven to 160°C/
325°F/Gas Mark 3. Grease and line
the base of a deep 20-cm/8-inch
round cake tin. Place the butter,
sugar and lemon rind in a bowl and
beat together until light and fluffy.
Gradually beat in the eggs. Gently
fold in the flour, alternating with
enough milk to give a soft, dropping
consistency.

2 Transfer the mixture to the
prepared tin and bake in the
preheated oven for 1¼–1½ hours,
or until risen and golden and a
skewer inserted into the centre
comes out clean.

3 Leave to cool in the tin for
10 minutes, then turn out onto a
wire rack and remove the lining
paper. Leave to cool completely.
To make the topping, brush the
honey over the cake and arrange
the fruit on top.

variation

*Traditionally, a Madeira cake is simply
decorated with a slice of candied peel on
top, which is placed on the cake after it
has been cooking for 1 hour.*

GINGERBREAD

THIS WONDERFULLY SPICY GINGERBREAD IS MADE BEAUTIFULLY MOIST BY THE ADDITION OF
CHOPPED FRESH APPLES. IT MAKES A PERFECT AFTER-DINNER TREAT, OR A DELICIOUS SNACK AT
ANY TIME OF THE DAY. IT IS VERY POPULAR WITH CHILDREN, SO GET YOUR SHARE WHILE YOU CAN.

makes
12 bars

preparation
25 minutes, plus
50 minutes'
cooling

cooking
35 minutes

ingredients
- 150 g/5 ½ oz butter, plus
  extra for greasing
- 175 g/6 oz soft
  brown sugar
- 2 tbsp black treacle
- 225 g/8 oz plain flour
- 1 tsp baking powder
- 2 tsp bicarbonate of soda
- 2 tsp ground ginger
- 150 ml/5 fl oz milk
- 1 egg, beaten
- 2 dessert apples, peeled,
  chopped and coated with
  1 tbsp lemon juice

1 Preheat the oven to 160°C/
325°F/Gas Mark 3. Grease a
23-cm/9-inch square cake tin and
line with baking paper.

2 Melt the butter, sugar and treacle
in a saucepan over a low heat and
leave the mixture to cool.

3 Sieve the flour, baking powder,
bicarbonate of soda and ginger into a
mixing bowl. Stir in the milk, beaten
egg and cooled buttery liquid,
followed by the chopped apples
coated with the lemon juice.

4 Mix everything together gently,
then pour the mixture into the
prepared tin and smooth the surface.

5 Bake in the preheated oven for
30–35 minutes, or until the cake has
risen and a fine skewer inserted into
the centre comes out clean.

6 Leave the cake to cool in the tin
before turning out and cutting into
12 bars.

variation
*If you enjoy the flavour of ginger, try
adding 25 g/1 oz finely chopped stem
ginger to the mixture in Step 3.*

CHOCOLATE CHIP MUFFINS

MUFFINS ARE ALWAYS POPULAR AND ARE SO VERY SIMPLE TO MAKE. THEY MAKE FABULOUS BITE-SIZED TREATS FOR CHILDREN AND ADULTS ALIKE – AND PERFECT FOR PARTIES TOO. OR WHY NOT POP THEM INTO LUNCH BOXES OR A PICNIC? THEY ARE SURE TO DELIGHT THE LUCKY RECIPIENTS.

makes
12

preparation
15 minutes,
plus 30 minutes'
cooling

cooking
25 minutes

ingredients
- 100 g/3½ oz soft margarine
- 225 g/8 oz caster sugar
- 2 large eggs
- 150 ml/5 fl oz whole-milk natural yogurt
- 5 tbsp milk
- 275 g/9½ oz plain flour
- 1 tsp bicarbonate of soda
- 175 g/6 oz plain dark chocolate chips

1 Preheat the oven to 190°C/375°F/Gas Mark 5. Line a 12-hole muffin tin with paper cases.

2 Place the margarine and sugar in a mixing bowl and beat with a wooden spoon until light and fluffy. Beat in the eggs, yogurt and milk until combined.

3 Sieve the flour and bicarbonate of soda together and add to the mixture. Stir until just blended.

4 Stir in the chocolate chips, then spoon the mixture into the paper cases and bake in the preheated oven for 25 minutes, or until a fine skewer inserted into the centre comes out clean. Leave to cool in the tin for 5 minutes, then turn out onto a wire rack to cool completely before serving.

variation

The mixture can also be used to make 6 large or 24 mini muffins. Bake mini muffins for 10 minutes or until springy to the touch.

MANHATTAN CHEESECAKE

THIS IS AN ABSOLUTELY STUNNING EXAMPLE OF A CLASSIC AMERICAN BAKED CHEESECAKE. THE
TRADITIONAL FRUITY BLUEBERRY TOPPING GIVES IT A WONDERFULLY DRAMATIC SPLASH OF
COLOUR. IT IS EASY TO PREPARE AND YOU CAN KEEP IT IN THE REFRIGERATOR UNTIL YOU NEED IT.

serves
8–10

preparation
20 minutes, plus
10 hours' cooling
and chilling

cooking
none

ingredients
- sunflower oil, for brushing
- 85 g/3 oz butter
- 200 g/7 oz digestive biscuits, crushed
- 400 g/14 oz cream cheese
- 2 large eggs
- 140 g/5 oz caster sugar
- 1½ tsp vanilla essence
- 450 ml/16 fl oz soured cream

BLUEBERRY TOPPING
- 55 g/2 oz caster sugar
- 4 tbsp water
- 250 g/9 oz fresh blueberries
- 1 tsp arrowroot

1 Preheat the oven to 190°C/
375°F/Gas Mark 5. Brush a
20-cm/8-inch springform tin with
oil. Melt the butter in a saucepan
over a low heat. Stir in the biscuits,
then spread in the tin. Place the
cream cheese, eggs, 100 g/3½ oz
of the sugar and ½ teaspoon of the
vanilla essence in a food processor.
Process until smooth. Pour over the
biscuit base and smooth the top.
Place on a baking tray and bake for
20 minutes until set. Remove from
the oven and leave for 20 minutes.
Leave the oven switched on.

2 Mix the cream with the remaining
sugar and vanilla essence in a bowl.
Spoon over the cheesecake. Return it
to the oven for 10 minutes, leave to
cool, then chill in the refrigerator for
8 hours, or overnight.

3 To make the topping, place
the sugar in a saucepan with
2 tablespoons of the water over
a low heat and stir until the sugar has
dissolved. Increase the heat, add the
blueberries, cover and cook for a few
minutes, or until they begin to
soften. Remove from the heat. Mix
the arrowroot and remaining water
in a bowl, add to the fruit and stir
until smooth. Return to a low heat.
Cook until the juice thickens and
turns translucent. Leave to cool.

4 Remove the cheesecake from the
tin 1 hour before serving. Spoon the
fruit topping over and chill until
ready to serve.

cook's tip
*If possible, it is best to leave the cheesecake
to chill in the refrigerator overnight at the
end of Step 2.*

CRUNCHY PEANUT BISCUITS

THESE RICH, CRUNCHY BISCUITS WILL BE POPULAR WITH CHILDREN OF ALL AGES, SINCE THEY
CONTAIN ONE OF THEIR FAVOURITE FOODS – PEANUT BUTTER. THEY ARE ALSO VERY NUTRITIOUS
BECAUSE THE PEANUTS ARE AN EXCELLENT SOURCE OF PROTEIN.

makes
20

preparation
15 minutes

cooking
15 minutes

ingredients
- 125 g/4 ½ oz butter,
  softened, plus extra
  for greasing
- 150 g/5 ½ oz chunky
  peanut butter
- 225 g/8 oz
  granulated sugar
- 1 egg, lightly beaten
- 150 g/5 ½ oz plain flour
- ½ tsp baking powder
- pinch of salt
- 75 g/2 ¾ oz unsalted
  natural peanuts, chopped

1 Lightly grease 2 baking trays. Beat the butter and peanut butter together in a large mixing bowl. Gradually add the granulated sugar and beat together well.

2 Add the beaten egg to the mixture, a little at a time, until it is thoroughly combined.

3 Sieve the flour, baking powder and salt into the peanut butter mixture. Add the peanuts and bring all of the ingredients together to form a soft

dough. Wrap in clingfilm and leave to chill for 30 minutes. Preheat the oven to 190°C/375°F/Gas Mark 5.

4 Form the dough into 20 balls and place them onto the prepared baking trays about 5 cm/2 inches apart to allow for spreading. Flatten them slightly with your hand.

5 Bake in the preheated oven for 15 minutes, or until golden brown. Transfer the biscuits to a wire rack and leave to cool.

cook's tip

For a crunchy bite and sparkling appearance, sprinkle the biscuits with demerara sugar before baking.

ALMOND BISCOTTI

BISCOTTI ARE HARD ITALIAN BISCUITS THAT ARE TRADITIONALLY SERVED AT THE END OF A MEAL FOR DIPPING INTO A SWEET WHITE WINE KNOWN AS VIN SANTO. THEY ARE EQUALLY DELICIOUS SERVED WITH COFFEE OR ACCOMPANIED BY VANILLA OR ALMOND-FLAVOURED ICE CREAM.

makes
20–24
preparation
20 minutes,
plus 20 minutes'
cooling
cooking
25 minutes

ingredients
- 250 g/9 oz plain flour, plus extra for dusting
- 1 tsp baking powder
- pinch of salt
- 150 g/5 ½ oz golden caster sugar
- 2 eggs, beaten
- finely grated rind of 1 unwaxed orange
- 100 g/3 ½ oz whole blanched almonds, lightly toasted

1 Preheat the oven to 180°C/ 350°F/Gas Mark 4, then lightly dust a baking sheet with flour. Sift the flour, baking powder and salt into a bowl. Add the sugar, eggs and orange rind and mix to a dough. Knead in the toasted almonds.

2 Roll out the dough into a ball, cut in half and roll out each portion into a log about 4 cm/1½ inches in diameter. Place on the floured baking sheet and bake in the preheated oven for 10 minutes. Remove from the oven and leave to cool for 5 minutes.

3 Using a serrated knife, cut the logs into 1-cm/½-inch thick diagonal slices. Arrange the slices on the baking sheet and return to the oven for 15 minutes, or until slightly golden. Transfer to a wire rack to cool and crispen.

variation

As an alternative to almonds, use hazelnuts or a mixture of almonds and pistachio nuts.

CHOCOLATE BROWNIES

YOU REALLY CAN HAVE A LOW-FAT CHOCOLATE TREAT. THESE MOIST BARS CONTAIN A DRIED FRUIT PURÉE, WHICH ENABLES YOU TO BAKE WITHOUT ADDING FAT. SO THEY ARE THE PERFECT GUILT-FREE FOOD FOR THE AVID SLIMMER – AS LONG AS YOU HIDE THEM FROM THE REST OF YOUR HOUSEHOLD.

makes
12

preparation
55 minutes, plus
1 hour's cooling
and setting

cooking
35–40 minutes

ingredients
- butter, for greasing
- 55 g/2 oz unsweetened stoned dates, chopped
- 55 g/2 oz ready-to-eat dried prunes, chopped
- 6 tbsp unsweetened apple juice
- 4 medium eggs, beaten
- 300 g/10½ oz dark muscovado sugar
- 1 tsp vanilla essence
- 4 tbsp low-fat drinking chocolate powder, plus extra for dusting
- 2 tbsp cocoa powder
- 175 g/6 oz plain flour
- 55 g/2 oz plain dark chocolate chips

ICING
- 125 g/4½ oz icing sugar
- 1–2 tsp water
- 1 tsp vanilla essence

1 Preheat the oven to 180°C/350°F/Gas Mark 4. Grease and line a 18 x 28 cm/7 x 11 inch cake tin with baking paper. Place the dates and prunes in a small saucepan and add the apple juice. Bring to the boil, cover and simmer for 10 minutes until soft. Beat to form a smooth paste, then leave to cool.

2 Place the cooled fruit in a mixing bowl and stir in the eggs, sugar and vanilla essence. Sift in 4 tablespoons of drinking chocolate, the cocoa and the flour, and fold in along with the chocolate chips until well incorporated.

3 Spoon the mixture into the prepared tin and smooth over the top. Bake in the preheated oven for 25–30 minutes until firm to the touch or until a skewer inserted into the centre comes out clean. Cut into 12 bars and leave to cool in the tin for 10 minutes. Transfer to a wire rack to cool completely.

4 To make the icing, sift the sugar into a bowl and mix with enough water and the vanilla essence to form a soft, but not too runny, icing.

5 Drizzle the icing over the chocolate brownies and leave to set. Dust with the extra chocolate powder before serving.

cook's tip
Make double the amount, cut one of the cakes into bars and open freeze, then store in freezer bags. Take out pieces of cake as required – they'll take no time to thaw.

GLOSSARY

THIS GLOSSARY IS NOT INTENDED TO BE EXHAUSTIVE BUT TO PROVIDE A CONCISE GUIDE TO KEY TERMS WITH WHICH A BEGINNER MAY NOT BE FAMILIAR. SOME OF THE BASIC COOKING TECHNIQUES AND INGREDIENTS, INCLUDING SEVERAL OUTLINED EARLIER IN THIS BOOK, ARE LISTED HERE FOR EASE OF REFERENCE.

A

Agar-agar Thickening and setting agent made from seaweed. A vegetarian alternative to Gelatine.

Al dente Italian term, literally meaning 'at the teeth', indicating desired texture of cooked pasta, soft on the outside but still firm and not overcooked inside.

Antipasto Italian term, literally meaning 'before pasta', denoting a hot or cold starter or 'hors d'oeuvres'.

Arborio rice Medium- to long-grain type of rice, from Northern Italy, that is ideal for risotto because it absorbs liquid while retaining a firm texture.

Arrowroot Starch extract of maranta root used to thicken sauces.

Aspic Clear jelly made from clarified meat, fish or vegetable stock mixed with gelatine. It is used to glaze or protect meat or fish and other foods or for savoury dishes set in a mould.

B

Bain-marie Method of cooking ingredients where they are placed in a dish, which is in turn placed in a shallow container of water and is gently heated in an oven or on a hob. This is used to melt ingredients, such as chocolate, without burning them.

Baking powder Raising agent used in baking cakes, biscuits and breads. It usually contains bicarbonate of soda, tartaric acid and dried starch or flour for absorbing moisture.

Balsamic vinegar Dark brown vinegar from Italy, made from fermented, reduced white grape juice, and aged in wooden barrels.

Basmati rice Small but long-grained type of rice grown in the Himalayan foothills. It is a creamy yellow with a nutty flavour and aroma.

Basting Spooning or brushing food during cooking with melted fat or stock to add flavour, colour and to prevent the food from drying out.

Bay leaf Aromatic herb used for flavouring meat, casseroles and soups, often in a bouquet garni.

Béarnaise sauce French sauce made from reduced vinegar, white wine, tarragon, black peppercorns and shallots, finished with egg yolks and butter.

Béchamel sauce Basic French, smooth white sauce made from flour stirred into a mixture of milk and butter.

Beurre manié French term meaning 'kneaded butter', a mixture of flour and softened butter, used to thicken sauces.

Bisque Thick, rich soup, made with cream and usually including shellfish.

Black butter Butter cooked over a low heat until dark brown and usually flavoured with vinegar or lemon juice, capers and parsley.

Black pepper Dried whole peppercorn, which is often crushed or ground to add flavour to food.

Blanching Technique of plunging food into boiling water then placing in cold water to stop the cooking process. This is used to loosen skins, or preserve colour and flavour.

Blind baking Partially cooking a pastry case before the filling is added. This involves cooking the pastry with a foil or paper lining and weighing down with cooking weights (such as baking beans). It avoids overcooking the pastry or making its base too moist when the filling is added.

Borsch or borscht Eastern European soup made with beetroot, cabbage and/or other vegetables and served hot or cold with soured cream.

Bouillabaisse Fish stew from southern France.

Bouquet garni Small group of herbs, usually parsley, bay leaf and thyme, tied together and used to flavour soups, casseroles and stocks in cooking, but removed before serving.

Brochette Cubes of meat or fish and vegetables cooked on a skewer.

Buttermilk Sour-tasting liquid remaining when milk has been churned to butter. It is often used in scones and soda breads.

C

Calvados Northern French dry spirit made from distilled cider and used to flavour meat dishes.

Canapés Small appetizers, often served with drinks.

Capers Sun-dried flower buds of a shrub from the Mediterranean and parts of Asia. They need to be rinsed to remove excess salt or brine, and are used to provide a piquant flavour to sauces or condiments, or as a garnish.

Caramelizing Heating sugar until it melts and turns brown, resetting as a hard glaze, or cooking chopped fruit or vegetables in water and sugar until they brown and glaze.

Cayenne pepper Ground spice powder with a hot flavour, made from the flesh and seeds of chilli pepper.

Chantilly cream Sweetened heavy whipped cream, often flavoured with vanilla, used as a topping for desserts, or folded into custards or cream for fillings.

Chiffonade Thin strips of shredded vegetables (usually sorrel or lettuce), used raw or lightly sautéed, often as a garnish.

Chilli Chilli peppers are small, come in many varieties and are characterized by their extremely hot seeds and flesh. Their potency can be reduced by removing their seeds, but this must be done carefully. It is important to avoid touching sensitive skin or eyes when handling chillies and to wash your hands thoroughly immediately afterwards.

Chinois Conical, fine-meshed sieve used to strain soups and sauces.

Choux pastry Light, double-cooked pastry used to make cakes and buns. It has a hard, crisp exterior and a hollow inside.

Clarified butter Unsalted butter heated slowly to evaporate the water content, and then strained to separate the milk solids. The clarified butter can then be used for cooking at higher temperatures than normal butter without burning.

Compote Dish of fruit, slowly cooked whole or in sugar.

Cornflour Fine, white, powdered starch extract of maize, used to thicken sauces. To avoid it forming lumps, the cornflour should be mixed with twice its weight in cold liquid before being added to the sauce, which should be continuously stirred until it boils.

Coulis Thick and smooth fruit or vegetable sauce. It may be served hot or cold.

Court-bouillon Spiced stock commonly used for cooking fish, seafood or vegetables.

Crème anglaise French term for rich custard cream, made with sugar, egg yolks and milk and flavoured with vanilla, and served hot or cold with dessert.

Crème fraîche French term for a thickened, tangy-flavoured cream made from pasteurized cows' milk.

Croûtons Small cubes of grilled, toasted or fried bread, which are then drained and cooled. Used to garnish salads or soups.

Crudités Raw seasonal vegetables, sometimes sliced or grated, usually served as an appetizer with a dipping sauce.

Custard A smooth mixture of eggs and milk that can be used as the basis for a savoury or sweet sauce or dish.

D

Dariole Small, steep-sided cylindrical mould for shaping pastry, or the pastry cooked in it.

Daube French dish of red meat, vegetables and seasoning, slowly braised in a red wine stock. It can also refer to the method of cooking meat, some vegetables or fish in a similar way.

Dauphinoise (à la) French term referring to the method of slowly baking in an oven with cream and garlic (such as potatoes).

Descaling Removing the scales from a fish by scraping the back of a knife along its surface, from the tail to the head.

Dropping consistency Required consistency of cake mix, where it reluctantly falls from the spoon.

E

Emulsifying Combining fats (for instance, butter or oil) and vinegar or citric juices together with a binding agent such as egg yolk.

Entrecôte French term, meaning 'between the ribs', referring to a tender beef joint, cut from the sirloin.

Escalope French term for very thin slice of meat or fish, often flattened for quick cooking.

Essence or Extract Concentrated extract or oil from foods such as fish, almonds, vanilla, coffee beans, or various plants, and used to flavour foods.

F

Filo pastry Very thin layers of pastry dough, often used in Greek or Middle Eastern dishes, which dry out and cook very quickly.

Fines herbes French term referring to a mixture of chopped aromatic herbs, usually chervil, tarragon, parsley and chives, used to flavour dishes.

Florentine In the style of a dish from Florence, usually referring to dishes served on a bed of cooked spinach. Also a small biscuit of dried fruit and nuts, coated in chocolate on one side.

Fond French term for Stock.

French dressing Cold sauce, made from olive oil and wine vinegar, seasoned with herbs and salt and pepper, and used to dress salads.

Fricassée Stew made from lightly frying white meat, such as chicken, and then cooking it in a white sauce with vegetables.

Fritter Piece of meat, fish or vegetable coated in batter and deep-fried until crisp and cooked.

Fromage frais Fresh, soft, low-fat cheese made from pasteurized cow's milk.

G

Galangal Spice related to ginger and used in south-east Asian cooking for flavour.

Garam masala Mixture of dry-roasted, ground spices, including cumin, coriander and turmeric, mixed to form a paste, or added to a dish for flavour just before the end of cooking.

Gelatine Setting agent derived from the protein of animal bones, used to set sweet or savoury jellies or thicken soups. Agar-agar is a vegetarian alternative, derived from red algae.

Ghee Type of clarified butter with a nutty, caramel-like flavour, created by simmering until the milk solids turn brown. It can be used for sautéing or frying at higher temperatures than normal butter without burning.

Gluten Flour protein, which gives dough elasticity and strength when mixed with water.

Granita Italian sorbet made from sweetened syrup flavoured with coffee or liqueur and often served as a refreshment.

Gratin Any dish topped with cheese or breadcrumbs, mixed with pieces of butter and heated until crisp and brown.

Gravy Sauce made from meat juices, mixed with a stock, wine or milk and thickened with flour. Also refers to the juices remaining in the pan after meat, fish or poultry has been cooked.

Griddle Flat, shallow, cast-iron pan, usually with ridges, for cooking food on a hob.

H
Harissa North African paste with a very hot flavour, made from chillies, garlic, cumin, coriander, mint and oil. It is usually served with couscous, and is used to flavour soups and stews.

Herbes de Provence Mixture of herbs traditionally used in the Provence region of southern France, usually consisting of basil, bay, marjoram, oregano, parsley, rosemary, tarragon and thyme.

Hoisin sauce Thick, reddish-brown, sweet and spicy Chinese sauce, made from a mixture of soya beans, garlic, chilli peppers and spices, commonly used as a table condiment or flavouring.

Hollandaise Rich, creamy and smooth sauce made from egg yolks, butter and lemon juice, and usually served on vegetables, fish or egg dishes.

Horseradish Herb grown for its leaves (for salads) and root. The pungent and spicy root is peeled and grated, and used to flavour sauces.

I
Infusing Imbuing a liquid (usually hot or boiling) with the flavours of herbs, spices, tea or coffee, by leaving them to stand in the liquid.

J
Jambalaya Spicy Creole rice dish traditionally including ham, sausage, chillies and tomatoes, but can also consist of any kind of meat, poultry or shellfish.

Julienne Shredded or thinly cut vegetables or citrus zest, commonly used as a garnish.

Jus French term for 'juice', referring to fruit or vegetable extract, or juice from meat.

K
Kedgeree Traditional British breakfast dish, originally deriving from India, consisting of rice, flaked fish (usually smoked haddock) and hard-boiled eggs.

Kneading Stretching and mixing dough by hand or mechanically, to make it smoother, softer, more elastic and pliable. The movement helps the gluten strands in the dough to stretch and enables the dough to retain gas bubbles and rise when cooked.

L
Lardons Small chunks of fat bacon or pork fat used to flavour dishes.

Lemon grass Root used in south-east Asian (especially Thai) cooking to impart a lemon flavour to sweet or savoury dishes.

Lyonnaise (à la) French term describing dishes including chopped onions. Lyonnaise sauce is made with sautéed onions and white wine and is then strained. It is usually served with meat or poultry dishes.

M
Mace Pungent spice made from the outer membrane of nutmeg, used to flavour various sweet and savoury dishes.

Macerating Soaking fruit in a liquid, such as brandy, to soften and add flavour.

Madeleine Small, buttery sponge cake, made with sugar, flour, butter and eggs, usually flavoured with lemon or almonds.

Marinating Soaking food in a seasoned liquid mixture, or marinade (usually containing oil, lemon or wine, herbs and spices), to tenderize and add flavour.

Marinière (à la) French term meaning 'in the style of a mariner', referring to cooking shellfish, or other seafood, in white wine and herbs. It can also refer to a dish garnished with mussels.

Mascarpone Thick, creamy and soft Italian cheese used in savoury and sweet dishes.

Mayonnaise Thick, creamy dressing made from oil, egg yolks, vinegar or lemon juice and seasoning.

Meringue Light, sweet dessert made by stiffly beating egg white and sugar together and baking.

Meunière (à la) French term meaning 'in the style of a miller's wife', referring to the method of cooking where the food (usually fish) is coated in flour, then shallow-fried in butter.

Mille-feuille French term for 'a thousand leaves', referring to a dessert made from puff pastry, whipped cream, jam or fruit.

Miso Paste made from soya beans and used as a flavouring in Japanese cookery, including soups, sauces and dressings.

Molasses By-product of refining sugar, molasses is a thick, dark brown syrup with a slightly bitter flavour.

Mornay sauce Béchamel sauce with grated cheese (usually Gruyère or Parmesan) added, often served with fish, egg or vegetable dishes.

Mustard Plant whose seeds have a piquant taste used in whole, ground or powdered form as a flavouring for seasoning, dressings, sauces and accompaniments.

N

Navarin French stew made from lamb or mutton, potatoes and other vegetables.

Noodles Thin Pasta strips, made with flour, water and egg or egg yolk.

O

Olive oil Rich oil extracted from pressed olives used for shallow frying, dressings, marinades and baking. Extra virgin olive oil is the purest form of the oil, taken from the first pressing of the olives.

P

Pancetta Italian bacon cured with salt and spices and used to flavour pasta, rice, soup or salad dishes.

Panna cotta Italian term meaning 'cooked cream', referring to a cold dessert made from a set custard of cream and gelatine, often flavoured with vanilla or caramel, for instance.

Papillote (en) French term meaning 'in a parcel', referring to a method of cooking food in a folded parcel of greaseproof

paper, to protect it from the high heat of the oven and help it retain moisture and flavour.

Parboiling Boiling food until half-cooked, in preparation for adding to other ingredients with shorter cooking times or to tenderize the food before roasting (as with potatoes).

Parmesan Hard, dry cheese, made from skimmed cow's milk, with a rich, sharp taste and used grated, usually after cooking, to flavour a dish, especially pasta and sauce.

Passata Smooth Italian-style tomato sauce.

Pasta Italian for 'paste', referring to the dough made from durum-wheat semolina, water and sometimes egg. Pasta comes in a wide variety of shapes and sizes and is served with sauces or soups.

Pectin Natural gelling agent extracted from ripe fruit and vegetables, and used in making jams and jellies.

Pesto Italian term meaning 'pounded', referring to a green sauce made from a blend of pine nuts, fresh basil, Parmesan cheese, garlic and olive oil. It is most commonly served with Pasta or as a dressing.

Pitta bread Middle-Eastern flat, hollow bread made from flour or whole-wheat flour and usually served with fillings or to accompany spicy dishes and dips.

Polenta Italian cornmeal porridge which can be eaten hot or, when cooled and firm, fried.

Prosciutto Italian term for a ham that has been seasoned, salt-cured and air dried, and served very thinly sliced, traditionally as an appetizer.

Puréeing Grinding or mashing fruit or vegetables to form a very smooth paste, manually by pressing the food through a sieve, or mechanically.

Q

Quenelle Small dumpling made from seasoned, minced meat, fish, or ground vegetables, bound with eggs and usually poached in stock.

Quiche Open pastry flan or tart, usually filled with an egg and milk custard and savoury ingredients.

Quinoa Small, bead-like grain, very rich in protein and mild in taste, which is cooked and served like rice.

R

Ragoût Thick, well-seasoned French stew consisting of meat, poultry, fish or vegetables, flavoured with wine.

Ratatouille French vegetable stew consisting of aubergines, courgettes, tomatoes, onions, sweet peppers and garlic simmered in olive oil.

Reducing Boiling a liquid, such as stock, wine or sauce, quickly to reduce its volume by evaporation, thicken it and concentrate the flavours.

Relaxing Leaving pastry to 'rest' after rolling in order to prevent it shrinking.

Ricotta Rich, creamy and smooth Italian cheese made from the curd of ewe's milk, used in many Italian dishes and as a stuffing for Pasta.

Rissole Sweet or savoury round pastry, filled with chopped meat or fish and breadcrumbs and cooked by frying or baking.

Risotto Italian rice dish, made by gradually mixing hot stock and rice during cooking to ensure that the rice absorbs the liquid. Traditionally, Arborio rice is used because of its capacity to absorb liquid and retain a firm texture.

Rösti Swiss term meaning 'crisp and golden', referring to a flat, round pancake of shredded potato, shallow fried on both sides until crisp and brown.

Rouille French term meaning 'rust', referring to a hot, chilli-flavoured red sauce usually served as a garnish with fish or fish stews.

Roulade French term, referring to a sweet or savoury rolled dish. The savoury dish may be a slice of meat, poultry or fish rolled around a stuffing, while the sweet dish is a filled and rolled sponge.

Roux Mixture of flour and fat, slowly cooked over a low heat, and used as a base for soups and sauces to thicken them.

S

Saffron Pungent and aromatic spice, yellow in colour, and available in whole or powdered form, which is used for colouring and flavouring dishes. The spice is derived from the stigmas of the saffron crocus and is very expensive.

Salsa Spanish and Mexican term meaning 'sauce', and specifically referring to a spicy, hot-flavoured, thick relish made from chillies and fruit, and served cold.

Salt Sodium chloride crystals, used for seasoning and preserving food. It is available in various forms, including sea salt and rock salt, from which cooking and table salt are derived.

Samosa Indian triangle-shaped pastry, filled with spiced meat or vegetables, and deep-fried.

Satay Indonesian speciality, consisting of meat, fish or poultry cubes, grilled on a skewer, and usually served with a spicy sauce.

Shortcrust pastry Crumbly pastry usually used for sweet or savoury pies and tarts.

Shucking To remove the edible part of food from its outer casing, such as removing an oyster from its shell, using a small, thick-bladed knife.

Sirloin Premium cut of tender beef, from the back, available as fillet steaks or joints for roasting.

Slaking Mixing a thickening agent with a liquid.

Smoothie Thick, smooth and cold drink made from blending fruit or vegetables, often with liquids, such as water, milk or ice cream.

Sorbet Smooth, semi-frozen water ice mixed with fruit juice or liqueur, and sometimes egg white or gelatine, and commonly served as a dessert.

Soy sauce Sauce commonly used in Chinese and Japanese cooking, made from fermented and boiled soya beans. It is used to flavour sauces, soups, marinades, meat, fish and vegetables.

Stock Flavoured, strained liquid made by cooking meat, fish, poultry and vegetables, with seasoning, in water, used for flavouring sauces, soups, stews or braised dishes.

Sweating Method of cooking ingredients, usually vegetables, in a little fat, slowly over a low heat so that they cook in their own steam without browning.

T

Tabasco sauce Hot-flavoured, spicy sauce made from Tabasco chilli peppers, vinegar and salt, and used to add flavour to sauces, meat or cocktails.

Tapenade Thick French paste made from black olives, capers, anchovies, lemon juice, olive oil and herbs, used to flavour sauces, marinades, stews, pasta or meat.

Tarte Tatin French apple tart made in a shallow dish by covering butter, sugar and apples with a pastry topping and baking until the ingredients caramelize. The tart is served upside down.

Terrine Pâté cooked in a small, fat-lined, deep-sided dish (also called terrine), and usually made from pieces of fish or meat.

Timbale Dish cooked in a mould (also called timbale), consisting of layers, usually of rice and vegetables.

Tisane Infusion of herbs in boiling water, drunk hot.

Tofu Curd of the soya bean, pressed into firm cheese-like blocks, which is bland in flavour but rich in iron and protein. Commonly used in oriental dishes, it can be cooked in soups, stir-fries, casseroles or sauces.

Turmeric Spice derived from the root of a ginger-related plant, with a yellow colour and bitter taste, used in oriental cooking to add colour and flavour.

V

Vanilla Sweet and fragrant flavouring extracted from the dried pods and seeds of the vanilla orchid, and used to flavour sweet and savoury foods.

Vichyssoise Rich and creamy soup, served cold, made from potatoes, leeks and cream, and garnished with chopped chives.

Vinaigrette Cold sauce made from a mixture of vinegar, oil and seasoning, normally used as a dressing for leaf salads or other cold dishes.

W

White sauce Basic smooth sauce, also known as Béchamel, made from flour stirred into a mixture of milk and butter.

Y

Yeast Microscopic, live fungus that converts its food, through fermentation, into carbon dioxide and alcohol and is therefore used in bread-making to make dough rise, or in brewing to make alcohol.

Z

Zabaglione Italian frothy dessert made by whisking egg yolks, wine and sugar together, while heating gently, and is served slightly warm.

Zest Fragrant outer rind of citrus fruit, grated or shredded and used to add flavour or as a garnish to a dish.

INDEX